# The Cuban Missile C

# The Cuban Missile Crisis

## Origins, Course and Aftermath

Jonathan Colman

EDINBURGH
University Press

Edinburgh University Press is one of the leading university presses in the UK. We publish academic books and journals in our selected subject areas across the humanities and social sciences, combining cutting-edge scholarship with high editorial and production values to produce academic works of lasting importance. For more information visit our website: www.edinburghuniversitypress.com

© Jonathan Colman, 2016

Edinburgh University Press Ltd
The Tun – Holyrood Road
12 (2f) Jackson's Entry
Edinburgh EH8 8PJ

Typeset in 11/14 Sabon by
Servis Filmsetting Ltd, Stockport, Cheshire,
and printed and bound in Great Britain by
CPI Group (UK) Ltd, Croydon CR0 4YY

A CIP record for this book is available from the British Library

ISBN 978 0 7486 9628 4 (hardback)
ISBN 978 0 7486 9630 7 (paperback)
ISBN 978 0 7486 9629 1 (webready PDF)
ISBN 978 0 7486 9631 4 (epub)

# Contents

# Acknowledgements

The Cuban Missile Crisis first caught my imagination when I worked as a research assistant to Len Scott – whose expertise about the crisis is unsurpassed – in the Department of International Politics at the University of Aberystwyth. Later, I was privileged to be able to attend a conference at Gregynog Hall, Wales, organised by Len and his colleagues in the Centre of Intelligence and International Security Studies at Aberystwyth and by the University of Cambridge Intelligence Seminar to mark the 50th anniversary of the missile crisis. As well as being highly congenial, the conference was a source of valuable knowledge about what went on in October 1962.

I would like to acknowledge with immense gratitude the help I have received with this book from the following friends and colleagues: Martin Alexander, Antonio Cerella, Mike O'Grady, Jeremy Richardson, Len Scott, Laura Stanley, Jake Widén and Oliver Wilkinson. Thanks are due to the staff at Edinburgh University Press for their helpful and professional attitude, and to the anonymous reviewers of the proposal and the manuscript for their insightful and constructive suggestions. Succession Picasso authorised the use of the painting on the cover. The work was the first in Pablo Picasso's four-part series 'The Rape of the Sabines', which he began at the height of the missile crisis and which borrowed from previous paintings by Nicolas Poussin and Jacques-Louis David to capture the atrocities of war.

Any limitations of the book are entirely my own responsibility. It is dedicated to my students, past, present and future.

*Jonathan Colman*
*Burnley, England, 2015*

# Abbreviations

| | |
|---|---|
| ABM | anti-ballistic missile |
| CAB | Cabinet records (TNA) |
| CC | Central Committee of CPSU |
| CIA | Central Intelligence Agency |
| CPCz | Communist Party of Czechoslovakia |
| CPSU | Communist Party of the Soviet Union |
| DCI | Director of Central Intelligence (CIA) |
| DEFCON | defence condition (US) |
| EEC | European Economic Community |
| ExComm | Executive Committee of the NSC |
| FKR | Soviet tactical cruise missile |
| FO | Foreign Office (Britain) |
| FRG | Federal Republic of Germany (West Germany) |
| *FRUS* | *Foreign Relations of the United States* series |
| GDR | German Democratic Republic (East Germany) |
| GRU | Soviet military intelligence |
| ICBM | intercontinental ballistic missile |
| JCS | US Joint Chiefs of Staff |
| JFK | John Fitzgerald Kennedy |
| KGB | Soviet political intelligence |
| MAD | mutual assured destruction |
| MLF | Multilateral Force |
| MRBM | medium-range ballistic missile |
| NAC | North Atlantic Council of NATO |
| NATO | North Atlantic Treaty Organisation |
| NPG | Nuclear Planning Group in NATO |
| NSAM | National Security Action Memorandum (NSC) |
| NSC | US National Security Council |

| | |
|---|---|
| POL | petrol, oil, lubricants |
| PREM | Prime Minister's Office (Britain) |
| RFK | Robert Francis Kennedy |
| SAC | US Supreme Air Command |
| SALT | Strategic Arms Limitation Talks |
| SAM | surface-to-air-missile |
| SED | Socialist Unity Party of Germany |
| SLBM | submarine-launched ballistic missile |
| SNIE | CIA Special National Intelligence Estimate |
| TASS | Russian news agency |
| TNA | The UK National Archives, Kew, Surrey |
| UN | United Nations |
| USAF | United States Air Force |
| USGPO | US Government Printing Office |
| USSR | Union of Soviet Socialist Republics |

# Introduction

The Cuban Missile Crisis was a six-day public confrontation in October 1962 between the United States and the Soviet Union over the presence of Soviet nuclear missiles in Cuba. It ended when the Soviets agreed to remove the weapons in return for a US agreement not to invade Cuba and a secret assurance that American missiles in Turkey would be withdrawn. The confrontation stemmed from the ideological rivalries of the Cold War, which had begun soon after the Second World War and involved each side jostling to secure military and political advantage. Along with the 'eyeball-to-eyeball' antagonism between the respective US and Soviet leaders John F. Kennedy and Nikita Khrushchev, and alongside a real threat of nuclear war, the crisis was a turning point given that, in its wake, American and Soviet leaders adopted more sober attitudes to East–West relations. At the same time, the Soviets pursued a nuclear build-up out of a desire never to find themselves compromised again by American power, and to negotiate arms limitation from a position of strength. The crisis accelerated the development of a more complicated, polycentric world, with some of Washington and Moscow's respective allies charting a more independent path after 1962 – partly because of a lack of consultation during the missile confrontation.

One writer suggested that the missile crisis was 'an event whose significance in international affairs almost defies hyperbole'.[1] Its undoubted importance has meant that practically every minute of the stand-off has been scrutinised intensely in a vast number of publications.[2] Crisis participants and journalists dominated the literature in the first few years after the missile crisis, and tended to laud Kennedy's response to the Soviet challenge. Famously, presidential aide Arthur Schlesinger described Kennedy's leadership as a 'combination of toughness and restraint, of will, nerve and wisdom, so brilliantly controlled, so matchlessly calibrated, that dazzled the world'.[3] Thus, the cool, heroic Kennedy, exhibiting immaculate judgement, forced the blustering Khrushchev to concede. Other works in this period often made for engaging reading but ranked less well as accurate historical accounts of the missile crisis, given the lack of primary sources, the Kennedy administration's tendency to 'spin' what went on, and the reverence accorded to the President after his murder in 1963. In particular, there was little awareness at this stage that he had agreed to remove US missiles from Turkey.

The 1970s and the 1980s saw a growing number of scholarly publications. Graham Allison presented a narrative of events and outlined three models of bureaucratic politics for understanding American policy. Some of the literature criticised the US administration; James Nathan noted in 1975 that 'the Kennedy administration's shimmering hour – the Cuban Missile Crisis – has just begun to have its luster tarnished by critics'.[4] Critics included Thomas Paterson, who wrote in 1978 that

> The president's desire to score a victory, to recapture previous losses, to flex his muscle accentuated the crisis and obstructed diplomacy . . . Kennedy gave Khrushchev no chance to withdraw his mistake or to save face . . . He left little room for bargaining but instead issued a public ultimatum and seemed willing to destroy . . . millions in the process.[5]

The greater openness that accompanied the end of the Cold War in the late 1980s expanded our knowledge of the missile crisis. In particular, there were several conferences involving crisis participants from the United States, the Soviet Union and Cuba, who were willing to share information and perspectives.[6] The new knowledge led to a growing acceptance that Khrushchev placed missiles in Cuba to defend the island from American aggression, which had been demonstrated by the US-sponsored attack by Cuban émigrés at the Bay of Pigs in April 1961. The conferences brought the long-overlooked Cuban perspective more to the fore.

This included explaining why Cuba's radical leader, Fidel Castro, chose to accept Soviet missiles – he wanted to protect the island and to strengthen the international socialist camp.[7] Furthermore, suspicions about the reason for the removal of the US Jupiter missiles in Turkey were confirmed.

The 1990s saw increased pace in the declassification of material from the John F. Kennedy Presidential Library, the US National Archives and the Central Intelligence Agency. The Kennedy Library released twenty-two hours of secret recordings of missile crisis conversations between the President and his 'ExComm' colleagues. Why Kennedy made the recordings, which began in July 1962, is uncertain, but they provide important insight into White House policymaking and into the views of individual advisers. Attorney General Robert F. Kennedy, for instance, emerged as a 'hawk' in the ExComm deliberations, in contrast to how he appeared in his posthumously published (1969) memoir *Thirteen Days*. In 1996 the US Department of State published around 900 pages of US documentation, including transcripts of the ExComm recordings, in a volume in the long-running *Foreign Relations of the United States* series.[8]

While there is a great deal of American documentation available, the picture is far from complete. Declassification often proceeds at a glacial pace because of political sensitivities, security concerns and limited resources. Most records of the US Joint Chiefs of Staff, the Defense Department, the Strategic Air Command and the US Air Force remain classified. The withheld material includes information about the U-2 reconnaissance aircraft that drifted into Soviet territory while on a routine air monitoring mission over the Arctic on the night of 26–7 October.[9] Some Soviet documents have been released since the end of the Cold War, with many being disseminated online through the Cold War International History Project and the National Security Archive.[10] These have illuminated, for example, differences of opinion between the Soviet Union and Cuba over the settlement of the missile crisis. However, the quantity of Soviet material available remains relatively modest. This means that there is limited knowledge of, for instance, how Soviet officials estimated the impact of nuclear weapons in Cuba on the balance of power, or how changing threat perceptions during the crisis might have influenced Khrushchev's conduct. Policy formation in Havana is still more obscure, as the Cuban government has proved especially parsimonious about releasing documents. To understand Cuban attitudes, thinking and initiatives, historians have to rely in large part on public speeches and statements – often decades after the event – from Fidel Castro and others, and on the records of other countries. Although the broad contours of Cuba's role are apparent, we cannot yet do full justice to Cuban concerns and contributions.

Whatever the limitations of the documentary record, there are no signs of the literature drying up. In recent years there has been a comprehensive general account of the missile crisis;[11] a growing focus on the perspectives of countries beyond the United States, the Soviet Union and Cuba;[12] and, since the fiftieth anniversary of the crisis, a crop of mainly specialised works.[13] This book conveys the latest interpretations of the origins, course and aftermath of the missile crisis, drawing on the secondary literature alongside documents from the United States, the Soviet Union, Cuba, Britain (the US partner in the vaunted 'special relationship') and other countries. Memoirs, including those of Robert F. Kennedy and Nikita Khrushchev, are used. Such sources are not to be treated uncritically because, as we have noted with the example of the former, they are often written with a view to publication and so tend to be self-serving.[14] Nonetheless, they can provide data and personal perspectives not otherwise available.

The book explores the culpability of the Eisenhower and Kennedy administrations for causing the crisis because of their hostility to the Castro regime, which had gained power in the Cuban Revolution of 1959. US policies ended up strengthening Castro by providing him with a powerful external enemy, and by encouraging ties between Cuba and the Soviet Union. Although the United States and the Soviet Union were the prime movers in the missile crisis, Cuba was a proud, independent and influential actor and not merely a superpower pawn. Early in 1962, for example, Castro exploited Soviet insecurities about losing their partner in the Caribbean to secure greater support from Moscow. Various longstanding myths about the crisis are dismissed, including the notion that on 24 October Soviet and American vessels were 'eyeball-to-eyeball' along the quarantine line that the US had established around Cuba when Khrushchev suddenly ordered a retreat. The account emphasises the danger of the confrontation. Kennedy estimated that the odds of nuclear war were 'somewhere between one out of three and even', while Khrushchev reflected that 'we were on the edge of nuclear war'.[15] Both leaders had their own reasons for emphasising the risks – Kennedy to assert the magnitude of his success in facing down the Soviet threat; Khrushchev to justify his decision to retreat. Other participants played down the threat of war,[16] but post-Cold War revelations have indicated that the two leaders had only a tenuous grip (and sometimes no grip at all) on operational matters, which could easily have spiralled out of control with devastating consequences.

Despite the extensive literature about the Cuban Missile Crisis, the global ramifications of what went on remain invisible other than in some of the more specialised texts. While placing American, Soviet and Cuban contributions at the centre of the discussion, this book stresses that the missile crisis was a world event. There was the threat of global cataclysm, and numerous countries were involved politically or militarily. The aftermath of the crisis is also poorly explored in many of the general accounts. It is argued in this book that the settlement of the confrontation during November was complex and messy, confounding the idea that President Kennedy had secured a firm victory, and that the crisis left a number of international legacies that would play themselves out over the next few years. These legacies included intra-bloc tensions and escalating conflict in Vietnam. It is emphasised, too, that the confrontation over Soviet weapons in Cuba ended formally only in 1970, when the terms of the settlement were clarified after Soviet efforts to construct a submarine base on the island.

Chapter 1 examines the US response to the emergence of Fidel Castro in Cuba, and covers Soviet–American relations under Kennedy. The second chapter considers Khrushchev's decision to place nuclear missiles in Cuba, and his efforts to deceive the US government about his actions. Chapter 3 explores the discovery

of the missiles, and the Kennedy administration's initial deliberations about how to respond. Chapter 4 examines the first part
of the confrontation, from Monday 22 to Thursday 25 October,
including military preparations and the implementation of the
quarantine. The subsequent chapter addresses the impact of the
crisis in the United Nations, Latin America, Europe and Asia.
Chapter 6 explores the most dangerous phase of the confrontation, from Friday 26 to Sunday 28 October. The final two chap-
ters cover the aftermath of the crisis, with Chapter 7 addressing
the settlement until the end of 1962, and Chapter 8 exploring
the after-effects up to 1970. The Conclusion sums up the arguments and suggests further avenues for research. The appendices
provide a chronology, a list of persons, biographies and a selection of documents with commentaries. The documents have been
selected to illuminate aspects of the origins, course and aftermath
of the missile crisis, and include US, Soviet, Cuban, British and
Chinese material.

It is appropriate to make a few points concerning terminol-
ogy. In the United States the confrontation of October 1962
was known as the 'Cuban Missile Crisis', in the Soviet Union
as the 'Caribbean Crisis' or the 'Cuba Crisis', and in Cuba as
the 'October Crisis'. Each term has a slightly different emphasis
and meaning. The American label implies that the Soviet Union
caused the crisis by placing nuclear missiles in Cuba. For Moscow,
though, the event was a superpower confrontation that happened
to be in the Caribbean; the absence of a reference to the missiles
avoided the question of Soviet culpability. The term 'Caribbean
Crisis' also played down the Cuban role. The Cubans referred to
the 'October Crisis' because in the early Castro years they had to
contend with a number of US invasion alarms. In the light of how
the Soviets negotiated an end to the crisis over Cuban heads, the
use of a home-grown term was also a matter of national pride.[17]
This work uses the term 'Cuban Missile Crisis' not to privilege
or endorse the American perspective, but simply because it is the
most widely recognised label.

## Notes

1. Frank C. Zagare, 'A Game-Theoretic History of the Cuban Missile Crisis', *Economies*, 2: 1, January 2014, p. 20.
2. For accounts of the literature, see Robert A. Divine, 'Alive and Well: The Continuing Missile Crisis', *Diplomatic History*, 18: 4, Fall 1994, pp. 551–60; Burton Kaufman, 'John F. Kennedy as World Leader', in Michael J. Hogan (ed.), *America in the World: The Historiography of American Foreign Relations since 1941* (Cambridge and New York: Cambridge University Press, 1995), pp. 342–9; William J. Medland, 'The Cuban Missile Crisis: Evolving Historical Perspectives', *The History Teacher*, 23: 4, August 1990, pp. 433–47; Don Munton and David Welch, *The Cuban Missile Crisis: A Concise History*, 2nd edn (Oxford and New York: Oxford University Press, 2012), pp. 107–16 (Munton and Welch provide a valuable account of film and documentary representations of the missile crisis as well as books and articles); Len Scott, 'Should We Stop Studying the Cuban Missile Crisis?', *International Relations*, 26: 3, September 2012, pp. 255–66; Randall B. Woods, 'Beyond Vietnam: The Foreign Policies of the Kennedy and Johnson Administrations', in Robert D. Schulzinger (ed.), *A Companion to American Foreign Relations* (Malden: Blackwell, 2006), pp. 341–8. For Russian perspectives, see Sergey Radchenko, 'The Cuban Missile Crisis: Assessment of New, and Old, Russian Sources', *International Relations*, 26: 3, September 2012, pp. 327–43.
3. Roger Hilsman, *To Move a Nation: The Politics of Foreign Policy in the Administration of John F. Kennedy* (Garden City, NY: Doubleday, 1967); Robert F. Kennedy, *Thirteen Days: A Memoir of the Cuban Missile Crisis* (New York: Norton, 1999); Pierre Salinger, *With Kennedy* (Garden City, NY: Doubleday, 1966); Arthur M. Schlesinger, Jr., *A Thousand Days: John F. Kennedy in the White House* (New York: Houghton Mifflin, 1965) (quotation p. 716); Theodore Sorensen, *Kennedy* (New York: Harper and Row, 1965). Other accounts from the period include Elie Abel, *The Missiles of October* (London: MacGibbon and Kee, 1969); and Henry M. Pachter, *Collision Course: The Cuban Missile Crisis and Coexistence* (New York: Praeger, 1963).
4. James A. Nathan, 'The Missile Crisis: His Final Hour Now', *World Politics*, 27: 2, January 1975, p. 256.

5. Graham Allison, *Essence of Decision: Explaining the Cuban Missile Crisis* (Boston: Little, Brown, 1971); Barton J. Bernstein, 'The Cuban Missile Crisis: Trading the Jupiters in Turkey?', *Political Science Quarterly*, 95: 1, Spring 1980, pp. 97–125; Herbert S. Dinerstein, *The Making of a Missile Crisis, October 1962* (Baltimore: Johns Hopkins Press, 1976); Thomas G. Paterson, 'Bearing the Burden: A Critical Look at JFK's Foreign Policy', *The Virginia Quarterly Review*, 54: 2, Spring 1978, pp. 193–212 (quotation p. 206).

6. For the conferences, see Bruce J. Allyn, James G. Blight and David A. Welch (eds), *Back to the Brink: Proceedings of the Moscow Conference on the Cuban Missile Crisis, January 27–28 1989* (Lanham, MD: University Press of America, 1992); James G. Blight, Bruce J. Allyn and David A. Welch (eds), *Cuba on the Brink: Castro, the Missile Crisis and the Soviet Collapse*, revised edn (New York: Rowman and Littlefield, 2002); James G. Blight and David A. Welch (eds), with foreword by McGeorge Bundy, *On the Brink: Americans and Soviets Reexamine the Cuban Missile Crisis* (New York: Noonday Press, 1990). Other post-Cold War works include Aleksandr Fursenko and Timothy Naftali, *'One Hell of a Gamble': Khrushchev, Castro, and Kennedy, 1958–64* (New York: Norton, 1997); Anatoli I. Gribkov and William Y. Smith, *Operation Anadyr: US and Soviet Generals Recount the Cuban Missile Crisis* (Chicago: Edition Q, 1994); Richard Ned Lebow and Janice Gross Stein, *We All Lost the Cold War* (Princeton, NJ: Princeton University Press, 1994); Carlos Lechuga, *In the Eye of the Storm: Castro, Kennedy, Khrushchev and the Missile Crisis*, translated by Mary Todd (Melbourne: Ocean Press, 1995); Jutta Weldes, *Constructing National Interests: The United States and the Cuban Missile Crisis* (Minneapolis: University of Minnesota Press, 1999); Mark J. White, *Missiles in Cuba: Kennedy, Khrushchev, Castro and the 1962 Crisis* (Chicago: Ivan R. Dee, 1998).

7. See Mark Laffey and Jutta Weldes, 'Decolonizing the Cuban Missile Crisis', *International Studies Quarterly*, 52, 2008, pp. 555–77, for the neglect of Cuba in the literature.

8. Available at US Department of State, *Foreign Relations of the United States Series* (Washington: USGPO), <https://history.state.gov/historicaldocuments> (last accessed 25 July 2015). Revised transcripts of the ExComm tapes, with commentary and analysis, are available in Ernest R. May and Philip D. Zelikow (eds), *The Kennedy Tapes: Inside the White House During the Cuban Missile*

*Crisis* (Cambridge, MA: Belknap, 1997). The recordings can be heard online at the Miller Centre, University of Virginia, John F. Kennedy Presidential Recordings, <http://millercenter.org/presiden tialrecordings/kennedy> (last accessed 25 July 2015).

9. Michael Dobbs, 'Why We Should Still Study the Cuban Missile Crisis', *United States Institute of Peace* Special Report, 1 June 2008, p. 5, <http://www.usip.org/sites/default/files/sr205.pdf> (last accessed 25 July 2015).

10. Available at the Cold War International History Project, Wilson Center, <http://www.wilsoncenter.org/program/cold-war-internatio nal-history-project> (last accessed 25 July 2015) and the National Security Archive, George Washington University, <http://www2. gwu.edu/~nsarchiv/> (last accessed 25 July 2015).

11. Michael M. Dobbs, *One Minute to Midnight: Kennedy, Khrushchev and Castro on the Brink of Nuclear War* (New York: Knopf, 2008).

12. For example, Leonardo Campus, *I sei giorni che sconvolsero il mondo: La crisi dei missili di Cuba e le sue percezioni internazionali* (Milan: Mondadori, 2014); David Gioe, Len Scott and Christopher Andrew (eds), *An International History of the Cuban Missile Crisis: A 50-Year Retrospective* (London: Routledge, 2014); L. V. Scott, *Macmillan, Kennedy and the Cuban Missile Crisis: Political, Military and Intelligence Aspects* (New York: St Martin's Press, 1999); Maurice Vaisse (ed.), *L'Europe et la Crise de Cuba* (Paris: Armand Collin, 1993).

13. For example, David M. Barrett and Max Holland, *Blind over Cuba: The Photo Gap and the Missile Crisis* (College Station, TX: Texas A&M University Press, 2012); David Coleman, *The Fourteenth Day: JFK and the Aftermath of the Cuban Missile Crisis* (New York: Norton, 2012); Alice L. George, *The Cuban Missile Crisis: The Threshold of Nuclear War* (New York and London: Routledge, 2013); David R. Gibson, *Talk at the Brink: Deliberation and Decision during the Cuban Missile Crisis* (Princeton, NJ: Princeton University Press, 2012); Sergo Mikoyan, *The Soviet Cuban Missile Crisis: Castro, Mikoyan, Kennedy, Khrushchev and the Missiles of November*, edited by Svetlana Savranskaya (Stanford, CA: Stanford University Press, 2012).

14. See Irina Paperno, 'What Can Be Done with Diaries?', *Russian Review*, 63: 4, October 2004, pp. 561–73.

15. Lebow and Stein, *We All Lost the Cold War*, p. 5; Sorensen, *Kennedy*, p. 705.

16. Len Scott, *The Cuban Missile Crisis and the Threat of Nuclear War* (London: Continuum, 2007), pp. 1–2.
17. James G. Blight and Philip Brenner, *Sad and Luminous Days: Cuba's Struggle with the Superpowers after the Missile Crisis* (Lanham, MD: Rowman and Littlefield, 2002), pp. 247–8.

# 1 The United States, the Cuban Revolution and the Cold War, 1959–61

Castro is not a communist but US policy can make him one.
*Nikita Khrushchev*

## The Emergence of Fidel Castro

President James Monroe's eponymous doctrine of 1823, in which he warned European powers not to seek new colonies in the New World, testified to what would become a longstanding concern on the part of the US government about the encroachment of rival influences to the south. Later in the century, after the closure of the western frontier and in a period of burgeoning economic power, the United States began to assert itself in the Caribbean, the Pacific and East Asia. In 1898 the country waged a brief and one-sided war against Spain in the name of liberating Cuba from Spanish rule. Although nominally independent, Cuba now found itself firmly in the American sphere. Even after American troops were withdrawn in 1903, the United States retained the use of a 45-square-mile naval base at Guantánamo, and maintained close supervision of Cuban affairs – not least through relying on pliant leaders. During the Second World War, Washington backed President Fulgencio Batista y Zaldívar, who then spent time in the United States only to return to Cuba to seize power by force in 1952. Although brutal and corrupt, Batista was hostile to communism and friendly to American interests. Elections in 1954 were marred by violence and intimidation perpetrated both by the regime and by opposition elements.[1]

One of the chief opposition groups was Fidel Castro's 26th

July Movement (the date commemorated an attack on a barracks in Santiago de Cuba in 1953), which took over a number of other rebel organisations. The Movement embodied nationalistic passions and appealed to workers, peasants and to elements of the middle class. The American domination of Cuban political and economic life was of particular concern to Castro and his associates. As well as backing the ruling elite, the United States dominated the Cuban economy. By 1958 there was $774 million of American investment in Cuba,[2] with two-thirds of the country's foreign trade being exchanged with the United States. US interests controlled a third of the sugar industry, all of Cuba's nickel resources, the electricity and telephone companies, and a large proportion of the railroads, cement plants, manufacturing, banking, oil-refining, resorts and casinos, and drugs and prostitution.[3]

To be sure, American economic dominance was not entirely detrimental to Cuba. A 1960 British analysis noted that the country

> would not now have so (for a Latin American country) exceptionally high a standard of living were it not for its development by American capital, the money spent by American tourists and the arrangement under which half its sugar is sold in the United States at twice the world price.[4]

The commercial relationship between Cuba and the United States had been 'mutually advantageous; in absolute terms the United States may latterly have had the best of the bargain but, in relation to the size of their respective economies, Cuba has profited far more'.[5] Yet there was still deep poverty in the country, encouraging resentment and rebellion. The US Embassy's commercial attaché stated that:

> Cuban farmers and their families with few exceptions are undernourished, inadequately clothed, illiterate or semi-literate, readily susceptible to a variety of diseases, and at the mercy of country merchants and middlemen whose prices are what the traffic will yield and whose interest rates are generally exorbitant.[6]

In the light of the Batista regime's growing brutality against an increasingly unified opposition, Ambassador Earl Smith in Havana noted that there were criticisms of the United States 'for supplying arms to the Cuban government' which used them not against any external enemy (for there were none), but to retain power.[7] Washington imposed an arms embargo to encourage Batista to carry out democratic reforms. However unsavoury, Batista was more appealing than Castro. The State Department had no faith that the 26th July Movement's 'top leadership . . . would show the qualities of integrity, moderation, and responsibility which will be needed to restore order and tranquility to Cuba'.[8] The triumph of Castro's rebellion in January 1959 generated great local acclaim. The US Embassy reported that after years of struggle the people of Havana gave him a 'hero's welcome . . . Hundreds of thousands lined the route to cheer him.'[9] Although the US government extended diplomatic recognition to Castro's regime, there were concerns about how he disdained 'Cuban alignment with US in [the] cold war and against Communism'.[10] Undoubtedly, Castro was ill-disposed towards his northern neighbour. During the summer of 1958 he told his secretary and confidante, Celia Sánchez, that, after the war against Batista ended, he was going to start a much bigger war, the war against the United States. It was his 'destiny'.[11]

For now, though, he needed to consolidate his position. In April 1959 he visited the United States at the invitation of the American Society of Newspaper Editors. He sought to use the visit to influence American public opinion, so that he might avoid a confrontation with the United States as he consolidated power.[12] Initially, President Eisenhower had wanted to deny Castro a visa, but the State Department thought it wiser for the President simply to absent himself from the Capitol.[13] Castro met instead with Vice-President Richard Nixon, and various other officials and congressional leaders. The visit enabled Castro to convey his ebullient personality to the general public, but he did not win over the US government. Nixon thought that Castro was either 'incredibly naive about Communism or under Communist discipline'. The Cuban leader's thinking about 'how to run a government or an economy are less developed than those of almost any world figure I have met in fifty countries'.[14] For his part, Castro felt that Nixon 'spent the whole time scolding me',[15] and he complained later that Eisenhower 'didn't even invite me for a cup of coffee, because I wasn't worthy'.[16] Yet a close associate of Castro noted that it did not seem to trouble him at the time,[17] and given that the visit was unofficial, the expectation of meeting the President was unrealistic. The nub, though, was that there had been no meeting of minds between the Cuban leader and his American hosts.

## Developing Cuban–Soviet Bonds

There was growing concern in the US government about Cuban links with the Soviet Union, as within weeks of Castro achieving power in 1959, Soviet representatives visited Havana. Soon Soviet Premier Nikita Khrushchev approved the supply of weapons from Soviet satellites to the Cuban armed forces,[18] and in February 1960, Deputy Premier Anastas Mikoyan led a trade delegation to Cuba. After a ten-day visit the Soviet Union agreed to provide $100 million worth of credit to Cuba and to buy Cuban sugar. The deal was not especially generous, but it was of great political significance, with Director of Central Intelligence (DCI) Allen Dulles remarking that the agreement 'marked the definite espousal of Castro by the USSR'.[19] Later, Moscow agreed to sell cut-price crude oil to Cuba, and by the end of the year the communist People's Republic of China granted interest-free credit and began extending agricultural support.[20] Increasingly, US officials saw Cuba as a portal for communist influence in Latin America, not least because the Havana regime sought to promote revolution in the region – the intention was to liberate neighbours from foreign imperialism and internal exploitation, and to secure allies. The National Security Council (NSC) reported that Cuba was 'being used as a base for the export of the communist-fidelista revolution', through providing 'funds, counsel to subversive activities . . . propaganda' and 'Spanish-speaking agents available for communist subversion and propaganda'.[21]

Domestically, the regime drastically cut rents and telephone electricity rates, gave more rights to workers and restricted the foreign ownership of land. Many of these initiatives came at the expense of US corporations. The US government condemned the execution of hundreds of Batista supporters in Cuba and the failure to hold free elections. American oil companies, after consulting Washington, refused to refine Soviet oil, so at the end of June Castro nationalised the companies' property in Cuba. President Eisenhower demonstrated his disapproval by cutting the quota of Cuban sugar purchases by 700,000 tons, and in October 1960 he imposed an economic embargo, banning American trade with Cuba apart from exports of medicine. The Castro regime's seizure soon afterwards of the remaining US properties and investments in Cuba showed how one hostile measure precipitated another, in a spiral of reciprocal antagonism. In January 1961, after the Cuban regime had asserted that most of the several hundred staff at the US Embassy in Havana were spies and saboteurs, the United States ended diplomatic relations with Cuba.[22] The Embassy suggested that by severing formal relations the US government would be better placed 'to strengthen and encourage the Cuban opposition, open the way for more vigorous economic and propaganda measures . . . and remove the distractions for US policy created by the attempt to operate a diplomatic mission in Cuba under existing circumstances'.[23]

Some aspects of American policies towards Castro's Cuba antagonised leading allies. The British, co-partners in the vaunted 'special relationship', supported the American government by providing diplomatic and intelligence reports from Havana after the closure of the US embassy,[24] but they resented US pressure to cease trade. In December 1960, a Foreign Office diplomat complained that 'The Americans did not consult us before they imposed their trade embargo.' The British were also concerned that the embargo helped to 'drive Cuba more rapidly and completely into economic dependence on the Sino-Soviet bloc'.[25] It seems clear that US policies were increasingly counterproductive. While it is unlikely that the United States and Cuba under Castro could ever have enjoyed lasting, cordial relations, given how poorly disposed the Cuban leader and his colleagues were to the United States, it is clear that if the US government had pursued policies of greater subtlety and restraint there would have been less chance of the Soviets gaining influence in Cuba.

This was certainly a possibility, as there were mutual reservations between the Soviet and Cuban governments. Nikita Khrushchev's son-in-law and editor of *Izvestiya*, Alexei Adzhubei, suggested in 1959 that Castro would be 'a typical Latin American dictato ... He's already been to the United States and is under its influence, so don't get any illusions.'[26] Khrushchev admired his 'personal courage' but thought that his fiery rhetoric 'didn't make much sense' tactically, as it would antagonise middle-class Cubans.[27] There were reservations on the Cuban side, too, stemming from national pride and independence. At a mass rally in July 1960 Castro expressed thanks for Soviet support, but added that his country 'does not depend on the preservation of its independence on Soviet rockets, but rather on the justice of her cause'. Minister of the Interior Ernesto 'Che' Guevara stated that 'any Soviet attempt to make Cuba a satellite would be resisted by Cuba to the last man'.[28] While the Havana regime valued Soviet patronage greatly, there were limits to how far it was willing to conform to Moscow's wishes.

## Planning to Overthrow Castro

Meanwhile, the White House had decided to try to bring down Castro. There were precedents for this, with CIA-facilitated 'regime changes' in Iran in 1953 and in Guatemala the following year. With the goal of replacing the Havana regime 'with one more devoted to the true interests of the Cuban people and more acceptable to the US', the CIA created a task force under Deputy Director for Plans Richard Bissell, and established a body known as the 5412 Committee – named after a NSC directive – to supervise the operation. Members included officials from the NSC, the State Department, the Pentagon and the CIA.[29] In April 1960, Bissell's task force produced a policy paper entitled 'A Program of Covert Action against the Castro Regime'. The paper recommended creating a force of Cuban exiles 'to organize, train, and lead resistance forces' in Cuba. The planning against Castro

('Operation Pluto') continued during the summer and autumn of 1960, but operational difficulties led Bissell's team to move from guerrilla infiltration towards a paramilitary invasion. The CIA now planned to use men training in Guatemala to conduct an amphibious landing in Cuba, secure a beachhead, and then establish a provisional government.[30]

In the 1960 election campaign, Democratic candidate John F. Kennedy urged a more vigorous waging of the Cold War, accusing the Republicans of neglecting American national security and allowing American international prestige to slip. He maintained that the Soviet arms build-up since the launch of the Sputnik satellite in 1957 and Eisenhower's reluctance to invest in the US defence effort had created a substantial 'missile gap' in favour of the Soviet Union. Although Eisenhower was rightly convinced that in fact the United States was in the lead, intelligence specialists were divided on the issue. Confidential White House briefings did not dispel Kennedy's sincere but politically expedient belief that it was the Soviet Union that was ahead.[31] Kennedy contended too that Moscow was outpacing the United States in the contest for influence in Asia and Africa. He had at first looked favourably upon Castro's overthrow of Batista, given the venality of the regime, but he grew concerned about Castro's links with communism.[32] In October, Kennedy's campaign staff suggested that he favoured unilateral intervention in Cuba. Republican contender Richard Nixon publicly rejected the idea. He was well informed about the CIA's plans for an attack, but had to keep the knowledge to himself. Following Kennedy's election victory in November, Eisenhower, Allen Dulles and Richard Bissell discussed the plans with the President-elect; Eisenhower wanted Kennedy to support the established Cuba policies.[33] After Kennedy endorsed Operation Pluto, plotting not only continued but did so with greater intensity.[34] He believed that the CIA had a vital role in neutralising the communist challenge in the developing world.[35] This is shown by how the Kennedy administration initiated 163 major CIA covert actions in less than three years, compared with 170 by President Eisenhower in eight years.[36]

Kennedy's famous inaugural address of 26 January 1961, with its declaration that the United States would 'pay any price, bear any burden, meet any hardship, oppose any foe to assure the survival and success of liberty', set the tone for a more resolute and activist foreign policy. In particular, it replied to Khrushchev's recent declaration of support for 'national liberation' warfare in the colonial and post-colonial world. Algeria, the Congo and Laos were Khrushchev's focus, while politically the declaration was – according to the CIA – 'intended in part to meet Chinese criticisms . . . that the USSR was in fact ruling out the use of force altogether in advancing the Communist cause'.[37] Nonetheless, Kennedy took the speech as a general challenge to the United States in the poorer parts of the world. One of the concerns after the revolution in Cuba was that communism would gain ground in other parts of Latin America. The region was, in the words of an official analysis, 'in a state of deep unrest. Most of its countries are economically undeveloped and socially backward. The distribution of land and other forms of national wealth greatly favours the propertied classes.'[38]

In March, the administration announced the Alliance for Progress, an organisation established to promote multi-billion dollar development in Latin America. The Alliance reflected Kennedy's sincere desire to help people in the region, which for him was entangled with the goal of preventing the spread of communism.[39] The youthful and dynamic figures of Castro and Kennedy – charismatic representatives of different 'new frontiers' – were competing for the same audiences, albeit with conflicting political visions. The Alliance for Progress achieved some success, at least in the short term. In the year after its launch, it facilitated improved tax administration, education programmes, agrarian reform and development planning.[40] Throughout the 1960s, though, economic growth for most Latin American economies was limited to about 2 per cent a year, and the organisation failed to reach any of its ninety-four statistical goals in health, education and welfare. In part, the Alliance ran adrift because the preoccupation with Castro led the US government to bolster elites who preferred to preserve the status quo rather than try to improve the quality of life for the masses.[41]

## The Bay of Pigs

Castro's revolutionary colleague Che Guevara commented on 14 April that the 'internal counterrevolution' had intensified to include damage to the Havana water system and power station and the destruction of several warehouses and a large store. The latter succumbed to 'special thermal bombs', a surviving one of which had a US Army stamp. Guevara suggested that, like its predecessor, the Kennedy administration sought to 'create the conditions for an internal explosion'.[42] The US role in the events about which Guevara complained is not very clear; there were independent counter-revolutionary groups within Cuba, as well as groups outside, that launched their own operations.[43] The US government did little to rein *them* in, and in some cases probably provided active support.

In the meantime, Operation Pluto faced difficulties. The CIA did not trust the exile force (fearing correctly that it had been infiltrated by Cuban intelligence), while key parts of the US government – including the US Embassy in Havana, CIA analysts, elements of the State Department, and the commander of the US Navy's Atlantic Fleet – had no role in the planning.[44] Some key officials harboured serious doubts. Presidential adviser Arthur Schlesinger maintained that 'No matter how "Cuban" the equipment and personnel, the US will be held accountable for the operation, and our prestige will be committed to its success'.[45] Under Secretary of State Chester Bowles believed that 'our national interests are poorly served by a covert operation of this kind at a time when our new President is effectively appealing to world opinion on the basis of high principle'.[46] Secretary of State Dean Rusk feared the consequences of military action against Cuba in the United Nations and in Latin America,[47] although he was reticent about conveying his reservations. He did not have a close relationship with Kennedy, and felt that his role was largely to execute rather than question presidential policies (he would be a much more effective presence in the ExComm discussions in October 1962). J. William Fulbright, head of the Senate Foreign Relations Committee, told Kennedy of the proposed invasion that 'To give this activity even covert support is of a piece with the hypocrisy and cynicism for which the United States is constantly denouncing the Soviet Union.'[48]

By contrast, Allen Dulles remained buoyant, asserting that there was an even better chance of success than there had been in Guatemala in 1954, with the overthrow of Jacobo Arbenz Guzman. When President Kennedy expressed reservations, Dulles speculated about what would happen to the thousand or more Cubans that the CIA had been training for months. They might, Dulles contended, end up wandering the hemisphere, complaining that the United States had lost its nerve. He intimated too that it would damage Kennedy politically if he cancelled an operation initiated by President Eisenhower, who had orchestrated the D-Day invasion of 1944.[49] Richard Bissell also played an important role in persuading Kennedy to proceed with the invasion.[50] Driven by the momentum, captured by his anti-Castro rhetoric during the 1960 campaign, and lacking the self-assurance to call a halt, Kennedy grew increasingly on edge. He told his advisers on 12 April that 'The minute I land one Marine, we're in this thing up to our necks. I can't get the United States into a war and lose it, no matter what it takes. I'm not going to risk an American Hungary. And that's what it could be, a fucking slaughter.'[51]

Instead of following his instinct and cancelling the operation, the President ordered steps to reduce the US role and so conceal the American hand. Cuban exiles would no longer land at the town of Trinidad as had been planned, but at the more sparsely populated and less prominent Bay of Pigs (Bahia de Cochinos, near the village of Playa Giron). 'Operation Pluto' had now become 'Operation Zapata', the name change reflecting the proximity of the Bay of Pigs to the Zapata Swamp. It was thought that the invaders could use the swamp area to adopt guerrilla tactics if they proved unable to establish a beachhead. Now, with Kennedy's operational changes, US naval vessels would be away from the landing area by dawn, and air support reduced.

As with all major 'covert' actions, maintaining secrecy posed a serious challenge. Since the end of 1960 Havana had gained a very strong sense of what was afoot, and in April 1961 Cuban intelligence noted that there was an American plan 'to overthrow the government of Cuba' by 'launching an invasion on a grand scale using mercenaries'.[52] Che Guevara thought that the new President was personally responsible for exposés in 'the Democrats' press' about 'the training of the Cuban counterrevolutionaries by the Eisenhower government . . . for an attack on Cuba', and that this meant that he 'does not want to associate himself with this kind of operations [sic]'. In fact, Kennedy had nothing to do with the press revelations, which meant that he had an opportunity to cancel the invasion in the light of how security had been compromised.[53] He declined that opportunity, while Guevara appeared not to appreciate that unauthorised leaks were a perennial problem for any US administration, and that American newspapers had their own agendas.

Almost every day until the invasion Fidel Castro spoke of the coming 'mercenaries' and exhorted the Cuban people to prepare for war,[54] while Guevara noted that even if an attack did take place the presence of 'large contingents of well-armed people's militia and the revolutionary army' meant that 'an operation of deploying paratroopers, even numbering several thousands [of] troops would be doomed to failure'.[55] In fact, there were only around 1,300 invaders, landing at the Bay of Pigs on 17 April. The attack did not go well. National Security Adviser McGeorge Bundy reported with telling understatement the following day that 'the situation . . . is not a bit good'. The defenders were a 'formidable enemy' possessing 'military know-how and vigor'.[56]

Arthur Schlesinger has argued that Richard Bissell had accepted Kennedy's modifications to Operation Zapata on the assumption that if the operation did not go to plan then the President would concede an expanded US role and would send the Marines. If that was Bissell's perception, then he had misjudged, given that strengthening the American role held no appeal at all for the President. He considered the test of the operation as being whether or not the people of Cuba would rise up against Castro, but it is clear that the Cuban leader was too widely supported.[57] Proportionately, the defenders suffered greater casualties, but the attackers were beaten within three days of the landing, with 114 killed and 1,189 captured. US officials were lost and bewildered at the rapid collapse of the operation. Chief of Naval Operations Admiral Arleigh Burke lamented that 'No-one knew what to do.'[58] Despite Kennedy's wishes, the American role in the botched invasion was abundantly clear, with Khrushchev complaining on 18 April that the 'armed bands invading [Cuba] were trained, equipped and armed in the United States of America'. He demanded an immediate end to the aggression.[59]

Fidel Castro cursed the 'miserable gringo imperialists' and 'millionaire parasites' in the United States who had 'organised the attack, planned the attack, trained the mercenaries, supplied the planes, supplied the bombs, prepared the airports – everyone knows it.' He described some of the invaders in bitter, class-conscious language: '194 ex-military personnel and henchmen; 100 owners of large landed estates; 24 large property owners; 67 landlords of buildings; 112 large merchants; 179 idle rich; 35 industrial capitalists; and 112 lumpens'.[60] After enduring rough conditions in captivity, the prisoners were freed in December 1962 in return for a large quantity of food and medical provisions.[61]

The failed invasion traumatised the administration. Chester Bowles noted that at an NSC meeting on 22 April, Attorney General Robert F. Kennedy 'took the lead ... slamming into anyone who suggested that we go slowly and try to move calmly and not repeat previous mistakes'.[62] Various internal inquests each made for tough reading. Colonel Jack Hawkins, Chief of the Paramilitary Staff of the CIA, blamed the politicians, believing that the effort to conceal US involvement had compromised the operation. In 'a cold war paramilitary operation' there was 'a basic conflict of interest between considerations of military effectiveness on the one hand and political considerations on the other'. Political restrictions were liable to damage military operations. Now the regime in Cuba was so 'firmly entrenched' it could not be overthrown by anything short of the 'overt application ... of United States military power'.[63] General Maxwell Taylor's Cuba Study Group reached similar conclusions.[64] Inspector General of the CIA Lyman Kirkpatrick maintained that there was a failure 'to appraise the chances of success realistically' and that 'an overt military operation' was beyond the CIA's capacities. Other CIA staffers would have none of this. Deputy DCI General Charles P. Cabell suggested that the Inspector-General's report 'misses objectivity by a wide margin. It ... presents a picture of unmitigated and almost wilful bumbling and disaster'.[65] Yet there was no avoiding the fact that Operation Zapata had been a profound setback for the US government – and above all for John F. Kennedy, just when he was finding his feet in the Oval Office. While the CIA and the military deserved some of the blame for what went on, his efforts to disguise American involvement had compounded existing flaws in planning.

Chester Bowles commented on 20 April that 'the President was really quite shattered . . . Here for the first time he faced a situation where his judgment had been mistaken.'[66] While privately he blamed himself for being 'stupid', Kennedy also condemned the CIA. Schlesinger recorded that 'The President said he could not understand how men like Dulles and Bissell, so intelligent and so experienced, could have been so wrong.'[67] Dulles and Bissell soon resigned, the public 'fall guys'. Kennedy felt too that the Joint Chiefs of Staff had played their part, by failing to press their reservations about the merits of the Bay of Pigs as a landing site.[68] At a press conference on 21 April, in which he covered a wide range of issues, the President stonewalled questions about the failure in Cuba, but he did admit that 'There's an old saying that victory has a hundred fathers and defeat is an orphan . . . I am the responsible officer of this government.'[69] This expression of personal responsibility demonstrated growing maturity. The Bay of Pigs was a bitter education, teaching the President a great deal about leadership and, in particular, about the judgement of military and intelligence officials. He realised beyond doubt that his advisers were entirely fallible and that there were occasions when it was better to make up one's mind more independently.

The US attack on Cuba horrified Nikita Khrushchev, but he admired how Kennedy took responsibility for what happened. He contrasted Kennedy's attitude with Eisenhower's refusal in 1960 to apologise for the overflight of the Soviet Union by Gary Powers in his U-2.[70] Despite his differences with the US government, Fidel Castro acknowledged that Kennedy had demonstrated strength of character by refusing to order the participation of US squadrons and troops, and, in common with Khrushchev, he respected how Kennedy had taken responsibility.[71] Nonetheless, Castro and his colleagues exploited the propaganda value of the invasion to the utmost, cracking down on the internal opposition and exalting the Soviet Union.[72] By the same token, the Bay of Pigs invasion tarnished the international standing of the US government. The CIA had briefed US Permanent Representative to the UN Adlai Stevenson about the attack, but only partially,[73] and had equipped him with photographs of a B-26 aircraft that the CIA had mocked up to look like a Cuban Air Force plane that had landed in Miami. The deception was intended to give the impression that the US government had nothing to do with the invasion, by making people think that the pilot had defected from the Cuban Air Force and, like others, had bombed his own airfields before escaping to the United States.[74] It seems that few were fooled. Patrick Dean, the British Permanent Representative to the UN, outlined a dramatic scene:

> Mr Stevenson was somewhat overwhelmed by the ferocity of attacks by Dr Roa [the Cuban representative] and his supporters, who scoffed at his assurances that the United States had committed no aggression against Cuba and that 'no offensive has been launched from Florida or from any part of the United States'. Had the invaders come from outer space, enquired Mr [Valerian] Zorin [of the Soviet Union]. To *his* knowledge, he went on amid satellite cheers, only one man had come from there, namely Major Gagarin.[75]

Stevenson complained to Rusk and Dulles that it was impossible to understand 'how we could let' an attack on Cuba 'take place two days before [a] debate on [the] Cuban issue' in the General Assembly.[76] Stevenson's colleagues in Washington had left him out on a limb, which Zorin had promptly sawn off.

For Arthur Schlesinger, the Bay of Pigs episode meant that 'We not only look like imperialists; we look like ineffectual imperialists; which is worse; and we look like stupid, ineffectual imperialists, which is worst of all.'[77] He noted when he visited Italy, France and the United Kingdom soon after the failed attack that there was 'a hunger for a rational explanation ... They could not believe that the US Government had been quite so incompetent, irresponsible and stupid as the bare facts of the operation suggested.' Washington was 'self-righteous' and 'trigger-happy', but goodwill towards the Kennedy administration had not evaporated completely: 'we have suffered a serious but by no means fatal loss of confidence in our intelligence and responsibility'.[78] Dean Rusk suggested a week later that European confidence in American leadership remained undiminished.[79] Allies were willing to give Kennedy the benefit of the doubt, not least because he was still finding his way. They believed correctly that the Bay of Pigs lesson would be a salutary one.

## Vienna and Berlin

Kennedy met Khrushchev in Vienna in June so that they could discuss Cold War issues and get the measure of one another. It was the first Soviet–American summit for two years, as a proposed Eisenhower–Khrushchev meeting in Paris in 1960 had collapsed amidst acrimony over the capture of Gary Powers. Khrushchev raised the issue of Cuba, asserting quite accurately that 'Castro is not a communist but US policy can make him one.' Kennedy admitted that the Bay of Pigs had been a mistake, but emphasised that Cuba posed a subversive threat to American interests.[80] Khrushchev mocked the suggestion that Cuba, a fraction of the size of the United States, could pose a threat. However, the question of Berlin dominated the discussions. Since the Second World War the Soviet Union and the Western allies had been unable to agree on Germany's future, so the country ended up divided between the Western-oriented Federal Republic of Germany (FRG; West Germany) and the communist German Democratic Republic (GDR; East Germany). Berlin, situated in the GDR, was also partitioned, with the western portion of the city providing a convenient exit route for thousands of East Germans seeking new lives in the more prosperous West. This was politically and economically costly to the communist authorities. At Vienna, Khrushchev renewed a threat he had first announced in 1958: to sign a treaty with the GDR that would bring the city under East German rule. The United States and its fellow occupying powers, Britain and France, would have to negotiate with the GDR to maintain access to Berlin, thus conferring diplomatic recognition on the East German regime and perpetuating the division of Germany. The GDR would not tolerate a Western presence on its territory, so the days of an Allied presence in Berlin would be numbered, at least without the using force. Kennedy had no desire to compromise the Western position, in part due to fear of being seen as weak. The President told Khrushchev that West Berlin was 'a symbol for Americans and . . . if we gave up our rights in Berlin we would be impeached by the American people'. However, the Soviet leader appeared to be in no mood for compromise, replying that 'If the US wants war over Germany let it be so'. The President concluded that 'it would be a cold winter'.[81]

Khrushchev recorded that at their last meeting Kennedy had been 'very gloomy. He was not just preoccupied but actually glum.'[82] The President, still shaken from the debacle in April, is said to have confided to the journalist James Reston that the summit had been 'the roughest thing in my life . . . [Khrushchev] thinks because of the Bay of Pigs that I'm inexperienced. Probably thinks I'm stupid. Maybe most important, he thinks that I had no guts.'[83] The Vienna conference gained notoriety in the United States, as indicated by a 1968 conversation between Secretary of Defense Clark Clifford and Dean Rusk:

> Clifford: . . . I think that President Kennedy's meeting in Vienna with Khrushchev was a calamity.
> Rusk: It was.
> Clifford: Boy, it was a real zero from President Kennedy's standpoint.[84]

The conference initiated a particularly tense phase of the Cold War, from the renewal of the Berlin crisis to the confrontation over the missiles in Cuba. However, recent historiography has tended to see the summit as far less calamitous and confrontational than it appeared at the time. The meeting facilitated progress on the diplomatic issue of Laos, which was neutralised the following year,[85] and the President conveyed American resolve in relation to Berlin. Although the conference had moments of acrimony, Kennedy and Khrushchev engaged abundantly in small talk and gained a better sense of one another as human beings.[86] Contrary to what Kennedy himself thought, Khrushchev left

Vienna with a favourable view of him. According to his memoirs, the Soviet leader respected how Kennedy had

> obviously studied all the questions we were likely to exchange views on, and he had absolutely full command of the material. This was not by any means what I had observed in the case of Eisenhower. This spoke in Kennedy's favor, of course, and in my eyes he grew in stature. Here was a counterpart to whom I could relate with enormous respect, even though we held completely different positions and in fact were adversaries. I valued his qualities.[87]

Obviously, Khrushchev was writing for posterity about a revered president, but Kennedy was indeed well-prepared at Vienna and, whatever his own misgivings, acquitted himself with calm professionalism. Nonetheless, this did not stop Khrushchev from renewing the pressure over Berlin. The US government feared that the Soviet Union would blockade access to West Berlin, as it had in 1948–9, or would even attack Western forces in the city. In a public address on 25 July Kennedy emphasised his determination to defend West Berlin, asking Congress for a $3.25 billion increase in military spending, and announcing the mobilisation of reservists and the provision of funding for a civil defence programme. Kennedy's measures, especially the civil defence preparations, were alarming but reflected his genuine fear of war.[88] He might, in fact, have gone further by accepting the counsel of former Secretary of State Dean Acheson to declare a state of national emergency.[89]

Recent research has suggested that the emigration problem was far more of an influence on Khrushchev than Kennedy's 25 July speech and the US defence build-up. His son Sergei has suggested that 'the salvo [Kennedy's speech] was fired in vain', since the Soviet leader had no real intention of signing a separate peace treaty with the GDR.[90] On the night of 13 August, the East German and Soviet authorities constructed a heavily guarded barrier around West Berlin, leaving just a few crossing points. The construction of the barrier – which would develop into the infamous Wall – had, however inelegantly, settled the issue of emigration at a stroke. Although advisers such as Dean Acheson pushed for a military response, the Bay of Pigs had taught Kennedy about the dangers of ill-conceived military action. He took the view that 'a wall is a lot better than a war', and quietly relinquished the longstanding assumption that the Western powers had the right of access to all of Berlin.[91]

Yet there remained scope for confrontation. A local dispute over access for an American diplomat and his wife to East Berlin escalated so that by 27 October American and Soviet tanks were poised 'eyeball-to-eyeball' at Checkpoint Charlie in the Friedrichstrasse. This was the first time that American and Soviet tanks had ever confronted one another. Seeking to avoid both escalation and a public climb-down, President Kennedy asked his brother Robert – who had emerged as the chief foreign policy adviser after the Bay of Pigs – to contact Moscow secretly through a contact at the Soviet embassy, press counsellor and intelligence official Georgi Bolshakov. RFK reported that 'the President would like them to take their tanks out of there in twenty-four hours'.[92] Khrushchev agreed, and the tanks withdrew. This 'back-channel' method of crisis resolution set a precedent for ending the missile crisis a year later.

## Operation Mongoose

There is evidence that Castro sought to improve his relationship with the United States as 1961 progressed,[93] but President Kennedy and his brother were not willing to compromise. When it had become clear that the Bay of Pigs operation was failing, Robert F. Kennedy had told JFK that 'The time has come for a showdown' with Cuba, 'for in a year or two the situation will be vastly worse'.[94] The Kennedy brothers considered that communism in the Western Hemisphere threatened US security, undermined US policies elsewhere and threatened to become an increasingly divisive issue in US domestic politics.[95] They believed, therefore, that the national interest, along with personal self-interest, demanded Castro's removal.

After Kennedy announced the end of US purchases of Cuban sugar, the Cuban leader declared that 'I am a Marxist–Leninist and I will continue to be a Marxist–Leninist until the last day of my life.'[96] It might be assumed that Moscow would relish this expression of ideological fraternity, but Soviet intelligence considered that the speech 'proceeded without sufficient preparation of the labouring classes, thus intensifying the class struggle in Cuba'. It alienated 'a significant portion of the petit bourgeoisie, the intelligentsia, the backward portions of the working class, and the peasantry, and also a series of Castro's revolutionary fighters, who were not ideologically ready for these changes'.[97] Despite their reservations, the Soviets showed no signs of shying away from the regime in Havana, for doing so would end an unprecedented opportunity to gain ground in the Western Hemisphere. According to Roger Hilsman of the State Department's Intelligence and Research Bureau, the Soviets had long sought 'to penetrate Latin America, because of that region's great strategic importance vis-à-vis the United States'.[98] There was enthusiasm that socialism was advancing peacefully, with Anastas Mikoyan telling Dean Rusk that 'You Americans must understand what Cuba means to us old Bolsheviks. We have been waiting all our lives for a country to go Communist without the Red Army, and it happened in Cuba. It makes us feel like boys again!'[99]

Although the US administration condemned Cuban subversion, there was no inhibition about trying to subvert the regime in Havana. On 3 November 1961, after delays caused by the preoccupation with Berlin, President Kennedy authorised a programme of covert action codenamed 'Operation Mongoose'. RFK was the prime mover. He conceived the programme as an effort to 'stir things up on the island with espionage, sabotage, general disorder, run & operated by Cubans themselves with every group but Batista-ites & Communists'. General Edward Lansdale, a veteran of covert activities in the Philippines and Vietnam, was made responsible for planning Mongoose. He sought to have 'the people themselves overthrow the Castro regime rather than US engineered efforts from outside Cuba'.[100]

A new body, the Special Group (Augmented), was established to control the Mongoose operation. Alongside Robert F. Kennedy, McGeorge Bundy and Maxwell Taylor, there were the following officials: Deputy Under Secretary of State for Political Affairs U.

Alexis Johnson, Deputy Secretary of Defense Roswell Gilpatric, Directory of Central Intelligence John McCone, and Chairman of the Joint Chiefs of Staff General Lyman Lemnitzer. Dean Rusk and Secretary of Defense Robert McNamara occasionally attended meetings. The CIA developed an operational force of around 400 people at its headquarters and at its Miami station.[101] The Miami station became the CIA's largest outpost in the world, and Mongoose burgeoned into the biggest postwar US covert operation yet undertaken.[102] The programme had its problems, though. It sought to foment a popular revolution, but this objective may have been conceived more in hope than confidence. Roger Hilsman saw 'no hard intelligence' of 'an internal political organization which would assure the support of the majority of the Cuban people against the Castro regime'.[103] A CIA analysis suggested that 'The regime's apparatus for surveillance and repression should be able to cope with any popular tendency toward active resistance.'[104] Arthur Schlesinger feared that the Cubans were being encouraged to take 'rash action'.[105] Operation Mongoose proved haphazard and inefficient. Robert F. Kennedy complained shortly before the discovery of the Soviet missiles in Cuba that the programme 'had been underway for a year, that the results were discouraging, that there had been no acts of sabotage, and even the one which had been attempted failed twice'.[106] The operation was sidelined during the missile crisis, and ended soon after.

## Murder Inc.

This darker side of American foreign policy in the Kennedy years included assassination efforts as well as sabotage and subversion. The CIA targeted Patrice Lumumba of the Congo and Rafael Trujillo of the Dominican Republic. Castro was also on the death list. Beginning in August 1960, the CIA worked with mobsters Sam Giancana of Chicago and John Rosselli from Los Angeles, both of whom had lost out when Castro took over in Cuba. The CIA agreed to pay $150,000 to Castro's killer. According to one official, the operation ended after the Bay of Pigs attack. However, an Agency report in 1967 noted that the 'CIA twice (first in early 1961 and again in early 1962) supplied lethal pills to US gambling syndicate members working on behalf of CIA in a plot to assassinate Fidel Castro'. Other efforts to kill him involved, farcically, exploding cigars, poison pens and wetsuits.[107] There is 'circumstantial evidence' that President Eisenhower knew of the plot to kill Castro,[108] but it is not clear whether or not he suggested assassination in the first place. As for John F. Kennedy, White House speechwriter Theodore Sorensen told the Senate during hearings in 1975 that while the CIA 'could somehow have been under the impression that they had a tacit authorization' to kill Castro, the idea of assassination was 'totally foreign' to Kennedy's 'character and conscience, foreign to his fundamental reverence for human life and his respect for his adversaries, foreign to his insistence upon a moral dimension in US foreign policy and his concern for this country's reputation abroad'.[109] In reality, it is very likely that Kennedy was no innocent. Richard Helms, DCI 1964–9, suggested that although there was 'nothing on paper' confirming that the President wanted Castro dead, 'there is certainly no question in my mind that he did'.[110]

It is very likely that President Kennedy knew broadly what was going on, but he appears to have been ambivalent about the idea of assassinating the Cuban leader. In November 1961, he asked Tad Szulc of the *New York Times*, 'What would you think if I ordered Castro to be assassinated?' Szulc replied that he thought it would be a terrible idea – to which Kennedy responded, 'I'm glad you feel the same way.'[111] Morality aside, Kennedy may have realised that murdering Castro might not have achieved much. CIA analyst Sherman Kent wrote in November 1961 that the death of the Cuban leader by assassination or by natural causes would have only a limited impact, because 'the regime has firm control of the country' and its 'principal surviving leaders would probably rally together in the face of the common danger'. Furthermore, 'a dead Castro, incapable of impulsive personal interventions in the orderly administration of affairs, might be more valuable to them as a martyr than he is now'.[112] Kennedy had misgivings about killing Castro, but it is telling that there is no record of him demanding an end to the efforts. What did

Castro know of the plotting against him? In 1978, he told a delegation from the House assassinations committee that 'For three years [until Kennedy's assassination] we had known there were plots against us.'[113] He knew that the United States was trying to bring down his regime, but he may not have known of the assassination efforts in particular, given the small number of individuals involved. All the same, Castro surely realised that if his regime was overthrown then his days would be numbered. Whether he was murdered while in power or soon after, it would make little difference.

## Notes

1. For US relations with Latin America and with Cuba, see Ernest R. May, *The Making of the Monroe Doctrine* (Cambridge, MA: Belknap Press, 1975); Lars Schoultz, *That Infernal Little Cuban Republic: The United States and the Cuban Revolution* (Chapel Hill, NC: University of North Carolina Press, 2009); Jay Sexton, *The Monroe Doctrine: Empire and Nation in Nineteenth-Century America* (New York: Hill and Wang, 2011); Gaddis Smith, *The Last Years of the Monroe Doctrine, 1945–1993* (New York: Hill and Wang, 1994).
2. Rubottom to Secretary of State, 17 January 1958, *Foreign Relations of the United States (FRUS) 1958–60 VI Cuba* (Washington, DC: USGPO, 1991), document 6, <https://history.state.gov/historical documents/frus1958-60v06> (last accessed 25 July 2015).
3. Alex von Tunzelmann, *Red Heat: Conspiracy, Murder, and Cold War in the Caribbean* (London and New York: Simon and Schuster, 2011), p. 156.
4. British Embassy Havana, annual review of Cuba for 1959, 20 January 1960, FO 371/148178, The National Archives, Kew, England (TNA).
5. Ibid.
6. Schoultz, *That Infernal Little Cuban Republic*, p. 54.
7. Ambassador in Cuba to the Secretary of State, 13 September 1957, *FRUS 1955–1957 VI American Republics, Multilateral; Mexico; Caribbean* (1987), document 294, <https://history.state.gov/historicaldocuments/frus1955-57v06/d294> (last accessed 25 July 2015).

8. Deputy Director of Intelligence and Research (Arneson) to the Secretary of State, 12 April 1958, *FRUS 1958–1960 Cuba* (1991), document 47, <https://history.state.gov/historicaldocuments/frus1958-60v06/d47> (last accessed 25 July 2015).

9. Embassy in Cuba to State Department, 9 January 1959, *FRUS 1958–1960 VI*, document 220, <https://history.state.gov/historicaldocuments/frus1958-60v06/d220> (last accessed 25 July 2015).

10. State Department to Embassy in Cuba, 22 April 1959, *FRUS 1958–1960 VI*, document 291, <https://history.state.gov/historicaldocuments/frus1958-60v06/d291> (last accessed 25 July 2015).

11. Ernesto R. Betancourt, 'Kennedy, Khrushchev, and Castro: A Participant's View of the Cuban Missile Crisis', *Society*, 35: 5, July–August 1998, p. 78.

12. Ibid. p. 79.

13. Schoultz, *That Infernal Little Cuban Republic*, p. 92.

14. Editorial note, *FRUS 1958–1960 VI*, <https://history.state.gov/historicaldocuments/frus1958-60v06/d287> (last accessed 25 July 2015).

15. William M. LeoGrande and Peter Kornbluh, *Back Channel to Cuba: The Hidden History of Negotiations between Washington and Havana* (Chapel Hill: University of North Carolina Press, 2014), p. 18.

16. James G. Blight, Bruce J. Allyn and David A. Welch (eds), with foreword by Jorge I. Dominguez, *Cuba on the Brink: Castro, the Missile Crisis, and the Soviet Collapse* (New York: Pantheon, 1993), p. 178.

17. Betancourt, 'Kennedy, Khrushchev, and Castro', p. 70.

18. Ibid. p. 79.

19. NSC meeting, 18 February 1960, *FRUS 1958–1960 VI*, document 456, <https://history.state.gov/historicaldocuments/frus1958-60v06/d456> (last accessed 25 July 2015).

20. NSC meeting, 29 December 1960, *FRUS 1958–1960 VI*, document 626, <https://history.state.gov/historicaldocuments/frus1958-60v06/d626> (last accessed 25 July 2015).

21. NSC paper, 'Cuba and Communism in the Hemisphere', 4 May 1961, *FRUS 1961–1963 X Cuba, January 1961–September 1962* (1997), document 202, <https://history.state.gov/historicaldocuments/frus1961-63v10/d202> (last accessed 25 July 2015).

22. Jim Rasenberger, *The Brilliant Disaster: JFK, Castro, and*

America's Doomed Invasion of Cuba's Bay of Pigs (New York: Scribner, 2011), pp. 76–7; Schoultz, That Infernal Little Cuban Republic, p. 140.

23. Embassy Cuba to State Department, 16 December 1960, FRUS 1958–1960 VI, document 623, <https://history.state.gov/historicaldocuments/frus1958-60v06/d623> (last accessed 25 July 2015).

24. Christopher Hull, 'Parallel Spheres: Anglo-American Cooperation over Cuba, 1959–61', Cold War History, 12: 1, February 2012, p. 63.

25. Ibid. p. 61.

26. Sergo Mikoyan, The Soviet Cuban Missile Crisis: Castro, Mikoyan, Kennedy, Khrushchev and the Missiles of November, edited by Svetlana Savranskaya (Stanford, CA: Stanford University Press, 2012), p. 57. Izvestiya was the newspaper expressing the official views of the Soviet government.

27. Michael M. Dobbs, One Minute to Midnight: Kennedy, Khrushchev and Castro on the Brink of Nuclear War (New York: Knopf, 2008), p. 149.

28. NSC meeting, 15 July 1960, FRUS 1958–1960 VI, document 558, <https://history.state.gov/historicaldocuments/frus1958-60v06/d558> (last accessed 25 July 2015).

29. 5412 Committee paper, 16 March 1960, FRUS 1958–1960 VI, document 481, <https://history.state.gov/historicaldocuments/frus1958-60v06/d481> (last accessed 25 July 2015).

30. Rebecca R. Friedman, 'Crisis Management at the Dead Center: The 1960–1961 Presidential Transition and the Bay of Pigs Fiasco', Presidential Studies Quarterly, 41: 2, June 2011, pp. 311–12.

31. Christopher A. Preble, 'Who Ever Believed in the "Missile Gap"? John F. Kennedy and the Politics of National Security', Presidential Studies Quarterly, 33: 4, December 2003, pp. 813–15.

32. Arthur Schlesinger, Jr., Journals 1952–2000 (London: Atlantic, 2007), p. 596.

33. Meeting with the President, 29 November 1960, FRUS 1958–1960 VI, document 613, <https://history.state.gov/historicaldocuments/frus1958-60v06/d613> (last accessed 25 July 2015).

34. Friedman, 'Crisis Management at the Dead Center', pp. 311–12.

35. Mark White, Kennedy: A Cultural History of an American Icon (London: Bloomsbury, 2013), pp. 58–68.

36. Tim Weiner, Legacy of Ashes: The History of the CIA (London: Penguin, 2007), p. 207.

37. National Intelligence Estimate, 2 May 1962, *FRUS 1961–1963 V Soviet Union* (1998), document 187, <https://history.state.gov/historicaldocuments/frus1961-63v05/d187> (last accessed 25 July 2015).

38. US policy towards Latin America, 3 July 1961, *FRUS 1961–1963 XII American Republics* (1996), document 15, <https://history.state.gov/historicaldocuments/frus1961-63v12/d15> (last accessed 25 July 2015).

39. Goodwin to Bundy, 26 April 1961, *FRUS 1961–1963 X Cuba, January 1961–September 1962* (1997), document 179, <https://history.state.gov/historicaldocuments/frus1961-63v10/d179> (last accessed 25 July 2015).

40. Turnage to Martin, 29 November 1962, *FRUS 1961–1963*, document 251, <https://history.state.gov/historicaldocuments/frus1961-63v12/d51> (last accessed 25 July 2015).

41. Stephen G. Rabe, *John F. Kennedy: World Leader* (Washington, DC: Potomac Books, 2010), p. 82; Stephen G. Rabe, *The Most Dangerous Area in the World: John F. Kennedy Confronts Communist Revolution in Latin America* (Chapel Hill: University of North Carolina Press, 1999), pp. 148–72, 196–7.

42. Conversation between Kudryavtsev and Guevara, 14 April 1961, *Cold War International History Project Bulletin*, 17/18, Fall 2012, pp. 162–3, <http://www.wilsoncenter.org/publication/bulletin-no-17-18> (last accessed 25 July 2015).

43. James G. Blight and Philip Brenner, *Sad and Luminous Days: Cuba's Struggle with the Superpowers after the Missile Crisis* (Lanham, MD: Rowman and Littlefield, 2002), p. 12.

44. Michael Dunne, 'Perfect Failure: The USA, Cuba and the Bay of Pigs, 1961', *The Political Quarterly*, 82: 3, July–September 2011, p. 453.

45. Schlesinger to Kennedy, 5 April 1961, *FRUS 1961–1963 V*, document 81, <https://history.state.gov/historicaldocuments/frus1961-63v10/d81> (last accessed 25 July 2015).

46. Bowles to Rusk, 31 March 1961, *FRUS 1961–1963 V*, document 75, <https://history.state.gov/historicaldocuments/frus1961-63v10/d75> (last accessed 25 July 2015).

47. Bundy to Kennedy, 8 February 1961, *FRUS 1961–1963 X*, document 39, <https://history.state.gov/historicaldocuments/frus1961-63v10/d39> (last accessed 25 July 2015).

48. Editorial note, *FRUS 1961–1963 X*, document 80, <https://history.state.gov/historicaldocuments/frus1961-63v10/d80> (last accessed

25 July 2015); Schoultz, *That Infernal Little Cuban Republic*, p. 153.

49. Arthur Schlesinger, Jr., 'Effective National Security Advising: A Most Dubious Precedent', *Political Science Quarterly*, 115: 3, Autumn 2000, pp. 347–51.

50. Schoultz, *That Infernal Little Cuban Republic*, p. 149.

51. Michael R. Beschloss, *The Crisis Years:* Kennedy and Khrushchev, 1960–1963 (New York: Harper Collins, 1991), p. 114.

52. Cuban G-2 (military intelligence), 'Report on Mercenary Camps and Bases in Guatemala, Nicaragua and Florida', 15 April 1961, *Cold War International History Project Bulletin*, 17/18, Fall 2012, pp. 169–80, <http://www.wilsoncenter.org/publication/bulletin-no-17-18> (last accessed 25 July 2015); Cuban Intelligence report, 15 April 1962, in ibid. pp. 181–6.

53. James G. Hershberg, 'Chatting with Che: Conversations in 1961 between Cuban Revolutionary Ernesto Guevara and the Soviet Ambassador in Havana – and a Brazilian Record of His Meeting in Punta del Este with JFK Aide Richard Goodwin', *Cold War International History Project Bulletin*, 17/18, Fall 2012, p. 158, <http://www.wilsoncenter.org/publication/bulletin-no-17-18> (last accessed 25 July 2015). See also LeoGrande and Kornbluh, *Back Channel*, pp. 44–7.

54. Rasenberger, *The Brilliant Disaster*, p. 171.

55. Conversation between Kudryavtsev and Guevara, 14 April 1961, *Cold War International History Project Bulletin*, 17/18, Fall 2012, pp. 162–3, <http://www.wilsoncenter.org/publication/bulletin-no-17-18> (last accessed 25 July 2015).

56. Bundy to Kennedy, 18 April 1961, *FRUS 1961–1963 X*, document 119, <https://history.state.gov/historicaldocuments/frus1961-63 v10/d119> (last accessed 25 July 2015).

57. James G. Blight and Peter Kornbluh (eds), *Politics of Illusion: The Bay of Pigs Invasion Reexamined* (Boulder, CO: Lynne Rienner, 1998), pp. 67–9.

58. Burke-Wilhide conversation, 18 April 1961, *FRUS 1961–1963 X*, document 121, <https://history.state.gov/historicaldocuments/frus 1961-63v10/d121> (last accessed 25 July 2015).

59. Khrushchev to Kennedy, 18 April 1961, *FRUS 1961–1963 V*, document 9, <https://history.state.gov/historicaldocuments/frus 1961-63v06/d9> (last accessed 25 July 2015).

60. Von Tunzelmann, *Red Heat*, pp. 241, 253–5.

61. See Thomas G. Smith, 'Negotiating with Fidel Castro: The Bay

of Pigs Prisoners and a Lost Opportunity', *Diplomatic History*, 19: 1, January 1995, pp. 59–86; LeoGrande and Kornbluh, *Back Channel*, pp. 47–50, 60–7.

62. NSC meeting, 22 April 1961, *FRUS 1961–1963 V*, document 166, <https://history.state.gov/historicaldocuments/frus1961-63v10/d166> (last accessed 25 July 2015).

63. A 'Record of Paramilitary Action Against the Castro Government of Cuba, 17 March 1960–May 1961', National Security Archive, George Washington University, <http://www2.gwu.edu/~nsarchiv/NSAEBB/NSAEBB353/> (last accessed 25 July 2015).

64. Cuba Study Group (Taylor) to Kennedy, 13 June 1961, *FRUS 1961–1963X*, document 233, <https://history.state.gov/historical documents/frus1961-63v10/d233> (last accessed 25 July 2015).

65. General C. P. Cabell, 'The Inspector-General's Report on the Cuban Operation', 15 December 1961, Central Intelligence Agency FOIA Electronic Reading Room, <http://www.foia.cia.gov/> (last accessed 25 July 2015).

66. Cabinet meeting, 20 April 1960, *FRUS 1961–1963 X*, document 158, <https://history.state.gov/historicaldocuments/frus1961-63v10/d158> (last accessed 25 July 2015).

67. Arthur M. Schlesinger, Jr., *A Thousand Days: John F. Kennedy in the White House* (New York: Houghton Mifflin, 1965), p. 290.

68. Memorandum for the record, 16 May 1961, *FRUS 1961–1963 X*, document 219, <https://history.state.gov/historicaldocuments/frus1961-63v10/d219> (last accessed 25 July 2015).

69. White, *Kennedy: A Cultural History*, p. 54; 'The President's News Conference', 21 April 1961, The American Presidency Project, <http://www.presidency.ucsb.edu/ws/?pid=8077> (last accessed 25 July 2015).

70. Richard Ned Lebow and Janice Gross Stein, *We All Lost the Cold War* (Princeton, NJ: Princeton University Press, 1994), p. 71.

71. Castro's remarks at the Havana conference, 11 January 1992, in Laurence S. Chang and Peter Kornbluh (eds), with foreword by Robert S. McNamara, *The Cuban Missile Crisis, 1962: A National Security Archive Documents Reader* (New York: The New Press, 1992).

72. Marchant to Home, 'Cuba: Annual Review for 1961', 11 January 1962, FO 371/162508, TNA [document 2, Appendix 4 in this volume].

73. Rasenberger, *The Brilliant Disaster*, p. 172; Weiner, *Legacy of Ashes*, p. 201.
74. William Ecker and Kenneth Jack, with introduction by Michael Dobbs, *Blue Moon over Cuba: Aerial Reconnaissance during the Cuban Missile Crisis* (Oxford: Osprey, 2012), p. 125.
75. Dean to Douglas-Home, 5 May 1961, FO 371/156183, TNA.
76. Mission in UN to Rusk and Dulles, 16 April 1961, *FRUS 1961–1963 X*, document 105, <https://history.state.gov/historicaldocuments/frus1961-63v10/d105> (last accessed 25 July 2015).
77. Schlesinger, *Journals*, p. 120.
78. Schlesinger to Kennedy, 3 May 1961, *FRUS 1961–1963 X*, document 96, <https://history.state.gov/historicaldocuments/frus1961-63v10/d196> (last accessed 25 July 2015).
79. Rusk to State Department, 10 May 1961, *FRUS 1961–1963 XIII Western Europe and Canada* (1994), document 104, <https://history.state.gov/historicaldocuments/frus1961-63v13/d104> (last accessed 25 July 2015).
80. Memorandum of conversation, 3 June 1961, *FRUS 1961–1963 V*, document 85, <https://history.state.gov/historicaldocuments/frus1961-63v05/d85> (last accessed 25 July 2015).
81. Memorandum of conversation, 4 June 1961, *FRUS 1961–1963 V*, document 89, <https://history.state.gov/historicaldocuments/frus1961-63v05/d89> (last accessed 25 July 2015); State Department paper, 12 June 1961, *FRUS 1961–1963 V*, document 95, <https://history.state.gov/historicaldocuments/frus1961-63v05/d95> (last accessed 25 July 2015); Memorandum of conversation, 26 June 1961, *FRUS 1961–1963 V*, document 102, <https://history.state.gov/historicaldocuments/frus1961-63v05/d102> (last accessed 25 July 2015).
82. Nikita Khrushchev, *Memoirs of Nikita Khrushchev. Volume 3: Statesman, 1953–1964*, edited by Sergei Khrushchev and translated by George Shriver (University Park, PA: Pennsylvania State University Press, 2007), p. 306. Kennedy's apparent gloom may have derived at least in part from his longstanding back problems.
83. David Reynolds, *Summits: Six Meetings that Shaped the Twentieth Century* (New York: Basic Books, 2007), pp. 207–10.
84. Record of meeting, 29 July 1967, *FRUS 1964–1968 XIV Soviet Union* (2000), document 282, <https://history.state.gov/historicaldocuments/frus1964-68v14/d282> (last accessed 25 July 2015).

85. See Lawrence Freedman, 'Laos and the Vienna Summit', in Gunter Bischof, Stefan Karner and Barbara Stelz-Marx (eds), *The Vienna Summit and its Importance in International History* (Lanham, MD: Lexington Books, 2014), pp. 243–63.

86. See Timothy Naftali, 'A Difficult Education'; Viktor Sukhodrev, 'The Personal Recollections of Khrushchev's Interpreter in Vienna' and Ted Sorensen, 'The Personal Recollections of a Presidential Adviser in Vienna', in Bischoff et al. (eds), *The Vienna Summit*, pp. 291–6, 349–54, 355–66.

87. Khrushchev, *Memoirs*, p. 305.

88. Philip Nash, 'Bear any Burden? John F. Kennedy and Nuclear Weapons', in John Lewis Gaddis, Philip H. Gordon, Ernest R. May and Jonathan Rosenberg (eds), *Cold War Statesmen Confront the Bomb: Nuclear Diplomacy Since 1945* (Oxford: Oxford University Press, 1999), p. 131.

89. Stephen G. Rabe, *John F. Kennedy: World Leader* (Washington, DC: Potomac Books, 2010), pp. 45–6.

90. See Vladislav M. Zubok and Hope M. Harrison, 'The Nuclear Education of Nikita Khrushchev', in Gaddis et al. (eds), *Cold War Statesmen*, p. 155.

91. Campbell Craig, 'Kennedy's International Legacy, Fifty Years On', *International Affairs*, 89: 6, November 2013, p. 1375.

92. Raymond L. Garthoff, 'The US–Soviet Tank Confrontation at Checkpoint Charlie', in Stephen J. Cimbala (ed.), *Mysteries of the Cold War* (Aldershot: Ashgate, 1999), p. 75.

93. See Editorial note, *FRUS 1961–1963 X*, document 279, <https://history.state.gov/historicaldocuments/frus1961-63v10/d279> (last accessed 25 July 2015); Goodwin to Kennedy, 22 August 1961, *FRUS 1961–1963 X*, document 256, <https://history.state.gov/historicaldocuments/frus1961-63v10/d256> (last accessed 25 July 2015).

94. Robert F. to John F. Kennedy, 19 April 1961, *FRUS 1961–1963 X*, document 157, <https://history.state.gov/historicaldocuments/frus1961-63v10/d157> (last accessed 25 July 2015).

95. Rabe, *The Most Dangerous Area*, p. 20.

96. Editorial note, *FRUS 1961–1963 X*, document 279, <https://history.state.gov/historicaldocuments/frus1961-63v10/d279> (last accessed 25 July 2015).

97. Aleksandr Fursenko and Timothy Naftali, *'One Hell of a Gamble': Khrushchev, Castro, and Kennedy, 1958–64* (New York: Norton, 1997), p. 161.

98. Hilsman to Rusk, 1 September 1962, *FRUS 1961–1963 X*, document 404, <https://history.state.gov/historicaldocuments/frus1961-63v10/d404> (last accessed 25 July 2015).

99. Dean Rusk, *As I Saw It: A Secretary of State's Memoirs* (New York: Norton, 1990), p. 245.

100. Editorial note, *FRUS 1961–1963 X*, document 270, <https://history.state.gov/historicaldocuments/frus1961-63v10/d270> (last accessed 25 July 2015).

101. Ibid.

102. James G. Hershberg, 'Before the "Missiles of October": Did Kennedy Plan a Military Strike against Cuba?', *Diplomatic History*, 14: 2, Spring 1990, p. 176.

103. Hilsman to Johnson, 20 February 1962, *FRUS 1961–1963 X*, document 305, <https://history.state.gov/historicaldocuments/frus1961-63v10/d305> (last accessed 25 July 2015).

104. National Intelligence Estimate, 21 March 1962, *FRUS 1961–1963 X*, document 315, <https://history.state.gov/historicaldocuments/frus1961-63v10/d315> (last accessed 25 July 2015).

105. Schlesinger to Kennedy, 5 September 1962, *FRUS 1961–1963 X*, document 413, <https://history.state.gov/historicaldocuments/frus1961-63v10/d413> (last accessed 25 July 2015).

106. Memorandum for the record, 16 October 1962, *FRUS 1961–1963 XI, Cuban Missile Crisis and Aftermath* (1996), document 19, <https://history.state.gov/historicaldocuments/frus1961-63v11/d19> (last accessed 25 July 2015).

107. Rasenberger, *The Brilliant Disaster*, pp. 81–2, 141–2; Memorandum for the record, 14 May 1962, *FRUS 1961–1963 X*, document 337, <https://history.state.gov/historicaldocuments/frus1961-63v10/d337> (last accessed 25 July 2015). See also Don Bohning, *The Castro Obsession: US Covert Actions Against Castro, 1959–65* (Washington, DC: Potomac Books, 2005), pp. 176–84; and Fabian Escalante, *The Cuba Project: CIA Covert Operations, 1959–62* (Melbourne: Ocean Press, 2004), pp. 123–8.

108. Rasenberger, *The Brilliant Disaster*, pp. 50, 143.

109. *Senate Reports Vol. 3–8, Alleged Assassination Plots Involving Foreign Leaders* (Washington, DC: USGPO, 1975), p. 120.

110. Dobbs, *One Minute to Midnight*, p. 154; Weiner, *Legacy of Ashes*, p. 216.

111. Memorandum for the record, 14 May 1962, *FRUS 1961–1963 X*, note 1, document 337, <https://history.state.gov/historicaldocuments/frus1961-63v10/d337> (last accessed 25 July 2015).

112. Kent to Dulles, 3 November 1961, *FRUS 1961–1963 X*, document 271, <https://history.state.gov/historicaldocuments/frus1961-63v 10/d271> (last accessed 25 July 2015).

113. Brian Latell, *Castro's Secrets: The CIA and Cuba's Intelligence Machine* (New York: Palgrave Macmillan, 2012), p. 172.

# 2 The Decision to Base Nuclear Missiles in Cuba, Spring–Summer 1962

It's a goddamn mystery to me.

*John F. Kennedy*

## The Decision

Historians have in recent years shown a much greater appreciation of how Cuban concerns and actions were important before,
during and after the missile crisis. US hostility demonstrated so
unambiguously at the Bay of Pigs and in continuing measures of
harassment led the regime in Havana to ask Moscow in August
1961 for a defence commitment of conventional missiles and
10,000 troops. Initially, there was little or no response, but in
February 1962 a dispute between Castro and Anibal Escalante,
a leading figure in the Cuban Communist Party, brought matters
to a head. Escalante supported the moderate Soviet approach in
revolutionary policy, while Castro was more radical. He ended
up exiling Escalante to Moscow, leading Khrushchev to conclude
that Cuba might break away from the Soviet Union. Cuba's
loss 'would have been a big blow to Marxist–Leninist doctrine
and would have thrown us far back in Latin America, lower-
ing our prestige there'.[1] It would also be a setback for Moscow
in the developing doctrinal dispute with communist China (the
'Sino-Soviet split'), and would damage Khrushchev's standing
at home.[2] The Soviet leadership decided in March 1962 that the
best way to keep Castro firmly in the Soviet camp while fortify-
ing the Cuban regime against American military action was to
create a strong self-defence capability. The Presidium approved

additional military supplies to Cuba to include conventional missiles, a training programme for the Cuban military, and a symbolic commitment of 3,000 Soviet troops.[3]

Why Khrushchev went further and decided to install nuclear missiles in Cuba has remained an area of intense speculation since the discovery of the weapons in October 1962. In November 1960, Castro had raised the question of extending the Soviet nuclear umbrella to Cuba, and during a visit to Moscow around the same time Che Guevara probed Khrushchev about the possibility of placing Soviet missiles in Cuba.[4] In April 1962, during a meeting with Defence Minister Rodion Malinovsky, Khrushchev asked, 'What about putting one of our hedgehogs down the Americans' trousers?'[5] Malinovsky considered that the issue was one for the politicians to decide. The idea of placing nuclear missiles in Cuba appears to have remained on Khrushchev's mind. He recollected that during a visit to Bulgaria from 14–20 May 1962 he was 'constantly preoccupied' about losing Cuba. He concluded, 'What if we were to come to an agreement with the government of Cuba and install missiles with atomic warheads there, but to do it in a concealed way, so that it would be kept a secret from the United States?' For now, he kept quiet about the idea: 'I couldn't even share these thoughts with [Bulgarian leader Todor] Zhivkov, because I hadn't discussed the matter with my own comrades.'[6] When he returned to the Soviet Union, Khrushchev learned of a conversation between Castro and the Soviet GRU (military intelligence) representative in Cuba, in which the Cuban leader made his military needs clear but also played hard to get.[7] This confirmed Khrushchev's fears about 'losing' Castro.

In Moscow, it was Khrushchev personally who was the prime mover behind the nuclear missiles scheme. He was in a strong position to implement his ideas, because of the impact of some of his administrative reforms in an already authoritarian environment. The CIA noted that in 1957 he had initiated a 'sharp reorganization of the Soviet Union's top political command', introducing new members according to their loyalty to him, and he more broadly operated within a 'totalitarian' system which 'inexorably funnels authority to a single point'.[8] Khrushchev had initiated a number of bold innovations, including 'the daring stroke of de-Stalinization' in 1956, the 'New Lands' agricultural initiative to increase crop yields, the challenge to the Western presence in Berlin 1958–61, cultivating a 'spirit of Camp David' after meeting President Eisenhower in 1959, and a 1960 plan to reorganise the Soviet military.[9] British Ambassador in Moscow Frank Roberts reflected later that on the Soviet side of the missile crisis, 'the controlling hand was that of Mr. Khrushchev himself . . . the crucial decisions at every stage were essentially his'.[10]

It has emerged recently that the Soviet installation of nuclear missiles outside the USSR had a precedent. In 1955, Khrushchev and Nikolai Bulganin had signed a decree initiating the stationing of nuclear missiles in the German Democratic Republic. Although there is limited evidence on the issue, the missiles – which were finally in place in 1959 – were probably aimed at Anglo-American 'Thor' missiles in Great Britain, US air bases in Western Europe, major Western European cities and possibly Atlantic harbours. It appears that the motive was to improve the Soviet Union's strategic position in the event of a conflict. Against a background of tensions over Berlin, Khrushchev told the US diplomat Averell Harriman in 1959 that

> It would take only a few Soviet missiles to destroy Europe: One bomb was sufficient for Bonn and three to five would knock out France, England, Spain and Italy. The United States would be in no position to retaliate because its missiles could carry a warhead of only ten kilograms whereas Russian missiles could carry 1,300 kilograms.[11]

The intelligence services of the United States, the Federal Republic of Germany, Great Britain and France learned of the deployment, but their governments decided not to respond. Certainly, for the United States, the missiles in East Germany were not to be taken lightly, but they did not pose a threat to American territory; nor was there the deep sensitivity that prevailed in relation to Soviet missiles in the Western Hemisphere. Furthermore, President Eisenhower was sanguine about Soviet nuclear capabilities, saying in 1960 that he would be far more worried about nuclear fallout from the United States' own weapons than Soviet retaliation.[12] It is not clear how far knowledge of the Soviet missiles in the GDR may have influenced policy towards West Berlin. In August 1959 the Soviet missile unit left the GDR in haste, moving the weapons to an area near Kaliningrad on the Baltic coast. Khrushchev's motives for the withdrawal are not clear, but they may have been connected with his desire for *détente* with the United States. How far the experience of placing missiles in the GDR shaped the 1962 decision is not known; nor is it apparent whether the Kennedy administration was aware of the brief presence of Soviet missiles in East Germany in 1959. If there was no such awareness, then the view that the Soviet Union had never placed nuclear missiles beyond its borders before may have encouraged the faulty view that it would not do so in Cuba.

## Motives

Khrushchev would always emphasise that the deployment of missiles in Cuba was intended to keep the country 'from being crushed' by another US attack.[13] In January 1962, Alexei Adzhubei reported after a conversation with John F. Kennedy that the President had compared Cuba with Hungary in 1956, where the Soviet Union had intervened militarily to crush a reformist government. Although the President probably made the comparison as a reminder of Soviet misdeeds, it was taken to mean that he was considering a second invasion of Cuba, this time using American troops. Adzhubei's report of the conversation was circulated within the Kremlin and the Communist Party.[14] In spring 1962 the US military began a series of exercises in the United States and in the Caribbean, including amphibious operations on an island fifty miles from Cuba against a symbolic regime called 'Ortsac' ('Castro').[15] A senior Soviet military commander, Igor D. Statsenko, who was in Cuba during the missile crisis, stated in a 1977 article that the US military exercises contributed to the missile deployment decision by raising fears of an invasion.[16] Anastas Mikoyan suggested that the 'manoeuvres could appear to be not an exercise but a sea cover for a strong blow against Cuba'.[17]

Some American officials have maintained that after the setback at the Bay of Pigs in April 1961 there were no further plans to invade Cuba. William Y. Smith, who served under General Maxwell Taylor in the Pentagon, noted in relation to the Caribbean manoeuvres in the summer of 1962 that the US military was 'doing everything possible to become ready so that they could attack *if* they were directed by civilian authority'. In other words, preparing for an invasion did not mean that one was inevitable, or even likely. Arthur Schlesinger stated unequivocally that the White House had no further intention of invading Cuba after the Bay of Pigs.[18] However, there is evidence that in late September and early October the Pentagon, acting at the behest of the President and the Secretary of Defense, intensified contingency planning for military action against Cuba. Why this was the case remains unclear, but it may have been connected with the 'Mongoose' anti-Castro measures that had been under way since 1961. Had these measures precipitated a popular revolt as intended, then the United States might have launched an invasion to push matters to a conclusion.[19] It seems, therefore, that an attack was not on the cards unless Operation Mongoose had first stimulated an uprising within Cuba. Nonetheless, the American muscle-flexing, harassment and hostility gave observers ample reason to think that the Bay of Pigs invasion would not be the last.

The Cuban defence motive that Khrushchev professed after the US administration had confronted him with the discovery of the missiles sat alongside a desire to redress the nuclear balance of power. This was a sensitive issue at the time. As noted in the previous chapter, during the election campaign of 1960 John F. Kennedy campaigned on the 'missile gap', maintaining that President Eisenhower had neglected national security and that the Soviet Union had taken the lead in the production of long-range nuclear missiles. However, as 1961 progressed it became increasingly clear from intelligence reports that the gap favoured the United States, not the Soviet Union. In a series of press conferences and interviews in autumn 1961, the President, Robert S. McNamara, Dean Rusk and Roswell Gilpatric asserted that the United States was quantitatively and qualitatively far ahead of the Soviet Union. For good measure, though, the administration announced a large military build-up, including extra funding for the Polaris submarine system and for land-based Minuteman

nuclear missiles.[20] The US revelations encouraged the Soviet Union
to end a three-year moratorium on atmospheric nuclear testing.
Between 30 August and 2 November 1961, the Soviets conducted
up to 39 tests, including an unprecedented 50-megaton detona-
tion. Khrushchev told the 22nd Party Congress in October that
'When the enemies of peace threaten us with force, they must be
and will be countered with force, and the more impressive force,
too.'[21] Soon President Kennedy authorised the US resumption of
atmospheric nuclear tests.

Khrushchev told Malinovsky in April 1962 that

> According to our intelligence we are lagging almost fifteen years
> behind the Americans in warheads. We cannot reduce that lead even
> in ten years. But our rockets on America's doorstep would drastically
> alter the situation and go a long way towards compensating us for the
> lag in time.[22]

Contemporary assessments tended to maintain that Khrushchev's
motive behind placing missiles in Cuba was to boost Soviet nuclear
power. Frank Roberts suggested that the chief aim was the 'accre-
tion of nuclear strength and bargaining power which the successful completion of the bases would have provided, and which
would have shifted the present balance of power substantially . . .
in the Soviet favour'.[23] A French assessment maintained that 'A
strong aerial defense, and if need be a naval defense', rather than
importing nuclear missiles, 'would have been sufficient' to defend
Cuba.[24] (US policymakers' perspectives are considered below.)
By placing strategic missiles on the island, Khrushchev sought to
fulfil two goals at once: defending Cuba while boosting the Soviet
Union's position in the nuclear arms race.

The assumption in the West was that Khrushchev's assertion
that he placed nuclear weapons in Cuba for the purpose of Cuban
defence was merely a post-facto rationalisation after he had been
forced to remove them while managing to secure a non-invasion
guarantee. Any view that Cuba *needed* defending from US aggression was given little credence. Khrushchev and his associates
did not publicly acknowledge the objective of strengthening the
balance of power not only because they were forced to withdraw

the missiles, but also because they did not want to make the tacit admission that the Soviet defence posture was deficient.[25] Nor would Castro have been impressed had Khrushchev told him that a key reason for placing missiles in Cuba and enmeshing the country in a dangerous superpower confrontation was to bridge the Soviet–American missile gap.[26] Later, though, Castro concluded that 'along with his love for Cuba Khrushchev wanted to fix the strategic parity in the cheapest way ... To defend Cuba it would have been sufficient to send six regiments of Soviet troops there, because the Americans would never have ever dared to open military activities against the Soviet troops'.[27]

There were those who played down the significance of the Soviet missiles. Robert McNamara thought that they did not make a difference, explaining that 'we had some five thousand strategic nuclear warheads, as against their three hundred'.[28] To this way of thinking, the presence of forty or so Soviet nuclear missiles and warheads in Cuba would be of little account militarily. Yet the military implications of the missiles could not be separated so easily from the political ones. President Kennedy suggested – in connection with whether or not the missiles altered the balance of power – that 'appearance contributes to reality'.[29] Khrushchev was as much concerned with the political as the military effect of placing missiles in Cuba, but there is evidence that the weapons did have an objective impact on the strategic balance. A State Department analysis during the missile crisis maintained that the weapons were of 'special significance' militarily because the Soviet Union had only around 75 operational intercontinental ballistic missiles (ICBMs), which meant that the missiles in Cuba would 'increase the first strike missile salvo which the USSR could place on targets in the continental United States by over 40%'.[30] Soviet analyses probably reached similar verdicts.

Placing missiles close to the United States would also take the sting out of US Jupiter missiles in Turkey, just across the Black Sea from the Soviet Union. In response to the launch of the Soviet space satellite *Sputnik* in October 1957, Washington sought to bridge the putative missile gap by proposing the deployment of American missiles in Europe. After a search for hosts, it was agreed by 1959 that Jupiter fleets would be stationed in Turkey and Italy, along with Thor missiles in Britain.[31] After formal negotiations had been concluded, the Turkish deployments were completed in March 1961. By this stage the Jupiters were obsolescent, but the Kennedy administration had continued with their emplacement to satisfy the Turkish government and to avoid giving the impression of vacillation. The presence of missiles in Turkey was politically awkward for Moscow, given their proximity. During the Cuban Missile Crisis, Khrushchev complained to Kennedy that 'Turkey adjoins us; our sentries patrol back and forth and see each other . . . You have placed destructive missile weapons [sic] . . . in Turkey, literally next to us.'[32] It should be understood that just as the US missiles in Turkey and elsewhere were intended for deterrence purposes, the Soviets did not intend using Cuba as a platform for a nuclear first strike. According to Castro, Khrushchev had 'an obsession' about never initiating nuclear war.[33] The thought of a nuclear exchange – which as he understood would cause 'hundreds of millions' of casualties – was abhorrent to him.[34]

Alongside the objectives of defending Cuba and boosting the Soviet Union's status in the nuclear balance of power, there were other factors which may have influenced Khrushchev's missiles-in-Cuba decision – although even in aggregate those reasons were not decisive; instead, they pushed him in a direction he already had good reason to travel. There was the international context. The Soviets had several recent Cold War achievements to their credit, including Cuba's entrance into the socialist world, and gaining leadership in the space race, with the Sputnik satellite in 1957 and by sending the first man into space in 1961.[35] At the same time, the picture was not one of unfettered progress. The CIA commented that 'the more rapid general advance of Communist fortunes which the Soviets seemed to have anticipated' around 1960 had 'failed to materialize'.[36] Khrushchev's revelations in 1956 about Stalin's brutal rule had tarnished the international allure of communism, as had the Soviet invasion of Hungary the same year. Democratic and market economies were prospering in Western Europe and Japan. There was a strained relationship with communist China, with Beijing advocating more militant policies and seeking leadership in the communist world. The Western presence in Berlin continued to frustrate the Soviet leader: it was 'a malignant growth on a healthy body'.[37] Installing missiles in Cuba offered Khrushchev a decisive opportunity to augment the recent Soviet successes and to counter the setbacks.

What did the Kennedy administration think about why Khrushchev had taken this fateful step? Even though understanding the Soviet leader's motives might have been valuable in suggesting how the missile crisis might be resolved, Kennedy and his advisers spent little time on this critical question, focusing instead on how to respond to a fait accompli.[38] Dean Rusk and Under Secretary of State George Ball thought that Khrushchev wanted a Cuba–Berlin 'bargain', removing the missiles in return for a settlement of the Berlin question.[39] Yet there is no evidence that Khrushchev installed the missiles with the express intention of sacrificing them in a Berlin trade, or in any deal: the costs and risks of the Cuban deployment greatly exceeded the value of sacrificing the missiles in any conceivable trade.[40] During the missile crisis Khrushchev would end up making a deal, but only under intense pressure. Deputy Under Secretary of State for Political Affairs Alexis Johnson suggested that stationing missiles in Cuba would help compensate for the Soviet deficiency in missiles capable of striking the United States.[41] McGeorge Bundy rejected the idea that the Soviets placed missiles in Cuba for defensive motives: 'it's very hard to reconcile that with what has happened'.[42] Former Ambassador to the Soviet Union Llewellyn Thompson came closest to understanding that defending Cuba was an important Soviet motive, when on 27 October he suggested that 'The important thing for Khrushchev . . . is to say, "I saved Cuba, I stopped an invasion."'[43]

What was President Kennedy's view? Although he was justified in recognising that the Soviets were generally cautious in their foreign policies, he was not at his most insightful when it came to understanding Khrushchev's Cuban initiative:

. . . it's a goddamn mystery to me. I don't know enough about the Soviet Union, but if anybody can tell me any other time since the Berlin blockade where the Russians have given us so clear provocation, I don't know when it's been, because they've been awfully cautious really.[44]

In sum, US policymakers were correct to note that the nuclear balance of power was of great concern to Khrushchev in his decision to place missiles in Cuba, but there was little awareness that the provocative character of American policy had given the Soviets good reason to believe that Cuba needed defending.

## Did Khrushchev Expect the US Government to Tolerate the Missiles?

It appears that Soviet politicians and analysts spent little time evaluating the possible American reaction to the presence of nuclear missiles in Cuba. In 1970, White House adviser Helmut Sonnenfeld told President Richard Nixon that the Soviets may have expected the US government to acquiesce to the presence of the missiles rather than take action. As there was only 'minimal camouflage accompanying the heavy Soviet military movements into Cuba ... the Soviets must at least have suspected that we had an idea of what they were doing'.[45] Khrushchev may have believed that

> as long as he did not flaunt his action in our face before the fall election we would remain passive and that, indeed, it was politically more important to us that nothing leaked out before November that the Soviets would acquire some 40-odd additional first-strike strategic launchers.[46]

Sonnenfeld asserted that Kennedy's 'public warnings against offensive deployments' were 'interpreted in Moscow as further signs of toleration, if not collusion' (the warnings are discussed in the next chapter). It is true that the efforts to disguise the missiles were minimal, but this was not intentional. Major-General Igor Demyanovich Statsenko, Commander of the 51st Missile Division, reported that Cuba's 'geographical and climatic conditions, population and lifestyle' made it 'impossible to sustain a lengthy concealment of the large number of the deploying troops and the varied and oversized equipment of the missile forces'.[47]

Khrushchev, appearing not to have thought matters through properly, did expect the administration to put up with the presence of the missiles when, as he intended, he revealed their installation after the November congressional elections. However, he did not take the Kennedy administration's warnings as signs of collusion. Although the CIA suggested that he might have drawn the wrong conclusions from the Bay of Pigs disaster in April 1961, from Kennedy's seeming weakness at the Vienna summit in June and from a US concession in relation to Laos in 1962,[48] we saw in the previous chapter that the President in fact cut a substantial figure in Khrushchev's eyes. The Soviet leader did not consider Kennedy to be a pushover. It is abundantly clear, though, that he underestimated the political significance to the US government of stationing nuclear missiles in Cuba. This was due to a failure to discuss the issue more widely; he did not even consult his ambassador in Washington, Anatoly Dobrynin, who knew the Kennedy administration better than did any other Soviet official. For the US government, the presence of Soviet missiles in Cuba was simply too provocative to be tolerated (see Chapter 3). All in all, Khrushchev's decision to deploy the missiles reflected what a former Western ambassador to Moscow described as 'an incurable political short-sightedness' that prevented him 'from foreseeing the remoter consequences of his words and actions'.[49]

## Securing Consent

Khrushchev needed the formal approval of the Soviet Presidium to pursue his missiles plan. Vladimir Malin, the Chief of the General Department of the Central Committee in the Kremlin, noted that straight after the visit to Bulgaria Khrushchev proposed the following steps in the Presidium:

> Come to an agreement with F[idel] Castro, conclude a military treaty regarding joint defense.
> Station nuclear missiles [there].

Carry this out secretly. Then declare it.
Missiles under our command.
This will be an offensive policy.[50]

The record of the meeting is limited, but there is evidence that the proposal did not meet with unanimous support. Anastas Mikoyan doubted that Castro would accept the stationing of nuclear missiles on Cuba, and felt that their presence could not be kept secret in any case.[51] (As noted earlier, Castro had asked for help defending his country, but he had not specifically requested the import of nuclear missiles.) Although the available documentation of the 1962 deliberations does not record his opposition, Presidium member Alexei Kosygin stated five years later that in relation to placing missiles on Cuba, 'I tried to keep Khrushchev from doing it.'[52] There were also reservations outside the Presidium. Khrushchev's international affairs adviser, Oleg Troyanovsky, believed that deploying missiles near the US border 'totally ignored the mood in the United States and the possible US reaction'.[53] This view demonstrated much more empathy with American politicians than did Khrushchev. He promoted his plan in a further session of the Presidium on 24 May, attended by twelve colleagues. There he got his way. Finally, on 10 June, after consultations with the Cuban government, the Presidium voted to confirm the preliminary decision.[54]

With a view to obtaining Castro's consent about the nuclear missiles, Khrushchev summoned KGB official Alexander Alexeyev from the Havana Embassy to Moscow. The Spanish-speaking Alexeyev got along well with Castro, who preferred dealing with him to dealing with Ambassador Sergei Kudryavtsev. Khrushchev told Alexeyev that he was to be appointed the new ambassador to Cuba, a decision 'linked with our decision to site nuclear-tipped missiles there'. Alexeyev was sceptical about the missile plan, suggesting that Castro would prefer to preserve his solidarity with other Latin American nations rather than permit Cuba to become a nuclear base, and he thought that the presence of Soviet nuclear missiles would perpetuate American hostility. The die was cast, though, with Alexeyev's reservations counting for little. However, Khrushchev decided that 'rather than tell Castro we have come to a decision, we ought perhaps to declare to him that to save the Cuban revolution it is imperative to take a bold step'.[55] Records of the conversations with Castro have not emerged, but he stated later that 'when we were told about the missiles, we believed that this was something that would strengthen the entire socialist camp . . . Secondarily, the missiles would contribute to our own defense.'[56] Therefore the Cuban leader was thinking about global socialism as well as Cuban national interest.

There were reservations among the Cuban leadership, though. Minister for the Armed Forces Raul Castro was 'convinced that we could not hide this fact from foreign intelligence, which was conducting activities on our soil, and that this fact would be known before it was officially announced'.[57] When during a visit to Moscow Che Guevara expressed worry about US reactions to the presence of nuclear missiles in Cuba, Khrushchev responded airily, 'You don't have to worry. There will be no big reaction from the US. And if there is a problem, we will send the Baltic Fleet.'[58] Khrushchev's statement reflected his blithe self-confidence, his misplaced assurance that the Americans would not discover the missiles, and his equally flawed view that the Administration would tolerate them. Unlike Khrushchev, the Cuban leadership also sought openness about the deployment. Fidel Castro proposed 'that Havana and Moscow formally and publicly agree to base missiles in Cuba through a legal agreement – just as the United States was doing on the soil of its allies in Europe'.[59] This proposal did not make any difference, so the Cubans swallowed their reservations and accepted the nuclear missiles. Captain Emilio Aragonés Navarro, a key figure in the Cuban military, noted that 'we were deferential to the Soviets' judgments, because, after all, they had superior information than we had. We trusted their judgment.'[60]

## Beyond Secrecy

Cuba's transition to a nuclear missile base took place in hermetic secrecy. Khrushchev told Foreign Minister Andrei Gromyko, who was one of the few knowledgeable Soviet officials, that 'We must deliver and deploy the missiles quietly, taking all precautions so as to present the Americans with an accomplished fact.' It was 'imperative to see that no information is leaked to the press before the end of the campaign for the American elections on November 4 if we are to avoid aggravating the situation there'.[61] Some of the details of the Soviet military operation emerged after the Cold War had ended. General Anatoli Gribkov, who oversaw the execution of the operation, noted that the General Staff detailed only five officers – four generals and a colonel – to make the plans. During the summer, the circle of those working on the project grew to include members of each of the services involved, but stringent secrecy still prevailed. The most senior officers brought into the project learned that Cuba was involved, but only a few were given details of what was planned. No secretaries were used to prepare memoranda. A colonel hand-wrote the proposal that was later adopted by the Defense Council. This way the initial decision grew into a detailed plan, and, still in handwritten form, it received Malinovsky's formal approval on 4 July and that of Khrushchev three days later.[62] The operation was codenamed Operation Anadyr, after a river flowing into the Bering Sea, the capital of the Chukotsky Autonomous District, and a bomber base in that region. It would be the largest and most complicated sea-borne operation in Soviet history. Major-General Igor Demyanovich Statsenko noted the schedule for achieving combat readiness:

> – regiments armed with R-12 [medium range ballistic missiles – MRBM] – by 11.01.62;
> – regiments armed with R-14 [intercontinental ballistic missiles – ICBM] – depending on the time of the completion of construction and installation works, in the period from 11.01.62 through 01.01.63.[63]

The choice of codename – Anadyr – was intended to suggest that the operation was a strategic exercise in the far north of the Soviet Union. The troops involved in the Cuban expedition were told they were going somewhere cold. To strengthen the deception, many units were equipped with winter gear. Personnel such as missile engineers who needed more detailed instructions were told only that they would be taking ICBMs to a site on Novaya

Zemlya in the Arctic. The deception was so thorough that even senior Soviet officers sent to Cuba did not know where they were going until they reached their destination.[64]

Major-General Statsenko indicated some of the secrecy that prevailed within Cuba:

> The missiles were unloaded from the ships only at night, under total blackout on the ships and in the ports. While the missiles were being unloaded, all external approaches to the ports were guarded by a specially assigned mountain rifle squadron consisting of 300 men, transferred from the Sierra Maestra. From then on, people from this squadron ensured the external security of the field deployment areas.[65]

Alongside the passive security surrounding Operation Anadyr, there were active steps to misdirect the US government. In July 1962, Soviet embassy official Georgi Bolshakov asked Robert F. Kennedy on behalf of Moscow to reduce the surveillance of Soviet shipping, on the grounds that it was causing annoyance. The administration fulfilled the request in the hope that Khrushchev would refrain from causing trouble over Berlin, the most sensitive issue in the run-up to the congressional elections.[66] On 11 September, the Soviet news agency TASS stated that 'The arms and military equipment sent to Cuba are designated solely for defensive purposes,' and that 'there is no need for the Soviet Union to shift its weapons for the repulse of aggression, for a retaliatory strike, to any other country, for instance, Cuba ... There is no need to search for sites for them beyond the boundaries of the Soviet Union.'[67] At the beginning of October, Bolshakov, acting under Moscow's instructions, told Robert F. Kennedy that the weapons that the Soviet Union had sent to Cuba were 'only ... of a defensive character'.[68] Soviet deception would antagonise the US government greatly, helping to turn the discovery of the missiles in Cuba into a dangerous confrontation.

## Notes

1. Nikita Khrushchev, *Memoirs of Nikita Khrushchev. Volume 3: Statesman, 1953–1964*, edited by Sergei Khrushchev and

translated by George Shriver (University Park, PA: Pennsylvania State University Press, 2007), pp. 325–6; Aleksandr Fursenko and Timothy Naftali, *'One Hell of a Gamble': Khrushchev, Castro, and Kennedy, 1958–64* (New York: Norton, 1997), pp. 169–70.

2. For the ideological rift between the People's Republic of China and the Soviet Union, which had begun to emerge in the late 1950s, see Lorenz M. Luthi, *The Sino-Soviet Split: Cold War in the Communist World* (Princeton, NJ: Princeton University Press, 2008).

3. Timothy Naftali, 'The Malin Notes: Glimpses inside the Kremlin during the Cuban Missile Crisis', *Cold War International History Project Bulletin*, 17/18, Fall 2012, pp. 299–300, <http://www.wilsoncenter.org/publication/bulletin-no-17-18> (last accessed 25 July 2015).

4. Fursenko and Naftali, *'One Hell of a Gamble'*, p. 70.

5. Dmitri Volkogonov, *The Rise and Fall of the Soviet Empire: Political Leaders from Lenin to Gorbachev* (London: Harper Collins, 1998), p. 236.

6. Khrushchev, *Memoirs*, pp. 325–6.

7. Nicola Miller, 'The Real Gap in the Cuban Missile Crisis: The Post-Cold War Historiography and the Continued Omission of Cuba', in Dale Carter and Robin Clifton (eds), *War and Cold War in American Foreign Policy, 1942–62* (Basingstoke: Palgrave, 2002), p. 223.

8. Current Intelligence Weekly Review, 26 January 1961, *Foreign Relations of the United States (FRUS) 1961–1963 V Soviet Union* (Washington, DC: USGPO, 1998), document 15, <https://history.state.gov/historicaldocuments/frus1961-63v05/d15> (last accessed 25 July 2015); Sergo Mikoyan, *The Soviet Cuban Missile Crisis: Castro, Mikoyan, Kennedy, Khrushchev and the Missiles of November*, edited by Svetlana Savranskaya (Stanford, CA: Stanford University Press, 2012), p. 166.

9. National Intelligence Estimate, 22 May 1963, *FRUS 1961–1963 V*, document 326, <https://history.state.gov/historicaldocuments/frus1961-63v05/d326> (last accessed 25 July 2015).

10. 'The Cuba Crisis: Its Course as Seen from Moscow', 7 November 1962, FO 371/162405, The National Archives, Kew, England (TNA).

11. Matthias Uhl and Vladimir I. Ivkin, '"Operation Atom": The Soviet Union's Stationing of Nuclear Missiles in the German Democratic Republic, 1959', *Cold War International History Project*, Issue 12/

13, Fall/Winter 2001, p. 303, <http://www.wilsoncenter.org/publication/bulletin-no-1213-fallwinter-2001> (last accessed 25 July 2015).

12. Ibid. pp. 299–307; Henry A. Kissinger, *Diplomacy* (New York: Simon and Schuster, 1994), p. 585.

13. Khrushchev, *Memoirs*, p. 327.

14. James Hershberg, 'A Trigger for Khrushchev's Deployment?', *Cold War International History Project Bulletin*, 17/18, Fall 2012, pp. 316–17, <http://www.wilsoncenter.org/publication/bulletin-no-17-18> (last accessed 25 July 2015).

15. Norman Polmar and John D. Gresham, *DEFCON-2: Standing on the Brink of Nuclear War during the Cuban Missile Crisis* (New York: John Wiley, 2006), p. 49.

16. James G. Hershberg, 'Before the "Missiles of October": Did Kennedy Plan a Military Strike against Cuba?', *Diplomatic History*, 14: 2, Spring 1990, p. 182.

17. Mikoyan's speech at the Military Council of General Pavlov's Group, 21 November 1962, in Mikoyan, *The Soviet Cuban Missile Crisis*, pp. 307, 470.

18. James G. Blight, Bruce J. Allyn and David A. Welch (eds), with foreword by Jorge I. Dominguez, *Cuba on the Brink: Castro, the Missile Crisis, and the Soviet Collapse* (New York: Pantheon, 1993), p. 161.

19. Hershberg, 'Before the "Missiles of October"', pp. 163–98.

20. Roger Hilsman, *To Move a Nation: The Politics of Foreign Policy in the Administration of John F. Kennedy* (Garden City, NY: Doubleday, 1967), p. 163; Christopher A. Preble, *John F. Kennedy and the Missile Gap* (Dekalb, IL: Northern Illinois University Press, 2004), pp. 164–5. The build-up was motivated by a desire to boost American prestige and to place the United States in a better position to negotiate arms limitation with the Soviet Union. Stephen G. Rabe, *John F. Kennedy: World Leader* (Washington, DC: Potomac Books, 2010), p. 32.

21. Editorial note, *FRUS 1961–1963 V*, document 126, <https://history.state.gov/historicaldocuments/frus1961-63v05/d126> (last accessed 25 July 2015); Vladislav M. Zubok and Hope M. Harrison, 'The Nuclear Education of Nikita Khrushchev', in Gaddis et al. (eds), *Cold War Statesmen Confront the Bomb*, p. 157; Viktor Adamsky and Yuri Smirnov, 'Moscow's Biggest Bomb: The 50-Megaton Test of October 1961 by Viktor Adamsky and Yuri Smirnov', *Cold War International History Project Bulletin*, 4, Fall 1994, pp. 3, 19–21,

&lt;http://www.wilsoncenter.org/publication/bulletin-no-4-fall-1994&gt;
(last accessed 25 July 2015).

22. Volkogonov, *The Rise and Fall of the Soviet Empire*, p. 236.

23. 'The Cuba Crisis: Its Course as Seen from Moscow', 7 November 1962, FO 371/162405, TNA.

24. Couve de Murville to various French diplomatic posts, 10 November 1962, *Cold War International History Project Bulletin*, 17/18, Fall 2012, p. 755, &lt;http://www.wilsoncenter.org/publication/bulletin-no-17-18&gt; (last accessed 25 July 2015).

25. Raymond Garthoff, *Reflections on the Cuban Missile Crisis* (Washington, DC: Brookings, 1987), p. 11.

26. Sergey Radchenko, 'The Cuban Missile Crisis: Assessment of New, and Old, Russian Sources', *International Relations*, 26: 3, September 2012, p. 330.

27. '"I Know Something About The Caribbean Crisis", Notes from a conversation with Fidel Castro, 5 November 1987, Some Details and Specifics of the Crisis Situation', *Cold War International History Project Bulletin*, 5, Spring 1995, pp. 88–9, &lt;http://www.wilsoncenter.org/publication/bulletin-no-5-spring-1995&gt; (last accessed 25 July 2015).

28. James G. Blight and David A. Welch (eds), with foreword by McGeorge Bundy, *On the Brink: Americans and Soviets Reexamine the Cuban Missile Crisis* (New York: Noonday Press, 1990), p. 23.

29. Abram Chayes, *The Cuban Missile Crisis: International Crises and the Role of Law* (New York: Oxford University Press, 1974), p. 3.

30. Garthoff to ExComm, 27 October 1962, in Garthoff, *Reflections*, p. 138.

31. See Philip Nash, *The Other Missiles of October: Eisenhower, Kennedy, and the Jupiters, 1957–1963* (Chapel Hill: University of North Carolina Press, 1997). On the Thors, see Stephen Twigge and Len Scott, 'The Other Other Missiles of October: The Thor IBMs and the Cuban Missile Crisis', *Electronic Journal of International History*, 3, 30 January 2012, &lt;http://sas-space.sas.ac.uk/3387/&gt; (last accessed 25 July 2015).

32. Khrushchev to Kennedy, 27 October 1962, *FRUS 1961–1962 XI Cuban Missile Crisis and Aftermath* (1996), document 91, &lt;https://history.state.gov/historicaldocuments/frus1961-63v11/d91&gt; (last accessed 25 July 2015).

33. Castro comments in Blight et al., *Cuba on the Brink*, p. 200.

34. Current Intelligence Weekly Review, 26 January 1961, *FRUS*

*1961–1963* V, document 15, <https://history.state.gov/historical documents/frus1961-63v05/d15> (last accessed 25 July 2015).

35. National Intelligence Estimate, 22 May 1963, *FRUS 1961–1963* V, document 326, <https://history.state.gov/historicaldocuments/frus 1961-63v05/d326> (last accessed 25 July 2015).

36. National Intelligence Estimate, 2 May 1963, *FRUS 1961–1963* V, document 187, <https://history.state.gov/historicaldocuments/frus 1961-63v05/d187> (last accessed 25 July 2015).

37. Khrushchev, *Memoirs*, p. 299.

38. Barton J. Bernstein, 'Reconsidering the Perilous Cuban Missile Crisis 50 Years Later', *Arms Control Today*, 2 October 2012, <https:// www.armscontrol.org/act/2012_10/Reconsidering-the-Perilous-Cuban-Missile-Crisis-50-Years-Later> (last accessed 25 July 2015).

39. White House meeting, 16 October 1962, *FRUS 1961–1963* XI, document 18, <https://history.state.gov/historicaldocuments/frus 1961-63v11/d18> (last accessed 25 July 2015); Off-the-record meeting on Cuba, 16 October 1961, *FRUS 1961–1963* XI, document 21, <https://history.state.gov/historicaldocuments/frus1961-63v11/d21> (last accessed 25 July 2015).

40. Arnold Horelick, 'The Cuban Missile Crisis: An Analysis of Soviet Calculations and Behavior', Memorandum RM-3779-PR, The Rand Corporation, September 1963, p. 11, <http://www.rand.org/ pubs/research_memoranda/RM3779.html> (last accessed 25 July 2015).

41. Off-the-record meeting on Cuba, 16 October 1961, *FRUS 1961– 1963* XI, document 21, <https://history.state.gov/historicaldocu ments/frus1961-63v11/d21> (last accessed 25 July 2015).

42. White House meeting, 16 October 1962, *FRUS 1961–1963* XI, document 18, <https://history.state.gov/historicaldocuments/frus 1961-63v11/d18> (last accessed 25 July 2015).

43. Ernest R. May and Philip D. Zelikow (eds), *The Kennedy Tapes: Inside the White House During the Cuban Missile Crisis* (Cambridge, MA: Belknap, 1997), p. 554.

44. Off-the-record meeting on Cuba, 16 October 1961, *FRUS 1961– 1963* XI, document 21, <https://history.state.gov/historicaldocu ments/frus1961-63v11/d21> (last accessed 25 July 2015).

45. Sonnenfeldt to Kissinger, 16 September 1970, *FRUS 1969–1976 XII Soviet Union, January 1969–October 1970* (2006), document 206, <https://history.state.gov/historicaldocuments/frus1969-76v12/d206> (last accessed 25 July 2015).

46. Ibid.

47. Report of Major-General Igor Demyanovich Statsenko, Commander of the 51st Missile Division, about the Actions of the Division from 07.12.62 through 12.01.1962, National Security Archive, George Washington University, <http://www2.gwu.edu/~nsarchiv/ NSAEBB/NSAEBB449/docs/Doc%201%20Igor%20Statsenko% 20After-action%20report.pdf> (last accessed 25 July 2015).
48. CIA report, 17 April 1964, *FRUS 1964–1968 XIV Soviet Union* (2000), document 26, <https://history.state.gov/historicaldocu ments/frus1964-68v14/d26> (last accessed 25 July 2015).
49. Ibid.
50. Protocol No. 32, Session of the CPSU Presidium, 21 May 1962, *Cold War International History Project Bulletin*, 17/18, Fall 2012, p. 303, <http://www.wilsoncenter.org/publication/bulletin- no-17-18> (last accessed 25 July 2015).
51. Khrushchev, *Memoirs*, p. 308.
52. Telephone conversation between Johnson and Eisenhower, 25 June 1967, *FRUS 1964–1968 XIV*, document 237, <https://history.state. gov/historicaldocuments/frus1964-68v14/d237> (last accessed 25 July 2015).
53. William Taubman, *Khrushchev: The Man and His Era* (New York: Norton, 2003), p. 530.
54. Protocol No. 32, Session of the CPSU Presidium, 21 May 1962, *Cold War International History Project Bulletin*, 17/18, Fall 2012, p. 303, <http://www.wilsoncenter.org/publication/bulletin-no-17-18> (last accessed 25 July 2015); Anatoli I. Gribkov and William Y. Smith, *Operation Anadyr: US and Soviet Generals Recount the Cuban Missile Crisis* (Chicago: Edition Q, 1994), pp. 14, 19.
55. Anatoly Dobrynin, *In Confidence: Moscow's Ambassador to America's Six Cold War Presidents, 1962–1986*, revised edn (Seattle: University of Washington Press, 2001), pp. 71–2.
56. Blight et al., *Cuba on the Brink*, p. 198.
57. Conversation between Gomulka (Poland) and Castro, 20 March 1965, *Cold War International History Project Bulletin*, 17/18, Fall 2012, p. 766, <http://www.wilsoncenter.org/publication/bulletin- no-17-18> (last accessed 25 July 2015).
58. Taubman, *Khrushchev*, p. 553.
59. Dobrynin, *In Confidence*, pp. 79–80.
60. Blight and Welch, *On the Brink*, p. 334.
61. Dobrynin, *In Confidence*, p. 72. The date of the elections was in fact 6 November.
62. Gribkov and Smith, *Operation Anadyr*, p. 24.

63. Report of Major-General Igor Demyanovich Statsenko, Commander of the 51st Missile Division, about the Actions of the Division from 07.12.62 through 12.01.1962, National Security Archive, George Washington University (note that the date format is month-day-year), <http://www2.gwu.edu/~nsarchiv/NSAEBB/NSAEBB449/docs/Doc%201%20Igor%20Statsenko%20After-action%20report.pdf> (last accessed 25 July 2015).
64. Gribkov and Smith, *Operation Anadyr*, pp. 36–8.
65. Report of Major-General Igor Demyanovich Statsenko, Commander of the 51st Missile Division, about the Actions of the Division from 07.12.62 through 12.01.1962, National Security Archive, George Washington University, <http://www2.gwu.edu/~nsarchiv/NSAEBB/NSAEBB449/docs/Doc%201%20Igor%20Statsenko%20After-action%20report.pdf> (last accessed 25 July 2015).
66. Fursenko and Naftali, *'One Hell of a Gamble'*, pp. 193–4.
67. Garthoff, *Reflections*, p. 15.
68. Fursenko and Naftali, *'One Hell of a Gamble'*, p. 219.

# 3 Discovering the Missile Bases, 14–22 October 1962

I now know how Tojo felt when he was planning Pearl Harbor.

*Robert F. Kennedy*

## Warning the Soviets

US intelligence realised in the summer of 1962 that there was a substantial build-up of Soviet conventional military forces in Cuba. The CIA noted that twenty-one ships docked in July. There was evidence of large equipment such as crates that could contain aeroplane fuselage or missile components. The Agency speculated that the activity could represent increased technical assistance to Cuban industry and agriculture, and/or the Cuban armed forces; the establishment of surface-to-air (SAM) missile sites; or the establishment of technical intelligence facilities targeted against important installations such as the Cape Canaveral airbase in Florida.[1] An assessment on 2 October indicated that the shipments included tanks, self-propelled guns and other types of ground force equipment. It was apparent that the bulk of the supplies, though, comprised SA-2 SAMs and supporting equipment. It was noted that the Soviets had established twenty-five SAM sites on Cuba. Additionally, three or four missile sites of a different type had been identified. These resembled known coastal defence missile sites elsewhere and were believed to accommodate Soviet anti-shipping missiles with a range of up to thirty-five miles. It was estimated that there were sixty older-type MIG fighter aircraft along with at least one MIG-21, which was of a more advanced design, plus others under assembly. It was thought that eventually the total of MIG-21s in Cuba could reach as many as thirty. The latest shipments included sixteen guided missile patrol boats equipped with short-range (up to seventeen miles) missiles.[2]

Knowledge of the Soviet conventional military build-up led the White House to consider issuing a public warning about placing nuclear weapons on Cuba, but the matter was not straightforward. On 1 September, Deputy Special Assistant for National Security Affairs Carl Kaysen was concerned that issuing a warning against deploying nuclear weapons would provide a tacit endorsement of deployments below that level. More importantly, warning the Soviets against deploying nuclear missiles close to US borders would give them a 'legalistic' excuse for complaining about US-controlled nuclear forces surrounding the Soviet bloc, which meant that 'a statement might very well have a reverse effect and help provide the justification for establishment of a nuclear capability in Cuba'.[3] Nonetheless, Kennedy did issue public warnings, on 4 and 13 September. He was, in part, responding to Congressional pressure. Senator Kenneth Keating (Republican, New York) maintained that the Soviet Union was placing offensive missiles in Cuba. Although Keating had no solid evidence for his ideas, his speeches were of considerable political importance.[4] His colleagues Homer Capehart (Republican, Indiana) and Everett Dirksen (Republican, Illinois) made similar charges.

On 4 September, President Kennedy warned the Soviets that the presence of 'offensive ground to ground missiles' in Cuba would cause 'the gravest issues'. Nine days later he made it clear that 'If at any time the Communist build-up in Cuba' should threaten American security, 'then this country will do whatever must be done'.[5] The administration underscored its concern by warning Ambassador Dobrynin privately that offensive weapons in Cuba would not be tolerated.[6] Thus the administration had distinguished between a willingness to tolerate the weapons that were known to be present already, and the unacceptability of weapons capable of striking the United States.[7] This distinction would shape the US response to the discovery of the missiles. What Khrushchev made of the administration's warnings is not known, but his missile initiative was past the point of no return. He was unlikely to reverse his decision in response to vague admonitions from the White House.

## Discovering the Nuclear Missile Bases

It became apparent decades later that the US authorities greatly underestimated the scale of the Soviet troop presence in Cuba, due to the lack of reliable sources. Sources indicate that in July, the Soviets had planned bringing a total of 50,874 men to the island, including personnel for field hospitals, bakeries, mechanical workshops and other support units. In September the plan was revised to eliminate a number of naval squadrons, in part due to their visibility. This left a proposed full contingent of 45,234. Of that number, 3,332 turned back in response to the US naval quarantine around Cuba imposed on 24 October. Actual Soviet troop strength by that time was 41,902.[8] The highest estimate of Soviet troop numbers during the crisis was 10,000, with the figure being raised retrospectively early in 1963 to 22,000. A more accurate assessment would have led the administration to demand the removal of the troops, which meant – fortuitously – that an intelligence failure had avoided complicating matters.[9] At the same time, the higher number of Soviet troops in Cuba meant that an invasion would have experienced unexpected resistance.[10]

Some commentators have emphasised the presence of a photographic 'intelligence gap' stemming from the absence of U-2 flights over Cuba in September and the first part of October.[11] Even before the discovery of the nuclear missile bases, Director of the CIA John McCone complained that the hiatus had 'placed the United States intelligence community in a position where it could not report with assurance the development of offensive capabilities in Cuba'.[12] Flights were deferred due to poor weather, and for political reasons: a U-2 had strayed over the Soviet island of Sakhalin in the north Pacific on 30 August, while another, operated by the Taiwanese, was lost over communist China a week later.[13] Such events were diplomatically awkward. Secretary of State Dean Rusk, recalling the furore about the capture of pilot Gary Powers from over the Soviet Union in May

1960, was anxious that 'everything should be done' to avoid a further incident.[14] On 8 October, in connection with a proposal to resume reconnaissance over Cuba, top CIA analyst Sherman Kent suggested that 'opinion in the free world would probably condemn the announcement as threatening a marked increase in international tensions', and the Cubans would raise the matter in the UN. The US government would probably find itself in a position of 'virtual isolation' on the issue.[15] Concerns of this type could not be disregarded. It is not in any case certain that more U-2 flights over Cuba would have provided information about the nuclear missile bases much before 14 October, as construction may not have been far enough advanced to enable detection by photography.[16] However, as some of the recent literature has explored, the administration was exceedingly touchy about the issue, engaging later in vigorous efforts to obscure the notion of compromised surveillance practices just when the Soviets were constructing their bases.[17]

It did not help that human agent coverage in Cuba was limited. A post-missile-crisis assessment suggested that there had been little forward planning for the installation of agents,[18] although the importance of such efforts would only become apparent later. The CIA had two main agent networks on Cuba, AMCOBRA and AMTORRID, and received numerous ad hoc reports from dozens of disgruntled Cubans arriving in Miami on a daily Pan Am flight. The new arrivals were debriefed at a specially established interrogation centre at Opa Locka, near Miami. Agents testified to the movement of equipment from the ports to Soviet sites on Cuba. However, many accounts of missile site construction were inaccurate, while others were simply fabricated by individuals seeking to provoke US action.[19] American intelligence specialists also faced the challenge of evaluating large volumes of information. In February 1963 John McCone told President Kennedy that of 3,500 agent and refugee reports, 'only eight in retrospect were considered as reasonably valid indicators of the deployment of offensive missiles to Cuba'.[20]

As early as April 1961, soon after the Bay of Pigs invasion, Walt Rostow of the State Department Policy Planning Council raised the possibility of the Soviets turning Cuba into a base for nuclear missiles,[21] but it was not an issue he pushed consistently. Around the same time, Robert F. Kennedy also expressed worries about the Soviets setting up a missile base in Cuba.[22] The following spring he voiced a similar concern, focusing on the potential benefits – not just the risks – of a deployment. In doing so, he showed greater empathy with the Kremlin's thinking than did most of his colleagues. Like Rostow, though, he raised the issue only sporadically. John McCone was one of the few in US foreign policy circles who showed a sustained concern that the Soviets would station nuclear weapons in Cuba; he reasoned that the SAM bases were intended to protect more than just conventional deployments. On 21 August, he suggested that Cuba was 'a possible location' for Soviet MRBMs.[23] On 16 September, he warned that 'we must carefully study the prospect of secret importation and placement of several Soviet MRBMs . . . Do not wish to be overly alarming [on] this matter but believe CIA and community must keep government informed of danger of a surprise.'[24]

However, McCone's views gained little traction in the bureaucracy, because his arguments were largely intuitive rather than backed by evidence. Moreover, his status as a card-carrying Republican may not have done him any favours, given that Republican politicians were criticising the administration about Cuba. Later, White House adviser Clark Clifford suggested that the DCI's 'warnings had been couched in highly emotional and impressionistic terms' rather than resting on firm evidence, 'and he never pushed the intelligence community into making a more intensive effort to corroborate his beliefs'.[25] Nonetheless, President Kennedy responded to his promptings when on 23 August he ordered a study of the implications of a Soviet nuclear missile base in Cuba, and how to react militarily to such a development.[26] On 9 October Kennedy met with his advisers to discuss gathering evidence through photographic reconnaissance.[27] The resumption of intelligence flights five days later helped to ensure that the evidence was soon at hand.

It is clear that relatively few in US foreign policy circles anticipated that the Soviet Union would turn Cuba into a nuclear missile base, as this step was seen as being uncharacteristically bold. The perception of Soviet caution was evident in a number of assessments. A joint CIA and State Department report in May 1961 suggested that the Soviet bloc would not 'provide offensive type missiles, nor nuclear weapons' to Cuba.[28] In January 1962 the CIA maintained that although the Soviet Union,

> Cuba and any other Caribbean state which fell under Communist control could be used by the USSR as areas in which to establish missile, submarine, or air bases, the establishment of any such Soviet bases is unlikely for some time to come.[29]

Even though the 'military and psychological value' of such bases would be substantial, the Soviets would probably not wish to take the risks involved.[30] The belief in Soviet risk aversion prevailed despite the mounting evidence of increased conventional military support for Cuba. On 25 August, Director of the State Department Bureau of Intelligence and Research, Roger Hilsman, suggested that the 'most likely explanation' for the 'unusually heavy Soviet shipments to Cuba' was that the Soviets were enhancing the Cuban regime's defensive capabilities. Hilsman did not mention that the build-up might include nuclear weapons, nor did he propose that the change in behaviour (that is, making a larger than anticipated military commitment) might require a re-examination of Soviet motivations.[31]

Presenting what became a notorious assessment, on 19 September Sherman Kent noted that the Soviet Union could 'derive considerable military advantage from the establishment of Soviet medium and intermediate range ballistic missiles in Cuba, or from the establishment of a Soviet submarine base there'. At the same time,

> Either development . . . would be incompatible with Soviet practice to date and with Soviet policy as we presently estimate it. It would indicate a far greater willingness to increase the level of risk in US–Soviet relations than the USSR has displayed thus far, and consequently would have important policy implications with respect to other areas and other problems in East–West relations.[32]

The logic was entirely accurate, but Kent had made the easy mistake of projecting past Soviet behaviour into the future, without considering the potential benefits as well as dangers of placing missiles on Cuba.[33] Moreover, he had assumed wrongly that Moscow was taking the advice of the Soviet embassy in Washington about the possible American reaction to missiles in Cuba. Kent thought that Ambassador Dobrynin would have warned Khrushchev about the dangers of a US riposte to missiles in Cuba, but (as noted in the previous chapter) Dobrynin was in the dark.[34] The general consensus in the US government, according to a contemporary analyst, was that 'good Bolsheviks will not engage in adventurism, adventurism being defined as the taking of even small risks of large catastrophes, such as the destruction of the citadel of Communism, the Soviet Union'.[35] A 1963 assessment of the performance of US intelligence noted 'the rigor with which the view was held that the Soviet Union would not assume the risks entailed in establishing nuclear striking forces on Cuban soil'.[36]

By the time U-2 flights resumed on 14 October, the surveillance programme had been moved from the CIA to Strategic Air Command, which had newer aircraft that could fly 5,000 feet higher and so were less vulnerable to attack from the ground. On 14 October, one of the flights provided decisive evidence of the development that few US officials had expected. Major Richard D. Heyser of the US Air Force flew north to south over the western part of the island, taking 928 photographs during his six minutes over Cuba. Specialists at the National Photographic Intelligence Centre concluded the following day that the Soviets were developing three medium-range missile sites at San Cristobal. Eight large MRBM transporters and four erector launchers in tentative firing positions were noted at the three locations. Additional U-2 missions on 15 October by Major Rudolf Anderson revealed a fourth MRBM site near San Cristobal, and two ICBM sites at Guanajay. Photographs also revealed twenty-one crates for Soviet IL-28 Beagle medium-range bombers at San Julian airfield.[37]

The end of the Cold War revealed a full picture of the Soviet nuclear presence on Cuba. It emerged that at the beginning of the missile crisis there were thirty-six R-12 MRBMs, with twenty-four launchers. The missiles had a range of 1,300 nautical miles, making them able to reach Washington DC and the southern US states, and they carried warheads with explosive yields from 200 to 700 kilotons. This was up to thirty-five times the power of the atomic bomb that destroyed Hiroshima in 1945. The R-12s were not yet operational. The proposed twenty-four R-14 ICBMs were still on their way to Cuba, on board the *Krasnodar* and the *Kasimov*. The R-14s had a range of 2,800 nautical miles, enabling them to strike anywhere in the United States apart from Seattle, and they carried warheads of one megaton. There were eighty FKR (*Frontiviye Krilatiye Raketi*) tactical (battlefield) cruise missiles, with an equal number of nuclear warheads each with a yield of 5–12 kilotons – the equivalent of the bomb that destroyed Hiroshima. These had a range of up to ninety miles and were deployed to coastal sites as well near the Guantánamo base. There were twelve 'Luna' missiles (NATO designation: Free Rocket Over Ground (FROG)) equipped with nuclear warheads. The weapons had a range of up to twenty-five miles and a yield of two kilotons. Soviet tactical nuclear weapons were capable therefore of destroying the Guantánamo base, US ships near Cuba and invading troops, creating a nuclear battlefield which could escalate into full-scale nuclear war. Furthermore, there were twenty-nine IL-28 bombers, of which six had been adapted to carry nuclear bombs.[38]

As the President's Foreign Intelligence Advisory Board noted, the United States had experienced 'near-total intelligence surprise ... with respect to the introduction and deployment of Soviet strategic missiles in Cuba'.[39] Yet what John McCone described as the 'imponderables of what the other fellow will or will not do' – that is, speculating about the enemy's intentions – is an eternal challenge for intelligence agencies.[40] Human intelligence material, despite its limitations, had helped to pinpoint the San Cristobal area as a suspected missile site.[41] Technical information from GRU agent Oleg Penkovsky, which the CIA had 'run' with the help of Britain's MI6 (see Chapter 5), helped with the interpretation of the U-2 photographs. Furthermore, contrary to the common view that the US government was entirely in the dark on the matter, there was a general and accurate sense that Soviet forces in Cuba would be armed with tactical nuclear weapons.[42] Ultimately, as McCone noted, 'Every major weapons system was detected, identified, and reported (with respect to numbers, location and operational characteristics) before any one of these systems obtained an operational capability.'[43] All told, it was a decent performance.

## Establishing ExComm

At 20:30 hours on 15 October, after the photographic analysts had completed their work, CIA Deputy Director Marshall S. Carter told McGeorge Bundy about the missile sites. Given the import of what had been uncovered, one might imagine that Bundy, who was much closer to Kennedy than was McCone, would convey the news to the President immediately. However, Bundy waited until early the next day before telling him, partly to permit him 'a quiet evening and a night of sleep' in 'preparation' for 'what would face you in the next days'.[44] A shocked Kennedy – who understood the reasons for the delay – responded to the news of the Soviet nuclear missiles by ordering the creation of an ad hoc advisory body of foreign affairs specialists, the Executive Committee of the National Security Council – 'ExComm'. The goal was, as he put it later, to decide how to eliminate the missiles 'while trying to avoid a nuclear exchange'.[45] ExComm had a precedent. After the North Korean attack on South Korea in 1950, President Truman asked Secretary of State Dean Acheson to convene a small group of advisers to meet with him at Blair House. The group ended up providing counsel throughout the war, assessing US interests and options. This advisory pattern continued during the crisis of French rule in Indochina in 1954, under President Eisenhower.[46]

The membership of ExComm drew mainly from the existing National Security Council. Its composition reflected the need for expertise pertinent to a military crisis in the Western Hemisphere involving the Soviet Union.[47] Alongside the Kennedy brothers, ExComm attendees included Under Secretary of State George W. Ball, National Security Adviser McGeorge Bundy, Secretary of the Treasury Douglas Dillon, Deputy Secretary of Defense Roswell Gilpatric, Vice-President Lyndon B. Johnson, Deputy Under

Secretary of State for Political Affairs Alexis Johnson, Secretary
of Defense Robert S. McNamara, Director of Central Intelligence
John McCone, Secretary of State Dean Rusk, Presidential Adviser
Theodore Sorensen, Chairman of the Joint Chiefs of Staff General
Maxwell Taylor, and Ambassador-at-Large Llewellyn Thompson.

Two other officials opted out after initial participation. Charles
Bohlen, a former ambassador to the Soviet Union, chose to take
up his new role as ambassador in Paris in order to avoid arous-
ing suspicion that a major crisis was imminent. Former Secretary
of State Dean Acheson left Washington on 21 October to brief
European leaders (see Chapter 5).[48] Three subcommittees were
established to support ExComm: a Berlin–NATO Subcommittee
under Paul Nitze of the Pentagon; an Advance Planning
Subcommittee under Walt Rostow of the State Department; and
a Communications Subcommittee under Jerome Wiesner of the
Defense Communications Agency and William H. Orrick of the
State Department. The sub-committees were responsible for planning for various contingencies and investigating different policy
options; for example, Nitze and his colleagues developed plans
for denuclearised zones in Latin America and Africa as a means
of resolving the crisis.[49]

## Rejecting Cuba–Turkey Parallels

Resisting the Soviet missiles in Cuba depended on rejecting the
idea that they were analogous with the American Jupiter missiles in
Turkey, which the Soviet Union had challenged only with words.
At times, though, the analogy appears to have been accepted.
Dean Rusk thought that Khrushchev 'may feel that it's important
for us to learn about living under medium-range missiles', just as
the Soviet Union lived in the shadow of such weapons. Llewellyn
Thompson predicted that Khrushchev would 'justify his actions
because of NATO missiles in Italy and Turkey'. John McCone
believed that Khrushchev sought to force the United States out of
its overseas bases and from Berlin. There was an acceptance that
the Jupiters were a logical target for attack if the United States
struck the Soviet missile bases in Cuba, with Robert Kennedy

saying on 16 October that if US air strikes destroyed the missiles in Cuba then it would be 'almost incumbent upon the Russians, then, to say, Well, we're going to send them in again, and if you do it again, we're going to do, we're going to do the same thing to Turkey, or . . . Iran'.[50]

President Kennedy accepted the analogy, albeit indirectly. In a strikingly obtuse statement on 16 October, he suggested that the Soviet move in Cuba was, in comparative terms, 'just as if we suddenly began to put in a major number of MRBMs in Turkey. Now that'd be goddamn dangerous.' McGeorge Bundy replied 'Well, we did, Mr President.'[51] Kennedy's comment is especially odd in light of how in August he had, out of concerns about the efficacy of the Jupiters, ordered a study into their removal (some of the early Cuban Missile Crisis literature suggested, mistakenly, that he had ordered their withdrawal).[52] However, he backed away from the analogy implicit in the 'goddamn dangerous' statement by saying that the decision to emplace the missiles was 'five years ago . . . during a different period'. For Kennedy and his advisers, US missiles in Turkey were defensive, while Soviet ones in Cuba were offensive – even though the weapons were much the same. Dean Rusk explained to US diplomats that US nuclear bases abroad were established in the face of 'Soviet expansion and aggression' including 'a series of open Soviet boasts and threats, beginning in 1957' after the launch of the Sputnik satellite. The purpose of US bases was to 'redress an imbalance created by Soviet aggressiveness and threatened expansion', while Soviet bases in Cuba had created 'a new and serious imbalance in [the] power situation, thus imperiling world peace'.[53] Evidently, American officials would only permit 'an imbalance' if it favoured the United States. Moreover, there was no appreciation that just as the US government had sought to defend Western Europe, the Soviet Union might feel a need to defend Cuba.

The Soviet secrecy and deception surrounding the stationing of missiles in Cuba greatly aggrieved US policymakers. Yet Washington was no stranger to underhand practices. Covert action had been a mainstay of US foreign policy since the Second World War, and recently the Kennedy administration had hoped to conceal its hand in the attack on Cuba in April 1961.

Nonetheless, for all the inconsistencies in US policy, it was reasonable for the administration to challenge the presence of the missiles in Cuba. It had warned Moscow against placing nuclear missiles there, and had met with deceit. On 25 October Kennedy told Khrushchev that the Soviet government had provided 'the most explicit assurance . . . both publicly and privately, that no offensive weapons were being sent to Cuba . . .' Relying on these 'solemn assurances', he had 'urged restraint upon those in this country who were urging action . . . And then I learned beyond doubt what you have not denied – namely, that all these public assurances were false.'[54] Furthermore, Soviet weapons in Cuba were of great importance in American domestic politics and relations with allies, and the presence of American missiles in Turkey did not have comparable consequences for the Soviet government.[55] Thus, placing missiles in Cuba, while in some ways comparable with US missiles in Turkey, was immensely more provocative. Kennedy expressed the case plainly in his 22 October public address: 'the secret, swift, and extraordinary buildup of Communist missiles' had taken place in 'an area well known to have a special and historical relationship to the United States and the nations of the Western Hemisphere, in violation of Soviet assurances, and in defiance of American and hemispheric policy'.[56]

## The Options

The early ExComm discussions settled on three chief options: diplomatic engagement with the Soviet Union, a naval blockade around Cuba to put pressure on the Soviets to remove the missiles, or an air strike with or without a ground invasion.[57] At this stage the longer-range R-14 missiles had not reached the island, and by 22 October, none of the R-12 missiles had been fuelled, targeted or mated with a warhead.[58] There was a concern that any strikes had to be carried out before the missiles became fully operational, with operational status being seen almost as a token of intent.[59] Robert McNamara noted that the 'danger of starting military action *after* they acquire a nuclear capability' was 'great',[60] given that the remaining weapons might be launched. Robert F. Kennedy was among those pushing vigorously for an air strike and an invasion: even though 'you're going to kill an awful lot of people, and we're going to take an awful lot of heat on it . . . we should just get into it, and get it over with, and take our losses'.[61] He suggested engineering a pretext for attack – a 'sinking *The Maine*' type incident.[62] RFK recalled in his memoir that during one of the early ExComm talks he passed a note to the President saying, 'I now know how Tojo felt when he was planning Pearl Harbor'.[63] His reference to Pearl Harbor has often been taken to indicate moral opposition to military action, but in the light of the ExComm records it is clear instead that the statement reflected his uncomfortable empathy with the instigator of a surprise attack.[64] The belligerence reflected a sense of betrayal that he felt upon learning that, contrary to assurances, Khrushchev had turned Cuba into a nuclear missile base.[65]

However useful it may have appeared to some, the analogy between attacking the nuclear missile bases in Cuba and the surprise Japanese attack on the United States naval base in Hawaii in 1941 was questionable: Dean Acheson suggested later that

> at Pearl Harbor the Japanese without provocation or warning attacked our fleet thousands of miles from their shores. In the present situation the Soviet Union had installed ninety miles from our coast – while denying that they were doing so – offensive weapons that were capable of lethal injury to the United States.[66]

Acheson was the most aggressive civilian adviser, urging that 'We should proceed at once with the necessary military actions and should do no talking. The Soviets will react some place. We must expect this; take the consequences and manage the situations as they evolve.' There should be 'no consultations with Khrushchev, Castro or our allies'.[67] McGeorge Bundy favoured an air strike to eliminate the bases in a quick, clean surgical operation that would confront 'the world with a fait accompli'.[68] Douglas Dillon advocated immediate military action.[69] John McCone suggested giving the Soviets twenty-four hours to begin dismantling and removing the missiles. If nothing happened 'we should make a massive surprise strike at air fields, MRBM sites and SAM sites concurrently'.[70] Maxwell Taylor supported an air strike, although he stopped short of an invasion.[71] Chief of the Air Staff Curtis LeMay told Kennedy that there was 'no choice except direct military action . . . blockade and political action will lead us right into war. This is almost as bad as the appeasement at Munich.' Chief of Naval Operations Admiral George Anderson and Chief of Staff for the Army Lieutenant General Earle Wheeler made similar arguments. The Joint Chiefs would remain consistent in advocating the use of force to eliminate the Soviet missiles.[72]

Robert McNamara advocated military preparations, but he was very conscious that matters could all too easily get out of hand:

> Now after we've launched fifty to a hundred sorties, what kind of a world do we live in? How, how do we stop at that point? I don't know the answer to this. I think tonight State and we ought to work on the consequences of any one of these courses of actions, consequences which I don't believe are entirely clear . . . At any place in the world.[73]

Initially, Dean Rusk favoured attacking Cuba but, like McNamara, he feared 'what the final outcome will be'. He favoured an effort to seek a 'settlement by political means'. Other ExComm members agreed that the surreptitious installation of the missiles was intolerable but favoured a diplomatic approach. George Ball argued that striking without warning was dangerous and morally unacceptable. Charles Bohlen 'strongly advocated diplomatic effort' because 'military action would rapidly escalate into an invasion'.[74]

Douglas Dillon later pointed out that figures who were reluctant to use military force were relative neophytes in dealing with international crises, while most of the hawks – such as himself and Acheson – had more experience. Because of this, the argument goes, they were more confident that using force would succeed in forcing the Soviets to back down.[75] Yet Dean Rusk, who had served in the State Department during the Cold War crises of the 1940s and early 1950s, favoured a political response;

while Robert F. Kennedy, with no involvement in foreign affairs before 1961, was belligerent. Different members of ExComm had their own ideas about the prospect of nuclear war. Hawks such as McCone and Dillon did not feel that it was likely, given the United States' conventional and nuclear military preponderance. By contrast, President Kennedy, Ball and McNamara felt that war was a real possibility. As noted in the Introduction to this work, Kennedy suggested after the confrontation that the chances of war had been somewhere between one in three, and even.[76] Ball feared that 'we might be about to blow up the world'.[77] While relishing the beautiful autumn evening on Saturday 27 October, McNamara wondered whether he would ever experience 'another Saturday night'.[78]

One of the oddities of the ExComm talks was that the prospect of nuclear war and how it would be waged was not discussed, even though on 22 October Kennedy had threatened the Soviets with a 'full retaliatory response' if they launched a nuclear attack.[79] The focus instead was on how to respond to the Soviet move. Yet few, if any, members of ExComm harboured illusions about what full-scale nuclear war would entail. Recently-released documents indicate that Kennedy's National Security Council underwent a harrowing briefing during the Berlin Crisis in July 1961. An analysis by the NSC's top-secret Net Evaluation Subcommittee stated that 'a nuclear exchange between the US and the USSR' would mean 'the shattering of the established political, military, and economic structure' of such 'scope and intensity' that it would 'practically defy accurate assessment'. All the same, the briefing depicted a Soviet surprise attack on the United States in the autumn of 1963 that began with submarine-launched missile strikes against Strategic Air Command bases. An estimated 48 to 71 million Americans were 'killed outright', while radioactive fallout would blanket up to 71 per cent of the nation's residences, bringing further casualties. In the Soviet Union and China respectively, by the end of one month 67 and 76 million people would have been killed. After the presentation, President Kennedy commented to Dean Rusk: 'And we call ourselves the human race.' Rusk himself thought it was 'an awesome briefing'.[80]

## The Blockade

Initially the President favoured initiating air strikes, but he came to recognise the disadvantages of attacking the missiles: it would be difficult to destroy them all; other, unknown missiles might be launched against the United States; a ground invasion would still be required; and matters could escalate out of control. Furthermore, the supposed resemblance to Pearl Harbor would be morally problematic.[81] (The parallel, however questionable, began to trouble Robert F. Kennedy, too, with him rejecting a strike on the missile bases on the grounds that 'A sneak attack was not in our traditions.'[82]) At the same time, some of the milder counsel did not impress the President, with him dismissing a suggestion from US representative to the UN Adlai Stevenson that the Guantánamo base would have to be conceded by saying that 'such action would convey to the world that we had been frightened into abandoning our position'.[83] Kennedy was keen to avoid war but, like most of his colleagues, he did wish to appear resolute in response to the highly provocative Soviet action of placing nuclear missiles in Cuba. This may help to explain why there was little or no discussion about making a private approach to Khrushchev, or about using economic pressure to shape Soviet policies. Nor was there discussion of making a démarche to Castro, reflecting the false assumption that he was nothing more than a Soviet puppet.[84] For all its limitations, though, ExComm represented a more orderly use of advisers than had taken place in the run-up to the Bay of Pigs attack, and its use showed how Kennedy had evolved as a manager of foreign affairs.

The chosen option – a naval blockade – would not prevent continued work on the missile sites using materials already in Cuba; as Dean Acheson commented, it was a 'method of keeping things out, not getting things out'.[85] However, a blockade did have its merits. It provided a middle ground between immediate recourse to dialogue and concessions on one hand, and violence on the other, while retaining the flexibility to move in either direction as matters unfolded. Ships heading towards the island would be stopped, boarded and searched for offensive weapons and other military resources. If a vessel was found to contain contraband, the commander would be told to head for another port, or the ship would be taken into custody.[86] The picket line (the 'Walnut Line') would be established 800 miles from Cuba, out of range of the IL-28 bombers. The administration referred publicly to a 'quarantine' rather than 'blockade', to avoid unfavourable associations with the Soviet blockade of Berlin in 1948–9, to evade questions of international law and to echo a 1937 speech from President Roosevelt in which he urged 'peace-loving nations' to 'quarantine the aggressors'.[87] The President would announce the quarantine proposal on television and radio on Monday 22 October.

## President Kennedy's Meeting with Gromyko

Until the President's public address, relations with the Soviets unfolded as usual. On 18 October, President Kennedy saw the Soviet Foreign Minister Andrei Gromyko in a meeting that been arranged before the discovery of the missiles. Gromyko maintained that Soviet assistance to the Castro regime was 'pursued solely' to enhance 'the defense capabilities of Cuba and to the development of Cuba'.[88] Kennedy felt that Gromyko 'told more barefaced lies than I have ever heard in so short a time. All during his denial that the Russians had any missiles or weapons, or anything else, in Cuba, I had the low-level pictures in the center drawer of my desk, and it was an enormous temptation to show them to him.'[89] As the response to the missile sites was still under discussion, Kennedy kept his own counsel. Later, Robert F. Kennedy explained the President's restraint to Dobrynin by saying that he was 'so shocked at Gromyko's presentation and his failure to recite these facts that he felt that any effort to have an intelligent and honest conversation would not be profitable'.[90]

Oblivious, Gromyko reported positively to Moscow that 'All that we know about the US position on the Cuban question warrants the conclusion that, by and large, the situation is quite satisfactory.'[91] For his part, Nikita Khrushchev considered that by stating, in effect, that 'we have no atomic missiles in Cuba' Gromyko was indeed 'lying', but the deceit was legitimate because 'he had orders from the Party'.[92] Gromyko's meeting

**79**

with President Kennedy gained some notoriety. Later, British ambassador in Washington Harold Caccia suggested that

> Something depends on the context and exact words used by the President and Gromyko. But it is a fine point for there is no doubt that Sir Harold Nicolson's injunction that truthfulness as observed by a diplomatist should include 'a constant anxiety to avoid, even inadvertently, leaving a false impression'.[93]

Gromyko did not actually deny the presence of nuclear weapons in Cuba, and he did not have the authority to reveal all even in the remote event that he had wanted to do so. At the same time, his performance on 18 October would always taint him in the eyes of the Kennedy administration.

## Towards the 22 October Address

On 22 October, prior to his television broadcast, the President briefed the non-ExComm members of his cabinet. These officials had realised over the previous few days that something was going on, but they were shocked about the discovery of the missiles.[94] With the help of Rusk, McNamara, McCone and Thompson, Kennedy also gave briefings to senior figures in Congress. Senator Richard Russell (Democrat, Georgia), Chairman of the Senate Armed Services Committee, urged military action, because Khrushchev had 'once again rattled his missiles; he can become firmer and firmer; we must react'. Even though he had opposed the Bay of Pigs invasion, Chairman of the Senate Foreign Relations Committee J. William Fulbright (Democrat, Arkansas) felt that 'The time has come for an invasion', as did Senator Bourke Hickenlooper (Republican, Iowa).[95] Kennedy rued the reflexively belligerent counsel he had received from the Congressmen; he reflected soon after that 'when you get a group of senators together, they are always dominated by the man who takes the boldest and strongest line. That is what happened the other day. After Russell spoke, no-one wanted to take issue with him.'[96] The idea that the senators were competing with one another was borne out the following day when, in conversation with McCone, Russell was more supportive of Kennedy's policies.[97] Both the Republican and the Democratic party leaderships issued statements of support. Kennedy also made a point of ensuring that he had the support of former presidents Herbert Hoover, Harry S. Truman and Dwight Eisenhower.[98] The President attached particular importance to the backing of the latter, given his status as an eminent military commander.

The administration took extraordinary precautions to conceal the existence of the crisis from the press until the public announcement planned for Monday 22 October. Not until the evening of 19 October – with Kennedy making an unscheduled return from the campaign trail to Washington, and Rusk cancelling a speaking engagement – did reporters become generally aware that something of great importance was going on.[99] Jeanne Sutherland, the wife of a British diplomat in Washington, noted that in the run-up to the 22 October address, 'The atmosphere became very oppressive . . . something very serious was obviously happening but nobody knew precisely what.'[100] The Cuban and Soviet governments realised that a major development was imminent, but could not be sure what. Although in the 1950s Soviet intelligence had installed a network of electronic 'bugs' in the US Embassy in Moscow when the building was under construction, the bugging did not yield much useful information during the missile crisis. US policy was made in the White House rather than the State Department and the US Embassy, and most Embassy officials did not have full knowledge about the discovery of the missiles in Cuba until 22 October.[101]

The KGB station in Washington had contacts among journalists (including John Scali of the American Broadcasting Company, whose contacts with the Soviets were sanctioned by the Federal Bureau of Investigation), and in foreign embassies including those of Argentina and Venezuela. The KGB also had agents in the French and Belgian foreign ministries, providing access to copies of cables from the French Ambassador in the United States, Herve Alphand, to Paris. All the same, Soviet intelligence had no top-level sources in the US government, which meant that during the missile crisis there was a reliance on mere gossip and speculation.[102] KGB official Alexander Feklisov wrote on several reports from the Washington station during the missile crisis, 'This report does not have any secret information.'[103] Soviet signals intelligence detected unusual activity among US communications in the days before Kennedy's speech, but could not explain the purpose of the activity. Similarly, the GRU became aware of heightened activity by the US Air Force and Navy in the Caribbean, and the Soviet military learned of an order from Robert McNamara that senior military officers should remain near the Pentagon to participate in a series of meetings. Nothing more was known.[104] Newspaper headlines such as 'Capital Crisis Air Hints at Developments on Cuba' in the *New York Times* on 22 October gave the Soviets further cause for concern.[105]

Deliberations began in the Kremlin about the developing crisis at about midnight in Moscow, midday Washington time, on 22 October. Khrushchev told the Presidium that 'It has become known that [Kennedy] is preparing some kind of address.' He noted that US naval vessels carrying soldiers were 'massing' in the Caribbean, but 'the heart of the matter is that we don't want to unleash a war. What we want is to cause a bit of a scare, to deter [US] forces with respect to Cuba.' There was discussion about authorising Soviet forces in Cuba to use tactical nuclear weapons against invading American forces, with Khrushchev and Defence Minister Malinovsky taking a hawkish position and backing this approach. However, deputy premier Anastas Mikoyan played a critical role in moderating the willingness to deploy the weapons, even though Khrushchev was intolerant of being challenged.[106] Now it was simply a matter of tense anticipation until President Kennedy's public address.

## Notes

1. CIA Memorandum, 20 August 1962, in Mary S. McAuliffe (ed.), *CIA Documents on the Cuban Missile Crisis* (Washington, DC: CIA History Staff, 1992), pp. 19–20.
2. Hilsman to Ball, 2 October 1962, *Foreign Relations of the United States (FRUS) 1961–1963 XI Cuban Missile Crisis and Aftermath*

(Washington, DC: USGPO, 1996), document 5, <https://history.state.gov/historicaldocuments/frus1961-63v11/d5> (last accessed 25 July 2015).

3. Jonathan Renshon, 'Mirroring Risk: The Cuban Missile Estimation', *Intelligence and National Security*, 24: 3, June 2009, p. 328; Kaysen to Clifton, 1 September 1962, *FRUS 1961–1962 X Cuba, January 1961–September 1962* (1997), document 402, <https://history.state.gov/historicaldocuments/frus1961-63v10/d402> (last accessed 25 July 2015).

4. Clark Clifford, *Counsel to the President: A Memoir* (New York: Random House, 1991), p. 357. See also Max Holland, 'A Luce Connection: Senator Keating, William Pawley, and the Cuban Missile Crisis', *Journal of Cold War Studies*, 1: 3, Fall 1999, pp. 139–67.

5. Editorial note, *FRUS 1961–1962 X*, pp. 1065–6, document 429, <https://history.state.gov/historicaldocuments/frus1961-63v10/d429> (last accessed 25 July 2015).

6. Richard Ned Lebow and Janice Gross Stein, *We All Lost the Cold War* (Princeton, NJ: Princeton University Press, 1994), p. 68.

7. Arnold Horelick, 'The Cuban Missile Crisis: An Analysis of Soviet Calculations and Behavior', Memorandum RM-3779-PR, The Rand Corporation, September 1963, <http://www.rand.org/pubs/research_memoranda/RM3779.html> (last accessed 25 July 2015).

8. Anatoli I. Gribkov and William Y. Smith, *Operation Anadyr: US and Soviet Generals Recount the Cuban Missile Crisis* (Chicago: Edition Q, 1994), p. 28.

9. Raymond L. Garthoff, 'US Intelligence in the Cuban Missile Crisis', in James G. Blight and David A. Welch (eds), *Intelligence and the Cuban Missile Crisis* (Abingdon: Frank Cass, 1998), pp. 28–9.

10. Blaine L. Pardoe, *The Fires of October: The Planned Invasion of Cuba during the Missile Crisis of 1962* (Stroud: Fonthill, 2012), p. 78.

11. See David M. Barrett and Max Holland, *Blind over Cuba: The Photo Gap and the Missile Crisis* (College Station: Texas A&M University Press, 2012).

12. McCone, 'Memorandum of Discussion with McGeorge Bundy', 5 October 1962, in McAuliffe (ed.), *CIA Documents*, pp. 115–17.

13. James R. Killian, 'Memorandum and Report for the President', 4 February 1963, in ibid. pp. 361–71.

14. Kirkpatrick, 'Memorandum for the Director', 1 March 1963, in ibid. pp. 61–2.
15. Sherman Kent, 'Implications of an Announcement by the President that the US Would Conduct Overheard Reconnaissance of Cuba', 8 October 1962, in ibid. pp. 115–17.
16. NSC meeting, 22 October 1962, *FRUS 1961–1963 XI*, document 41, <https://history.state.gov/historicaldocuments/frus1961-63v11/d41> (last accessed 25 July 2015).
17. Barrett and Holland, *Blind over Cuba*, pp. 22–39.
18. James R. Killian, 'Memorandum and Report for the President', 4 February 1963, in McAuliffe (ed.), *CIA Documents*, pp. 361–71.
19. Michael M. Dobbs, *One Minute to Midnight: Kennedy, Khrushchev and Castro on the Brink of Nuclear War* (New York: Knopf, 2008), p. 122; Lehman, Memorandum for DCI, 'CIA Handling Kirkpatrick, Memorandum for the Director, "CIA Handling of the Soviet Buildup in Cuba"', 14 November 1962, in McAuliffe (ed.), *CIA Documents*, p. 99.
20. John A. McCone, 'Memorandum for the President', 28 February 1963, in ibid. p. 374.
21. Rostow, 'Notes on Cuba Policy', 24 April 1961, in Laurence Chang and Peter Kornbluh (eds), with foreword by Robert S. McNamara, *The Cuban Missile Crisis, 1962: A National Security Archive Documents Reader* (New York: The New Press, 1992), pp. 16–17.
22. Arthur M. Schlesinger, Jr., *Robert Kennedy and His Times* (New York: Ballantine Books, 1979), p. 471.
23. Renshon, 'Mirroring Risk', pp. 329–30.
24. Ibid. pp. 330–1.
25. Clifford, *Counsel*, pp. 357–8.
26. NSAM 181, 23 August 1962, *FRUS 1961–1962 X*, document 386, <https://history.state.gov/historicaldocuments/frus1961-63v10/d386> (last accessed 25 July 2015).
27. Rostow, 'Notes on Cuba Policy', 24 April 1961, pp. 16–17.
28. Editorial note, *FRUS 1961–1963 V Soviet Union* (1998), document 58, <https://history.state.gov/historicaldocuments/frus1961-63v05/d58> (last accessed 25 July 2015).
29. Special National Intelligence Estimate, 17 January 1962, *FRUS 1961–1963 XII American Republics* (1996), document 91, <https://history.state.gov/historicaldocuments/frus1961-63v12/d91> (last accessed 25 July 2015).
30. Ibid.

31. Renshon, 'Mirroring Risk', p. 328.
32. Special National Intelligence Estimate (SNIE 85-3-62), 19 September 1962, in McAuliffe (ed.), CIA Documents, p. 93.
33. Renshon, 'Mirroring Risk', pp. 315–38.
34. Len Scott, 'Eyeball to Eyeball: Blinking and Winking, Spyplanes and Secrets', *International Relations*, 26: 3, September 2012, p. 357; Dino Brugioni, *Eyeball to Eyeball: The Inside Story of the Cuban Missile Crisis*, edited by Robert F. McCort (New York: Random House, 1991), p. 147.
35. Horelick, 'The Cuban Missile Crisis', p. 34.
36. James R. Killian, 'Memorandum and Report for the President', 4 February 1963, in McAuliffe (ed.), *CIA Documents*, pp. 361–71.
37. Pardoe, *The Fires of October*, pp. 71–2; Editorial note, *FRUS 1961–1963 XI*, document 16, <https://history.state.gov/historical-documents/frus1961-63v11/d16> (last accessed 25 July 2015).
38. Aleksandr Fursenko and Timothy Naftali, *Khrushchev's Cold War: The Inside Story of an American Adversary* (New York: Norton, 2006), pp. 468–9; Gribkov and Smith, *Operation Anadyr*, pp. 26–7; Svetlana Savranskaya and Thomas Blanton (eds), with Anna Melyakova, 'Last Nuclear Weapons Left Cuba in December 1962: Soviet Military Documents Provide Detailed Account of Cuban Missile Crisis Deployment and Withdrawal', National Security Archive, George Washington University, <http://www2.gwu.edu/~nsarchiv/NSAEBB/NSAEBB449/> (last accessed 25 July 2015).
39. James R. Killian, 'Memorandum and Report for the President', 4 February 1963, in McAuliffe (ed.), *CIA Documents*, pp. 361–71.
40. McCone to Kennedy, 28 February 1962, in ibid. pp. 373–6.
41. Lehman to DCI, 'CIA Handling of the Soviet Buildup in Cuba', 14 November 1962, in ibid. p. 99.
42. On the Kennedy administration's knowledge about the tactical nuclear weapons see David G. Coleman, 'The Missiles of November, December, January, February ... The Problem of Acceptable Risk in the Cuban Missile Crisis Settlement', *Journal of Cold War Studies*, 9: 3, Summer 2007, pp. 5–48.
43. McCone to Kennedy, 28 February 1962, in McAuliffe (ed.), *CIA Documents*, pp. 373–6. On the performance of US intelligence see Max Holland, 'The Politics of Intelligence Postmortems: Cuba, 1962–1963', *International Journal of Intelligence and Counterintelligence*, 20: 3, Fall 2007, pp. 415–52.
44. Editorial note, *FRUS 1961–1963 XI*, document 16, <https://

history.state.gov/historicaldocuments/frus1961-63v11/d16> (last accessed 25 July 2015).

45. Kennedy's Remarks to the NSC Meeting, 22 January 1963, *FRUS 1961–1963 XIII Western Europe and Canada* (1994), document 168, <https://history.state.gov/historicaldocuments/frus1961-63v13/d168> (last accessed 25 July 2015).

46. Dan Caldwell, 'The Cuban Crisis and the American Style of Crisis Management', RAND/UCLA Center for the Study of Soviet International Behavior, March 1989, <http://www.rand.org/pubs/notes/N2943.html> (last accessed 25 July 2015).

47. David R. Gibson, *Talk at the Brink: Deliberation and Decision during the Cuban Missile Crisis* (Princeton, NJ: Princeton University Press, 2012), pp. 51–2.

48. Dean Acheson, 'Homage to Plain Dumb Luck', in Robert A. Divine (ed.), *The Cuban Missile Crisis* (New York: Wiener, 1988), p. 192. Acheson criticised the ExComm discussions as being 'repetitive, leaderless and a waste of time', but he only attended the sessions on 17 October, when the President was out on the campaign trail.

49. Memorandum for the record, 25 *October 1962, FRUS 1961–1963 X-XI-XII Microfiche Supplement, American Republics; Cuba 1961–1962; Cuban Missile Crisis and Aftermath*, document 398, <http://history.state.gov/historicaldocuments/frus1961-63v10-12mSupp/d398> (last accessed 25 July 2015).

50. Meeting at the White House, 16 October 1961, *FRUS 1961–1963 XI*, document 18, <https://history.state.gov/historicaldocuments/frus1961-63v11/d18> (last accessed 25 July 2015).

51. Off-the-record meeting on Cuba, 16 October 1962, *FRUS 1961–1963 XI*, document 21, <https://history.state.gov/historicaldocuments/frus1961-63v11/d21> (last accessed 25 July 2015); Philip Nash, *The Other Missiles of October: Eisenhower, Kennedy, and the Jupiters, 1957–1963* (Chapel Hill: University of North Carolina Press, 1997), p. 121.

52. NSAM 181, 23 August 1962, *FRUS 1961–1962 X*, document 386, <https://history.state.gov/historicaldocuments/frus1961-63v10/d386> (last accessed 25 July 2015); Nash, *The Other Missiles*, p. 110.

53. Telegram to all diplomatic and consular posts, 24 October 1962, *FRUS 1961–1963 X-XI-XII*, document 390, <http://history.state.gov/historicaldocuments/frus1961-63v10-12mSupp/d390> (last accessed 25 July 2015).

54. Kennedy to Khrushchev, 25 October 1962, *FRUS 1961–1962 XI*, document 68, <https://history.state.gov/historicaldocuments/frus 1961-63v11/d68> (last accessed 25 July 2015).
55. Lebow and Stein, *We All Lost the Cold War*, p. 79.
56. Radio and Television Report to the American People on the Soviet Arms Buildup in Cuba, 22 October 1962, John F. Kennedy Presidential Library and Museum, <http://www.jfklibrary.org/ Asset-Viewer/sUVmCh-sB0moLfrBcaHaSg.aspx> (last accessed 25 July 2015) [document 4, Appendix 4 in this volume].
57. For a full account of the planning for military action, see Pardoe, *The Fires of October*.
58. Gribkov and Smith, *Operation Anadyr*, p. 6.
59. Stephen Twigge and Len Scott, 'The Other Other Missiles of October: The Thor IBMs and the Cuban Missile Crisis', *Electronic Journal of International History*, 3, 30 January 2012, <http://sas-space.sas.ac.uk/3387/> (last accessed 25 July 2015).
60. Off-the-record meeting on Cuba, 16 October 1962, *FRUS 1961– 1963 XI*, document 21, <https://history.state.gov/historicaldocu ments/frus1961-63v11/d21> (last accessed 25 July 2015).
61. Meeting at the White House, 16 October 1962, *FRUS 1961–1963 XI*, document 18, <https://history.state.gov/historicaldocuments/ frus1961-63v11/d18> (last accessed 25 July 2015); Sheldon M. Stern, *The Cuban Missile Crisis in American Memory: Myths versus Reality* (Stanford, CA: Stanford University Press, 2012), p. 42.
62. Off-the-record meeting about Cuba, 16 October 1962, *FRUS 1961–1963 XI*, document 21, <https://history.state.gov/historical documents/frus1961-63v11/d21> (last accessed 25 July 2015). In February 1898 an explosion on board the *SS Maine* in Havana harbour, caused allegedly by the Spanish, helped to precipitate an American declaration of war against Spain. The American victory brought an end to Spanish rule in Cuba, and the beginning of US domination of the country until 1959.
63. Robert F. Kennedy, *Thirteen Days: A Memoir of the Cuban Missile Crisis* (New York: Norton, 1999), p. 37.
64. Len Scott, David Gioe and Christopher Andrew, 'Introduction', in David Gioe, Len Scott and Christopher Andrew (eds), *An International History of the Cuban Missile Crisis: A 50-Year Retrospective* (London: Routledge, 2014), p. 2.
65. Mark White, 'Fifty Years On: The Cuban Missile Crisis Revisited and Reinterpreted', Lecture Series Paper No. 9, Institute for the

Study of the Americas, 2012, <http://sas-space.sas.ac.uk/4748/1/markwhite.pdf> (last accessed 25 July 2015).

66. Acheson, 'Homage to Plain Dumb Luck', pp. 188–9.
67. Memorandum for the file, 17 October 1962, *FRUS 1961–1963 XI*, document 23, <https://history.state.gov/historicaldocuments/frus1961-63v11/d23> (last accessed 25 July 2015).
68. Record of meeting, 19 October 1962, *FRUS 1961–1963 XI*, document 31, <https://history.state.gov/historicaldocuments/frus1961-63v11/d31> (last accessed 25 July 2015).
69. Memorandum for the file, 19 October 1962, *FRUS 1961–1963 XI*, document 28, <https://history.state.gov/historicaldocuments/frus1961-63v11/d28> (last accessed 25 July 2015).
70. Memorandum for discussion, 17 October 1962, *FRUS 1961–1963 XI*, document 26, <https://history.state.gov/historicaldocuments/frus1961-63v11/d26> (last accessed 25 July 2015).
71. Memorandum for the file, 17 October 1962, *FRUS 1961–1963 XI*, document 23, <https://history.state.gov/historicaldocuments/frus1961-63v11/d23> (last accessed 25 July 2015).
72. Scott, 'Eyeball to Eyeball', pp. 352–3.
73. Off-the-record meeting on Cuba, 16 October 1962, *FRUS 1961–1963 XI*, document 21, <https://history.state.gov/historicaldocuments/frus1961-63v11/d21> (last accessed 25 July 2015).
74. Memorandum for the file, 19 October 1962, *FRUS 1961–1963 XI*, document 28, <https://history.state.gov/historicaldocuments/frus1961-63v11/d28> (last accessed 25 July 2015).
75. James Blight and David A. Welch (eds), with foreword by McGeorge Bundy, *On the Brink: Americans and Soviets Reexamine the Cuban Missile Crisis* (New York: Noonday Press, 1990), pp. 215–19.
76. Raymond L. Garthoff, *A Journey through the Cold War: A Memoir of Containment and Coexistence* (Washington, DC: Brookings, 2001), p. 181.
77. George W. Ball, *The Past has Another Pattern: Memoirs* (New York: Norton, 1982), pp. 297–8.
78. Len Scott, *The Cuban Missile Crisis and the Threat of Nuclear War* (London: Continuum, 2007), p. 2.
79. Scott, 'Eyeball to Eyeball', p. 353.
80. '1961 Report of the Net Evaluation Subcommittee National Security Council', undated, available at National Security Archive Electronic Briefing Book No. 480, <http://www2.gwu.edu/~nsarchiv/nukevault/ebb480/#_ednref11> (last accessed 25 July

2015); Dean Rusk, *As I Saw It: A Secretary of State's Memoirs* (New York: Norton, 1990), pp. 246–7.

81. NSC meeting, 22 October 1962, *FRUS 1961–1963 XI*, document 41, <https://history.state.gov/historicaldocuments/frus1961-63v11/d41> (last accessed 25 July 2015).

82. Record of Meeting, 19 October 1962, *FRUS XI*, document 31, <https://history.state.gov/historicaldocuments/frus1961-63v11/d31> (last accessed 25 July 2015).

83. NSC meeting, 20 October 1962, *FRUS 1961–1963 XI*, document 34, <https://history.state.gov/historicaldocuments/frus1961-63v11/d34> (last accessed 25 July 2015).

84. James A. Nathan, 'The Missile Crisis: His Final Hour Now', *World Politics*, 27: 2, January 1975, p. 268; Mark Laffey and Jutta Weldes, 'Decolonizing the Cuban Missile Crisis', *International Studies Quarterly*, 52, 2008, p. 563. Later, the administration made an approach to Castro through intermediaries – see Chapter 5. For the limitations of ExComm, see Barton J. Bernstein, 'Reconsidering the Perilous Cuban Missile Crisis 50 Years Later', *Arms Control Today*, 2 October 2012, <https://www.armscontrol.org/act/2012_10/Reconsidering-the-Perilous-Cuban-Missile-Crisis-50-Years-Later> (last accessed 25 July 2015).

85. Acheson, 'Homage to Plain Dumb Luck', p. 190.

86. Katzenbach to Attorney General Kennedy, 23 October 1962, *FRUS 1961–1963 X-XI-XII*, document 374, <https://history.state.gov/historicaldocuments/frus1961-63v10-12mSupp/d374> (last accessed 25 July 2015).

87. NSC meeting, 21 October 1962, *FRUS 1961–1963 XI*, document 38, <https://history.state.gov/historicaldocuments/frus1961-63v11/d38> (last accessed 25 July 2015); Robert Weisbrot, *Maximum Danger: Kennedy, the Missiles and the Crisis of American Confidence* (Chicago: Dee, 2001), p. 131; Abram Chayes, *The Cuban Missile Crisis: International Crises and the Role of Law* (New York: Oxford University Press, 1974), p. 10. Traditionally, a blockade was seen as an act of war. While the blockade of Cuba deprived the Soviet Union of freedom of the seas, it fell short of preventing the import of non-military supplies. It was therefore something of a grey area legally.

88. Memorandum of conversation, 18 October 1962, *FRUS 1961–1963 XI*, document 29, <https://history.state.gov/historicaldocuments/frus1961-63v11/d29> (last accessed 25 July 2015).

89. Ernest R. May and Philip D. Zelikow (eds), *The Kennedy*

*Tapes: Inside the White House During the Cuban Missile Crisis* (Cambridge, MA: Belknap, 1997), p. 169.

90. Robert Kennedy to JFK, 24 October 1962, *FRUS 1961–1963 XI*, document 53, <https://history.state.gov/historicaldocuments/frus 1961-63v11/d53> (last accessed 25 July 2015).

91. Anatoly Dobrynin, *In Confidence: Moscow's Ambassador to America's Six Cold War Presidents, 1962–1986*, revised edn (Seattle: University of Washington Press, 2001), p. 77.

92. Conversation between the delegations of the CPCz and the CPSU, 30 October 1962, *Cold War International History Project Bulletin*, 17/18, Fall 2012, p. 402, <http://www.wilsoncenter.org/publica tion/bulletin-no-17-18> (last accessed 25 July 2015).

93. Caccia minute, 31 October 1962, FO 371/162401, The National Archives, Kew, England (TNA).

94. Brugioni, *Eyeball to Eyeball*, pp. 353–4.

95. Memorandum for the file, 24 October 1962, *FRUS 1961–1963 XI*, document 43, <https://history.state.gov/historicaldocuments/ frus1961-63v11/d43> (last accessed 25 July 2015).

96. Arthur M. Schlesinger, Jr., *A Thousand Days: John F. Kennedy in the White House* (New York: Houghton Mifflin, 1965), p. 694.

97. Memorandum for the file, 23 October 1962, *FRUS 1961–1963 X-XI-XII*, document 371, <https://history.state.gov/historicaldoc uments/frus1961-63v10-12mSupp/d371> (last accessed 25 July 2015).

98. NSC meeting, 22 October 1962, *FRUS 1961–1963 XI*, document 41, <https://history.state.gov/historicaldocuments/frus1961-63v11/d41> (last accessed 25 July 2015).

99. Washington (David Ormsby-Gore) to Foreign Office, 9 November 1962, CAB 21/5581, TNA.

100. Jeanne Sutherland, *From Moscow to Cuba and Beyond* (London: Radcliffe, 2010), p. 152.

101. Embassy in the Soviet Union to State Department, 24 May 1964, *FRUS 1964–1968 XIV Soviet Union* (2000), document 32, <https://history.state.gov/historicaldocuments/frus1964-68v14/d32> (last accessed 25 July 2015).

102. Aleksandr Fursenko and Timothy Naftali, 'Soviet Intelligence and the Cuban Missile Crisis', in James G. Blight and David A. Welch (eds), *Intelligence and the Cuban Missile Crisis* (Abingdon: Frank Cass, 1998), pp. 67–71.

103. See also Christopher Andrew, 'Remembering the Cuban Missile Crisis: Memoirs, Oral History and *Lieux Mémoire*', in David

Gioe, Len Scott and Christopher Andrew (eds), *An International History of the Cuban Missile Crisis: A 50-Year Retrospective* (London: Routledge, 2014), pp. 14–17.

104. Fursenko and Naftali, 'Soviet Intelligence and the Cuban Missile Crisis', p. 78.
105. Fursenko and Naftali, *Khrushchev's Cold War*, p. 470.
106. Alexander Fursenko, 'Night Session of the Presidium of the Central Committee, 22–23 October 1962', translated by Yuri M. Zhukov, *Naval College War Review*, 59: 3, Summer 2006, pp. 132–5.

# 4 Confrontation, 22–25 October 1962

On the relationships between the heads of our governments . . . a lot really does depend.

*Anatoly Dobrynin*

## Kennedy's 22 October Address

Shortly before the President's 22 October public address, Dean Rusk briefed Ambassador Dobrynin about the discovery of the missiles in Cuba and outlined the US response. Naturally, the Ambassador was deeply concerned: the 'downright provocative' American actions could bring 'grave consequences'. The White House should have raised the matter with Andrei Gromyko a few days earlier when he had met with the President, instead of making a dramatic and confrontational public address.[1] As noted in Chapter 2, Dobrynin knew nothing about the stationing of the missiles on Cuba. He and the Soviet Permanent Representative to the UN Valerian Zorin had been told simply to 'answer any questions about missiles in Cuba by saying that the Soviet Union supplied Cuba with "defensive weapons" only, without going into any details whatever'. Dobrynin and Zorin both thought that any Soviet missiles in Cuba were conventionally armed and could not reach American territory. Dean Rusk later told Dobrynin that the White House had debated whether to demand his recall for 'deliberately misleading' the administration, but it was realised that he 'lacked detailed information' and so it would be 'unfair' to accuse him of 'duplicity'.[2] Moreover, Robert F. Kennedy maintained close contact with the Ambassador throughout the crisis, seeing him as a voice of reason and an important means of communicating with the Kremlin.

In the United States, there was a moment of absurdity just before the President's address to the nation at 19:00 hours on 22 October. State Department diplomat G. Lewis Schmidt recalled that a TV had been brought into the office for the benefit of him and his colleagues. Just before the President's scheduled appearance there was a commercial 'for Doublemint Gum ... Two attractive look-alike young women scantily dressed began cavorting across the screen, singing "Double your pleasure, double your fun; Doublemint, Doublemint, Doublemint Gum."' Then, abruptly, the President appeared, announcing 'his determined response to Soviet effrontery that, for all we knew, could end in nuclear holocaust!'[3] In his address, Kennedy sought to outline the apparent threat to the security of the United States and the Western hemisphere, to justify the reasonableness of the American response and to demonstrate resolution without aggression. He stated that, contrary to Soviet statements, Cuba now hosted missiles that posed 'a clear and present danger' to the security of the United States and Latin America. He invoked the apparent lesson of the 1930s: 'aggressive conduct, if allowed to go unchecked and unchallenged, ultimately leads to war'. Any nuclear missile launched from Cuba would generate a 'full retaliatory response upon the Soviet Union'. This statement – threatening nuclear war – demonstrated the gravity of the situation, but fortunately the Soviet authorities had no wish at all to initiate such a chain of events. Kennedy stated that the US government was to implement 'a strict quarantine on all offensive military equipment under shipment to Cuba'. He also referred to the 'captive people of Cuba', with the speech reaching the island through the use of 'special radio facilities'. He shared the Cuban people's 'aspirations for liberty and justice for all', so differentiating between the general populace and the regime, and implying falsely that Castro had no popular support.[4]

Theodore Sorensen had drafted the speech. Unused was a briefer and still more solemn version, in which the President was to state that the USAF had struck 'to remove a major nuclear weapons build up from the soil of Cuba'.[5] Sorensen later denied having written the alternative address: the author's identity was a 'minor mystery'. He claimed that he would not have drafted such a speech himself, given that he opposed attacking Cuba.[6] Fortunately the alternative version, whoever was responsible, was surplus to requirements – for now.

The text of Kennedy's address reached Moscow in the early hours of Tuesday 23 October. Nikita Khrushchev thought that it was West German intelligence that had uncovered the Soviet missile bases, and had told the US government.[7] But there was no foundation for this view, which is a comment on the quality of information he was receiving. Khrushchev concluded that the President's speech was 'not a [declaration of war] against Cuba, but some kind of ultimatum.' In a letter that was released to the press and broadcast on the radio as well as sent directly to the US government, Khrushchev maintained that the weapons (there was no admission that they were nuclear missiles) were intended purely to deter an attack on Cuba; and that the quarantine violated 'international norms of freedom of navigation on the high seas'.[8]

In the face of the American challenge, the Soviets dedicated much energy to understanding American policies and attitudes – making efforts of a type that had not featured in relation to the possible impact of stationing missiles in Cuba. There was a broad knowledge – probably from US press reports – of the decision-making apparatus in the White House. The KGB suggested that a 'small group of men (around 10)', including Robert F. Kennedy and some Pentagon officials, had taken the quarantine decision.[9] In his own assessment, Dobrynin surmised that Kennedy and his advisers had several goals in relation to Cuba. The first was to 'take up the gauntlet' posed by Soviet 'military deliveries' to the island, in order to reestablish the international 'correlation of forces'. Dobrynin felt, rightly, that the Soviet military presence in the Western Hemisphere was a major embarrassment to the United States. The American attitude to Cuba also had to be understood in a broader context, according to the Ambassador: the US government sought to end 'the development of events in the whole world, which are generally disadvantageous to the USA'. In particular, fears of a Soviet–East German peace treaty, which would end the American presence in Berlin, encouraged the administration to stand firm over Cuba.[10]

Dobrynin neglected to mention the deception surrounding the installation of missiles in Cuba that was a particular source of antagonism. Furthermore, deliberations in ExComm did not reflect any concern or perception that the United States was falling behind in the Cold War. Dobrynin's assessment of the individual ExComm advisers was questionable, to say the least – he recognized that Robert F. Kennedy was one of the 'the most militant' of the President's advisers, but he also thought that Douglas Dillon was 'restrained and . . . cautious'.[11] The evidence does not reveal much about how Soviet views of the likelihood of an attack on Cuba developed during the missile confrontation, otherwise we might have a clearer understanding of how and why Khrushchev's thinking evolved, from a seemingly unyielding position to agreeing to remove the missiles.

## Kennedy and Khrushchev

Although they could not control every outcome, the actions of the principals would be critical in navigating the confrontation safely. As Dobrynin put it, 'On the relationships between the heads of our governments, on which history has placed special responsibility for the fate of the world, a lot really does depend; in particular, whether there will be peace or war.'[12] Although they had obviously had their differences – above all over Berlin, and now Cuba – the two leaders had taken the measure of one another in Vienna in June 1961, and gained a fuller sense of mutual understanding from over a year's worth of correspondence on a wide range of issues.[13] It was essential to maintain confidence and communication, given the danger. Robert F. Kennedy told Dobrynin on 24 October that his brother still had 'trust and confidence' in the Soviet leader, despite the denials about the missiles. He reminded Dobrynin that the President had complied rapidly when Khrushchev had once asked him to remove US troops from Laos.[14] Kennedy junior seems to have felt that the American action in Laos imposed a reciprocal obligation on Khrushchev to remove the missiles from Cuba, although there is no indication that the Soviet leader shared this view.

There was the question of how well John F. Kennedy and Nikita Khrushchev would bear up. Despite an assiduously cultivated image of vigour and dynamism,[15] Kennedy had long battled illness, including a back injury and a glandular complaint, and relied on a daily cocktail of medications. However, he held up well both physically and psychologically throughout the missile crisis. He demonstrated continued clarity of thought and remained courteous and pleasant with subordinates, with Rusk describing him as 'as calm as an iceberg'.[16] The President maintained a regular routine, sleeping regular hours, eating a proper diet, swimming regularly, and taking hot baths for relaxation, all helping him to deal with the profound stress of the confrontation.[17] As for Khrushchev, he is known to have suffered from a range of physical problems including excess weight, kidney trouble, high blood pressure and a liver ailment.[18] There is no indication that he was taking any medications that might have impeded his thinking, but another assessment indicated that he suffered from irritability, forgetfulness even about recent events, and stubbornness. He had also become subject to depression and ill-temper. Fortunately, Khrushchev's wife, Nina, was said to have a moderating influence on his personality – so she may have been an unsung hero of the crisis, keeping Nikita steady amidst the storm.[19] Both Kennedy and Khrushchev would endure the most extraordinary pressures and tensions, although as the week progressed it would be the nerves of the latter that grew the most frayed.

## Military Affairs and Home Fronts

### The United States

ExComm had agreed on 16 October to increase the alert status of US military forces. From 20 October, US aircraft left their home bases throughout the United States to strengthen air defence units in the southeast.[20] At the very hour of the President's speech on 22 October, US military forces across the globe moved to

DEFCON-3. Although American nuclear forces had been placed in a state of readiness on several occasions since the establishment of the DEFCON system in 1959, the missile crisis would represent both the highest state of readiness for nuclear war that US military forces have ever attained and the longest period of time (one month) that they had maintained an alert.[21] With the move to DEFCON-3, sixty-six B-52s took to the air, equipped with nuclear bombs and flight plans that could take them over the Soviet Union, and twenty-two other planes equipped with nuclear air defence weapons were soon aloft near the Florida coast.[22] There was a substantial movement of American troops to the southeast of the United States. According to the British consul in Miami, the atmosphere was 'very much like southern England before D-Day' in 1944. He thought that 'some form of military action was imminent'. Heavy military convoys had been going into Tampa; several troop trains had passed through Miami bound south; and military air transport had been leaving the civil airport in Miami at intervals of up to one per minute.[23]

American preparations included reinforcing the Guantánamo base in Cuba with additional units of Marines; Robert McNamara reported on 22 October that 'about 7,000 additional men have been placed there in the last several days'.[24] US fighter bombers at bases in the Europe and Asia were alerted and armed.[25] On 24 October, when the quarantine was implemented, the Pentagon increased the alert status to DEFCON-2, just short of readiness for general war. At his own initiative, Commander-in-Chief of Strategic Air Command Thomas Powers transmitted uncoded messages to Supreme Air Command (SAC) commanders indicating that the alert process was unfolding as scheduled. He sought to ensure that the Soviet Union knew of SAC's readiness, thereby acting as a deterrent,[26] although what his superiors made of his initiative is not known. According to his son, Khrushchev saw the move to DEFCON-2 as a bluff, but he still took it into consideration.[27] By 24 October, there was an increase in the number of Polaris SLBMs (submarine launched ballistic missiles) on alert from the regular peacetime level of forty-eight to the full force of 112 missiles. Increased numbers of forward-based aircraft in the Pacific and Europe were prepared with nuclear weapons.[28]

The American people responded to the crisis with a blend of patriotism and anxiety. Independent polls indicated that 84 per cent backed the quarantine and that only 4 per cent opposed it; but 20 per cent believed that 'some shooting' would occur and another 20 per cent felt that the Third World War was inevitable.[29] There was panic buying of tyres, cars and gasoline (clearly, many citizens were thinking of fleeing to remote areas). Prices on Wall Street fell substantially, although firms that built atomic shelters were swamped with orders.[30] Public concerns about the possibility of nuclear war – especially in relation to the crisis over Berlin in 1961 – meant that by the time of the missile crisis, existing shelters, public or private, could house about one-third of the population. However, the civil defence programme that had been announced during the Berlin crisis had not gained much ground because of fears over its effectiveness and about creating panic, while most of the public shelters lacked essential provisions such as food and water. During the confrontation, Kennedy expressed interest in evacuating key areas of the United States, but this came to nothing because of concerns about creating public alarm.[31]

There were plans to protect US government employees from nuclear war. If an attack was imminent, Kennedy and leading officials would be transported to Mount Weather, a bunker hidden in the Blue Ridge Mountains in Virginia fifty miles away from Washington. The facility could house 200 people for thirty days. Similarly, members of Congress had their own bunker in White Sulphur Springs, West Virginia. Generally, though, the attempt to preserve the continuity of government had serious limitations, not least because sufficient advance warning was needed and because the plans were in many respects out of date.[32] There was another difficulty. Dean Rusk noted that the programme was

> psychologically impossible. One has to have an alternative govern-
> ment in place made up of people who had nothing to do with the
> events which unfold. In first place, people in the government are not
> going to abandon all their colleagues and their families to get in a
> helicopter and go charging out to West Virginia ... In the second
> place, the first band of shivering survivors who get their hands on the

President and the Secretary of State following such a situation will hang them to the nearest tree.[33]

While top US officials had a bolthole if the worst came to the worst, it did nothing to ease their burdens.

### The Soviet Union

A lack of documentation has meant that relatively little is known about Soviet and Warsaw Pact military preparations. However, there is evidence that on October 23 Soviet authorities cancelled all leave and gave orders to 'raise the battle readiness and vigilance of all troops'.[34] There is also evidence that on 24 October, Soviet nuclear forces were placed on a higher state of nuclear alert.[35] While civil defence measures in the Soviet Union were more extensive than in the United States, this was due in part to a desire to control as well as to protect the population.[36] Moscow officials strove to convey an air of normality, to avoid causing panic and to demonstrate that they remained in command. On 23 October, Khrushchev and four of his colleagues made a point of attending the opera.[37] British ambassador in Moscow Frank Roberts reported on 24 October how he and the US ambassador, Foy Kohler, dined with Vice Minister for Foreign Affairs Arkadiy Sobolev, noting that Sobolev and the other Soviet guests 'were restrained and friendly and avoided controversial topics'.[38] Relative calm prevailed in the Soviet Union, not least due to sheer ignorance. An American diplomat in Leningrad suggested that people there 'to the best of my knowledge, were absolutely unaware of what was going on'.[39] A French service attaché in Minsk reported that during the confrontation over Berlin the Soviet authorities had striven to create a crisis atmosphere as 'they were making the running'. Now that they were reacting to American actions, 'excessive emotion might ... have proved embarrassing'.[40]

Later in the week, there was a carefully choreographed public protest outside the US Embassy. An American diplomat noted how women and children were unloaded from trucks in nearby streets and collected signs denouncing American colonialism and imperialism. Hundreds of troops moved into side streets near the embassy to make sure the demonstration did not get out of control. The protestors disbanded promptly on police orders after exactly four hours, and water-spraying trucks cleaned the road straight after.[41] The protests were token ones, orchestrated closely by the Soviet authorities. In keeping with the general sense of composure in the Moscow establishment, there was no animosity towards individual representatives of the United States or its allies. Frank Roberts knew of 'no manifestations of personal unfriendliness to members of the United States Embassy or other Western diplomats'.[42]

### Cuba

In a ninety-minute television and radio counterpart to President Kennedy's address, President Castro assailed the quarantine as 'a violation against the sovereign rights of our people and all people', and argued that the Soviet weapons were defensive. He maintained that 'anyone who comes to inspect Cuba better come in full combat gear'.[43] The British ambassador in Havana, Herbert Marchant, reported that the speech was 'a skilful performance' that was 'unusually free of emotion and histrionics'. Castro appeared 'calm and confident and chuckled at some of his own scornful sallies against America'.[44] The address played an important role in maintaining Cuban morale, with Castro showing himself as

> desperate but determined, often most convincing when his argument was most dishonest. Bloody his head certainly was but it was unbowed and I could not help but feeling that if the counter revolution could throw up a leader of half his weight . . . victory might well be theirs.[45]

The ambassador noted that although the people of Havana had been 'buying up stocks of such things as paraffin, petroleum, coffee . . . there has been no frenzied rush on the shops'. There was 'an unnatural calm here as on the edge of a cyclone. This is partly the result of the government's policy to keep the temperature down and morale up by continuing as far as possible . . .

business as usual'. It also stemmed from 'a mood of dazed anxiety
... the average man and woman' had no 'burning desire to die
for the cause'.[46] Ambassador Alexei Alekseev contended that
Soviet prestige in Cuba had 'climbed to unprecedented heights.
The actions of the USSR government in its defense of Cuba are
completely convincing the people of the failure of the American
provocations.'[47] There were in fact many people in Cuba who
maintained greater sympathy for the Americans than they did for
the Soviets, and even for the Castro regime. Nearly half the 3,000
or so local employees at the Guantánamo base showed up for
work on Tuesday 23 October, and even more turned up the following day. Many of the Cubans had been working at the naval
base for years and opposed Castro. They provided information
about Cuban and Soviet troop deployments to the Marines and
welcomed the possibility of an American invasion.[48]

Alekseev reported on 23 October that the Cuban government
had decided to mobilize the popular militia of 350,000 people, to
fend off an invasion.[49] Castro had particular confidence in Cuba's
30mm anti-aircraft guns, which were 'very effective weapons
against landings, and have an enormous value, as they serve to
fight on the coast, against infantry, airplanes, and everything; they
are the weapons that can demolish the highest number of tactical
aircraft'. He ordered 30mm gun batteries to be concentrated in
several locations, and 'that when a plane passes over these, flying
low, "fry it".' He considered that it was 'necessary to start to fire
some shots, because the [Americans] have a mess stirred up'.[50]
In the event, it would be the Soviets who would shoot down an
American aircraft.

## The Berlin Non-Crisis

US policymakers feared that in the light of the quarantine of
Cuba, or especially in the event of military attacks on the island,
the Soviets might move against American positions in Iran, Turkey
or South Korea, or – above all – Berlin.[51] Some Soviet diplomats
did feel that the time was right to exploit American vulnerability in the city. Vasili Kuznetsov, First Deputy Foreign Minister,

pressed for action against West Berlin in retaliation for the Cuba quarantine.[52] On 23 October Anatoli Dobrynin recommended 'hinting to Kennedy in no uncertain terms' about the possibility of action 'against the Western powers in West Berlin',[53] although he may have had nothing more in mind than a bluff. While the Soviet Union had conventional superiority in Europe, Soviet officials did not wish to complicate an already fraught situation – Khrushchev told Kuznetsov that he 'could do without' his 'sort of advice'.[54] Anastas Mikoyan explained to the Cuban leadership later that 'We did not intend to act on Berlin . . . It was known through diplomatic channels that Kennedy did not want to make matters more serious.'[55] Hence, the city that had been the centre of Soviet–American antagonisms from 1958 to 1961 had no part in the crisis of October 1962.

## The Quarantine

On 22 October Robert McNamara outlined the procedures to deal with Soviet ships as they approached the quarantine line:

> Our orders are to hail the incoming vessels, both Soviet and non-Soviet surface and submerged, to stop them, to search them, to divert those carrying designated goods, offensive weapons initially, to ports of their choosing. If they refuse to stop, disable them and then to take them in as prizes.[56]

There was ample scope for matters to get out of hand. President Kennedy told British Prime Minister Harold Macmillan that 'Our Naval Commanders are instructed to use the minimum of force, but I know of no sure escape from the problem of the first shot.'[57] McNamara, seeing the quarantine mainly as a form of political communication to Khrushchev rather than a 'textbook military operation', strove to maintain close control over its implementation. He asked Chief of Naval Operations Admiral George Anderson for clarification about how local commanders would implement the quarantine. They did not see eye to eye. McNamara recollected that after a testy conversation, he told Anderson that:

'You're not going to fire a single shot at anything without my express permission, is that clear?' ... That is when he made his famous remark about how the Navy had been running blockades since the days of John Paul Jones, and if I would leave them well alone they would run this one successfully as well.[58]

Anderson gave his reluctant agreement that 'no force would be applied without my permission'. However, his version of the encounter was less dramatic, and he suggested that the mention of John Paul Jones was a later embellishment. Anderson did say, though, that 'Mr Secretary, you go back to your office and I'll go back to mine and we'll take care of things.' This did not go down well with McNamara.[59] Whatever was said, the White House was determined that crisis management was to be left in civilian hands. Furthermore, although some military leaders had reservations about White House policies, the loyalty of the military was never remotely in question.

Even before the discovery of the missiles, various figures had mooted the idea of quarantine as a means of putting pressure on Moscow in the context of the military build-up in Cuba. In September, Khrushchev had told the Austrian Vice Chancellor Bruno Pitterman that he had instructed Soviet ships en route to Cuba to ignore quarantine warnings and to respond in kind if fired upon.[60] On 24 October Khrushchev struck a resolute stance when he told Kennedy that 'violation of the freedom to use international waters and international airspace is an act of aggression'. He could not 'instruct the captains of Soviet vessels bound for Cuba to observe the orders of American naval forces blockading that Island', and would authorise 'the measures we deem necessary and adequate to protect our rights'.[61] It soon emerged, though, that a number of Soviet vessels sailing towards Cuba had retreated without challenging the quarantine. In *Thirteen Days*, Robert F. Kennedy recorded John McCone saying during the morning of 24 October that 'some of the Russian ships have stopped dead in the water ... Six ships previously on their way to Cuba at the edge of the quarantine line have stopped or turned back toward the Soviet Union'.[62] Famously, Dean Rusk responded to the news by telling McGeorge Bundy that 'We're eyeball-to-eyeball and the other fellow just blinked.'[63] Apart from wanting to avoid escalation, Khrushchev sought to prevent the loss of any of the missile technology on board the Soviet vessels. He was not to know that there were no collection plans or operations being levied for the boarding parties.[64]

The retreat of the Soviet vessels has generated confusion, especially in relation to an alleged encounter between the *Essex* and the *Kimovsk*. The *Essex* was due to intercept the *Kimovsk* at 10:30–11:00 a.m. Washington time on 24 October. Journalists told the story of a near-confrontation on the quarantine line. However, it has emerged only recently that the *Kimovsk* was nearly 800 miles away from the *Essex*. The *Kimovsk* and another 'high interest' ship – the *Yuri Gagarin* – had turned back the previous day, after receiving urgent instructions from Moscow. Later, when the facts emerged, the White House let the record of the 'eyeball-to-eyeball' scenario stand, to preserve the image of cool determination.[65] The Soviets continued to hold back from challenging the quarantine. President Kennedy reported to Harold Macmillan on 25 October that

> today we figure now [that] fourteen ships turned around. They were probably the ones with the aggressive cargo. One tanker [the *Bucharest*] we stopped; we asked where it was going it said it was coming from the Black Sea to Cuba and the cargo was oil.[66]

The *Bucharest* sailed on unhindered, as at this stage only vessels carrying military equipment were to be intercepted.

In early October the Soviets had deployed three Project 641 (NATO designation: Foxtrot) and one Project 611 (Zulu) submarines 'to strengthen the defense of the island of Cuba'. Each was armed with twenty-two torpedoes, and each vessel had a nuclear warhead for one of the torpedoes. Although Khrushchev was keen to reduce the danger of the crisis, on 22–3 October he gave an order to 'Let the four submarines move ahead.'[67] However, Moscow had decided that it would be too dangerous to have the submarines cross the quarantine line, and ordered that they should stay two days away from Cuba. Communications with the submarines were limited, though, which meant that the commanders did not know about the US signalling procedures, and that they did not receive instructions to alter course.[68] Furthermore, the vessels were of an old design, and were subject to oxygen shortages and unbearable heat during periods of prolonged submersion, thus straining the composure of crews immensely in already tense circumstances. The American authorities did not know of the troubles afflicting the submarines, but were very concerned about them nonetheless. On 23 October, McNamara told ExComm that there was a submarine 'near the more interesting ships' (the *Kimovsk* and the *Yuri Gagarin*). He stated that 'in the event of intervention by a submarine' while a surface vessel was being intercepted 'the submarine might have to be destroyed'.[69]

The US navy was given procedures for signalling the Soviet submarines to surface. McNamara explained to ExComm on 24 October that practice depth charges would be used to convey a warning:

> when our forces come upon an unidentified submarine, we will ask it to come to the surface for inspection by transmitting the following signals, using a depth charge of this type and also using certain sonar signals which they may not be able to accept and interpret. Therefore, it is the depth charge that is the warning notice and the instruction to surface.[70]

President Kennedy recognised the danger of the submarine commanders concluding from the depth charges that they were under attack, not least because McNamara's procedures deviated from standard international practice for surfacing unidentified submarines. Robert F. Kennedy reported that when hearing McNamara's briefing, the President raised his hand 'to his face and covered his mouth. He opened and closed his fist. His face seemed drawn, almost gray.'[71] He saw the potential for a dangerous clash between American ships and Soviet submarines, but realised that the danger could not be avoided if the quarantine was to be enforced. Details of the signalling system were transmitted to the Soviet government through the US Embassy in Moscow on 25 October. It was stated that all signalling devices were harmless. However, there was no receipt of the signalling procedures, and the captains of the vessels were not told of them.[72] On 27 October, already the most dangerous day of the crisis, the US Navy would have the first of three direct encounters with the submarines.

## Washington DC: Considering the Options

Although Soviet ships with military cargoes held back from challenging the quarantine, there was a desire in ExComm to move matters forward before the missiles in Cuba became operational. On 25 October Kennedy noted that there were three chief options: a diplomatic settlement; extending the quarantine to provide for the interception of POL (petrol, oil, lubricants); and launching an air strike on the missile bases.[73] Dean Rusk continued to advocate diplomacy and dialogue, expressing hope for initiatives in relation to UN Secretary-General U Thant and in relation to Brazilian efforts to act as an intermediary (see Chapter 5).[74] He also suggested that the United States might 'buy the charter and cargo of tramp steamers going to Cuba. We could pay either the captain or the owner of the ship whatever he asks to defect with his ship.' This would intensify 'the pressure on the Cubans without further use of military force'.[75] The suggestion went no further, but it was part of Rusk's extensive and imaginative contributions to the ExComm deliberations, which historians have at last begun to acknowledge. At the time, there were those who did not credit him with having anything to say, because he was often seen as rather reticent. Sir Kenneth Strong, head of Britain's Joint Intelligence Bureau, who was in Washington from 13 to 25 October, suggested to Prime Minister Macmillan later that he 'did not know what view Rusk had taken' during the ExComm talks, and was not even sure about 'whether he had a view or not'.[76] Robert F. Kennedy suggested in *Thirteen Days* that after expressing support for air strikes the Secretary of State 'had other duties during this period of time and frequently could not attend our meetings'. Given the stakes, this was tantamount to an accusation of irresponsibility and negligence.[77] In reality, Rusk was an important voice in favour of a non-violent resolution of the crisis.[78]

Robert McNamara favoured extending the quarantine by adding jet fuel and petroleum to 'the list of product embargoes'. This would demonstrate further resolution without being unduly provocative. Robert F. Kennedy – once more belying the pacific image presented in *Thirteen Days* – veered towards an air strike, arguing that it was better to 'react by attacking the missiles already in Cuba' than to confront the Soviets 'by stopping one of their ships'. Douglas Dillon, anticipating that the Soviets would soon challenge the quarantine, 'preferred that the confrontation take place in Cuba rather than on the high seas'.[79] President Kennedy saw merit in temporising, 'stretching things out' for another day or so, as 'We've got some credit on our side', with ships having turned around. Furthermore, because 'the UN is involved in this now [see Chapter 5] . . . I don't want to have a fight with a Russian ship tomorrow morning, and a search of it at a time when it appears that U Thant has got the Russians to agree not to continue'. Without the continued suspension of Soviet shipping, then there was the problem of 'the possible sinking of [a] ship tomorrow afternoon'.[80]

## Khrushchev: Looking for an Exit

During the night of 24–5 October, a bartender in the National Press Club in Washington approached Anatoli Gorsky, a TASS correspondent. Dobrynin, duly apprised of what had gone on, reported that the bartender 'whispered that he had overheard a conversation of two prominent American journalists' – Robert Donovan and Warren Rogers of the *New York Herald Tribune* – 'that the President had supposedly taken a decision to invade Cuba today or tomorrow night'. Dobrynin noted that 'there is information that an order has been issued to bring the armed forces into maximum battle readiness including readiness to repulse nuclear attack'.[81] It turned out that Rogers and Donovan had been discussing the prospect of reporters being sent to Cuba if an invasion took place. Even though the 'intelligence' suggesting an imminent invasion was simply gossip, Dobrynin had judged it fit to send to Moscow, which meant that it ended up on Khrushchev's desk.

There were further indications that an invasion was looming, with Ambassador Alekseev stating that 'information has been received by us and the Czechs from unverifiable sources on the possibility of an interventionist landing or a bombing of Cuban military targets on 26–27 October'.[82]

Such intimations edged Khrushchev towards compromise, as emerged in several ways. On 24 October, Khrushchev told an American businessman, William E. Knox, who had happened to be in Moscow, that he would be 'delighted to visit the President or for the President to visit him for a rendezvous at sea or anywhere else. A summit was desirable'. In the meeting with Knox, he also provided his first admission that the Soviet Union had stationed nuclear missiles on Cuba.[83] Soviet expert Averell Harriman told Dean Rusk that Khrushchev was 'sending us desperate signals to get us to help take him off the hook', including an order to the Soviet ships to change course; a message to the British pacifist and philosopher Bertrand Russell in which Khrushchev said that the Soviet Union would do all that it could to prevent nuclear war; and how after his visit to the opera on Monday he made a point of speaking with an American singer, in a gesture of goodwill.[84] In the Presidium on 25 October, the Soviet leader mocked his adversary while expressing a willingness to retreat:

> The Americans say that the missile installations in Cuba must be dismantled. Perhaps this will need to be done. This is not capitulation on our part. Because if we fire, they will also fire. There is no doubt that the Americans became frightened, this is clear. Kennedy was sleeping with a wooden knife.[85]

Khrushchev explained the 'wooden knife' metaphor by saying that 'when a man goes bear hunting for the first time, he takes with him a wooden knife so that it will be easier to clean his trousers'. More politely, the Soviet leader added that

> we have now made Cuba a country that is the focus of the world's attention. The two systems have clashed. Kennedy says to us, take your missiles out of Cuba. We respond: 'Give firm guarantees and pledges that the Americans will not attack Cuba.' That is not a bad [trade].[86]

This – and more – was what he obtained, but matters would get worse before they got better.

## Notes

1. Telegram from Soviet Ambassador to the USA Dobrynin to the USSR MFA, 22 October 1962, *Cold War International History Project Bulletin*, 5, Spring 1995, pp. 69–70, <http://www.wilson center.org/publication/bulletin-no-5-spring-1995> (last accessed 25 July 2015).
2. Anatoly Dobrynin, *In Confidence: Moscow's Ambassador to America's Six Cold War Presidents, 1962–1986*, revised edn (Seattle: University of Washington Press, 2001), p. 74. See also Memorandum from Attorney General to President Kennedy, 23 October 1962, *Foreign Relations of the United States (FRUS) 1961–1963 XI Cuban Missile Crisis and Aftermath* (Washington, DC: USGPO, 1996), document 53, <https://history.state.gov/histor icaldocuments/frus1961-63v11/d53> (last accessed 25 July 2015).
3. G. Lewis Schmidt oral history interview conducted by Allen Hansen, 8 February 1988, Association for Diplomatic Studies and Training (ADST), Foreign Affairs Oral History Program, Arlington, VA, <http://www.adst.org> (last accessed 25 July 2015).
4. Radio and Television Report to the American People on the Soviet Arms Buildup in Cuba, 22 October 1962, John F. Kennedy Presidential Library and Museum, <http://www.jfklibrary.org/ Asset-Viewer/sUVmCh-sB0moLfrBcaHaSg.aspx> (last accessed 25 July 2015) [document 4, Appendix 4 in this volume]; Jutta Weldes, *Constructing National Interests: The United States and the Cuban Missile Crisis* (Minneapolis: University of Minnesota Press, 1999), p. 189.
5. 'Alternative draft of JFK's speech on 22 October 1962', in Mark J. White (ed.), *The Kennedys and Cuba: The Declassified Documentary History* (Chicago: Dee, 1999), p. 208.
6. Theodore Sorensen, *Counsellor: A Life at the Edge of History* (New York: Harper, 2008), p. 294.
7. Conversation between the delegations of the CPCz and the CPSU, 30 October 1962, *Cold War International History Project Bulletin*, 17/18, Fall 2012, p. 401, <http://www.wilsoncenter.org/publica tion/bulletin-no-17-18> (last accessed 25 July 2015).

8. Alexander Fursenko, 'Night session of the Presidium of the Central Committee, 22–23 October 1962', translated by Yuri M. Zhukov, *Naval College War Review*, 59: 3, Summer 2006, pp. 134–5; Khrushchev to Kennedy, 23 October 1962, in *FRUS 1961–1963 XI*, document 48, <https://history.state.gov/historicaldocuments/frus1961-63v11/d48> (last accessed 25 July 2015).

9. Aleksandr Fursenko and Timothy Naftali, 'Soviet Intelligence and the Cuban Missile Crisis', in James G. Blight and David A. Welch (eds), *Intelligence and the Cuban Missile Crisis* (Abingdon: Frank Cass, 1998), p. 78.

10. Dobrynin to the Soviet Ministry of Foreign Affairs, 23 October 1962, *Cold War International History Project Bulletin*, 5, Spring 1995, pp. 70–1, <http://www.wilsoncenter.org/publication/bulletin-no-5-spring-1995> (last accessed 25 July 2015).

11. Dobrynin to the Soviet Ministry of Foreign Affairs, 23 October 1962, *Cold War International History Project Bulletin*, 8/9, Winter 1996–7, p. 287, <http://www.wilsoncenter.org/sites/default/files/CWIHP_Bulletin_8-9.pdf> (last accessed 25 July 2015).

12. Dobrynin to the USSR MFA, 24 October 1962, *Cold War International History Project Bulletin*, 5, Spring 1995, pp. 71–3, <http://www.wilsoncenter.org/publication/bulletin-no-5-spring-1995> (last accessed 25 July 2015).

13. Arthur M. Schlesinger, Jr., *Robert Kennedy and His Times* (New York: Ballantine Books, 1979), p. 529.

14. Memorandum from Attorney General to President Kennedy, 23 October 1962, *FRUS 1961–1963 XI*, document 53, <https://history.state.gov/historicaldocuments/frus1961-63v11/d53> (last accessed 25 July 2015).

15. See Mark White, *Kennedy: A Cultural History of an American Icon* (London: Bloomsbury, 2013), on the importance of 'image' for JFK.

16. James Blight and David A. Welch (eds), with foreword by McGeorge Bundy, *On the Brink: Americans and Soviets Reexamine the Cuban Missile Crisis* (New York: Noonday Press, 1990), p. 180 [see also document 9, Appendix 4 in this volume for Kennedy's demeanour].

17. Dino Brugioni, *Eyeball to Eyeball: The Inside Story of the Cuban Missile Crisis*, edited by Robert F. McCort (New York: Random House, 1991), p. 450.

18. Current Intelligence Weekly Review, 20 April 1962, *FRUS 1961–1963 V Soviet Union* (1998), document 183, <https://history.state.gov/historicaldocuments/frus1961-63v05/d183> (last accessed 25 July 2015).

19. Brugioni, *Eyeball to Eyeball*, p. 449.
20. Anatoli I. Gribkov and William Y. Smith, *Operation Anadyr: US and Soviet Generals Recount the Cuban Missile Crisis* (Chicago: Edition Q, 1994), p. 138.
21. Scott D. Sagan, *The Limits of Safety* (Princeton, NJ: Princeton University Press, 1993), p. 62.
22. Gribkov and Smith, *Operation Anadyr*, p. 138.
23. Situation in Florida, 26 October 1962, FO 371/162391, The National Archives, Kew, England (TNA).
24. Ernest R. May and Philip D. Zelikow (eds), *The Kennedy Tapes: Inside the White House During the Cuban Missile Crisis* (Cambridge, MA: Belknap, 1997), p. 260.
25. Brugioni, *Eyeball to Eyeball*, p. 367.
26. Laurence Chang and Peter Kornbluh (eds), with foreword by Robert S. McNamara, *The Cuban Missile Crisis, 1962: A National Security Archive Documents Reader* (New York: The New Press, 1992), p. 371.
27. Len Scott, *The Cuban Missile Crisis and the Threat of Nuclear War* (London: Continuum, 2007), p. 130.
28. Sagan, *The Limits of Safety*, pp. 62–5.
29. James N. Giglio, *The Presidency of John F. Kennedy* (Lawrence: University Press of Kansas, 2006), pp. 205–6.
30. Brugioni, *Eyeball to Eyeball*, p. 375.
31. Alice L. George, *Awaiting Armageddon: How Americans Faced the Missile Crisis* (Chapel Hill: University of North Carolina Press, 2003), p. 62; Memorandum for the files, 23 October 1962, *FRUS 1961–1963 XI*, document 51, <https://history.state.gov/historical documents/frus1961-63v11/d51> (last accessed 25 July 2015).
32. George, *Awaiting Armageddon*, p. 45.
33. Blight and Welch, *On the Brink*, p. 184.
34. Webcast of Robert S. Norris, 'The Cuban Missile Crisis: A Nuclear Order of Battle, October/November 1962', Cold War International History Project, 24 October 2012, <http://www.wilsoncenter.org/event/cuban-missile-crisis-nuclear-order-battle> (last accessed 25 July 2015).
35. Sagan, *Limits of Safety*, p. 144.
36. George, *Awaiting Armageddon*, p. 60.
37. Raymond L. Garthoff, *Reflections on the Cuban Missile Crisis* (Washington, DC: Brookings, 1987), p. 41.
38. Moscow to Foreign Office, 24 October 1962, PREM 11/3690, TNA.

39. Hans N. Tuch oral history interview conducted by G. Lewis Schmidt, 4 August 1989, ADST, <http://www.adst.org> (last accessed 25 July 2015).
40. Moscow to Foreign Office, 4 November 1962, FO 371/162394, TNA.
41. Michael M. Dobbs, *One Minute to Midnight: Kennedy, Khrushchev and Castro on the Brink of Nuclear War* (New York: Knopf, 2008), p. 202.
42. Moscow to Foreign Office, 4 November 1962, FO 371/162394, TNA.
43. Tomas Diez Acosta, *October 1962: The 'Missile' Crisis as Seen from Cuba* (New York: Pathfinder, 2002), pp. 224–56.
44. Havana to Foreign Office, 24 October 1962, FO 371/1623777, TNA.
45. The Cuban Crisis, 10 November 1962, FO 371/162408, TNA.
46. Havana to Foreign Office, 26 October 1962, FO 371/162380; Havana to Foreign Office, 24 October 1962, FO 371/162377, TNA.
47. Alekseev to USSR Foreign Ministry, 25 October 1962, *Cold War International History Project Bulletin*, 8/9, Winter 1996–7, p. 287, <http://www.wilsoncenter.org/publication/bulletin-no-89-win ter-1996> (last accessed 25 July 2015).
48. Dobbs, *One Minute to Midnight*, p. 129.
49. Alekseev to USSR Foreign Ministry, 23 October 1962, *Cold War International History Project Bulletin*, 8/9, Winter 1996–7, p. 283, <http://www.wilsoncenter.org/publication/bulletin-no-89-win ter-1996> (last accessed 25 July 2015).
50. Record of Meeting of Fidel Castro and Military Chiefs, 24 October 1962, *Cold War International History Project Bulletin*, 17/18, Fall 2012, pp. 136–8, <http://www.wilsoncenter.org/publication/bulle tin-no-17-18> (last accessed 25 July 2015). For a full account of Cuban preparedness see Blaine L. Pardoe, *The Fires of October: The Planned Invasion of Cuba during the Missile Crisis of 1962* (Stroud: Fonthill, 2012), pp. 179–90.
51. Department of State to Certain Diplomatic Missions, *FRUS 1961– 1963 V*, document 141, <https://history.state.gov/historicaldocu ments/frus1961-63v15/d141> (last accessed 25 July 2015).
52. Scott, *Cuban Missile Crisis*, p. 61.
53. Dobrynin to the USSR Foreign Ministry, 23 October 1962, *Cold War International History Project Bulletin*, 5, Spring 1995, p. 71, <http://www.wilsoncenter.org/publication/bulletin-no-5-spring- 1995> (last accessed 25 July 2015).

54. Raymond L. Garthoff, 'US Intelligence in the Cuban Missile Crisis', in Blight and Welch, *Intelligence and the Cuban Missile Crisis*, p. 31.
55. Meeting of the Secretary of the CRI with Mikoyan in the Presidential Palace, 4 November 1962, *Cold War International History Project Bulletin*, 8/9, Winter 1996–7, p. 340, <http://www.wilsoncenter. org/publication/bulletin-no-89-winter-1996> (last accessed 25 July 2015).
56. May and Zelikow, *The Kennedy Tapes*, p. 259.
57. Ibid. p. 283.
58. Blight and Welch, *On the Brink*, pp. 63–4.
59. Pardoe, *The Fires of October*, pp. 165–6.
60. Moscow to Foreign Office, 23 October 1962, FO 371/162375, TNA.
61. Khrushchev to Kennedy, 24 October 1962, *FRUS 1961–1963 XI*, document 61, <https://history.state.gov/historicaldocuments/frus 1961-63v11/d61> (last accessed 25 July 2015).
62. Robert F. Kennedy, *Thirteen Days: A Memoir of the Cuban Missile Crisis* (New York: Norton, 1969), p. 71.
63. Dean Rusk, *As I Saw It: A Secretary of State's Memoirs* (New York: Norton, 1990), p. 237.
64. Aleksandr Fursenko and Timothy Naftali, *Khrushchev's Cold War: The Inside Story of an American Adversary* (New York: Norton, 2006), p. 477; Michael B. Petersen, 'A Trial by Fire: Military Intelligence Reform and the Cuban Missile Crisis', in David Gioe, Len Scott and Christopher Andrew (eds), *An International History of the Cuban Missile Crisis: A 50-Year Retrospective* (London: Routledge, 2014), p. 125.
65. Dobbs, *One Minute to Midnight*, pp. 87–9, 91.
66. Kennedy–Macmillan telephone conversation, 25 October 1962, *FRUS 1961–1963 XI*, document 74, <https://history.state.gov/ historicaldocuments/frus1961-63v11/d74> (last accessed 25 July 2015).
67. Protocol No. 60 Session of 22–23 October 1962, *Cold War International History Project Bulletin*, 17/18, Fall 2012, p. 307, <http://www.wilsoncenter.org/publication/bulletin-no-17-18> (last accessed 25 July 2015).
68. Fursenko and Naftali, *Khrushchev's Cold War*, p. 480.
69. Record of Action of EXCOMM meeting, 24 October 1962, *FRUS 1961–1963 XI*, document 55, <https://history.state.gov/historical documents/frus1961-63v11/d55> (last accessed 25 July 2015).

70. May and Zelikow, *The Kennedy Tapes*, p. 355.
71. Fursenko and Naftali, *Khrushchev's Cold War*, p. 481; Kennedy, *Thirteen Days*, pp. 69–70.
72. Svetlana V. Savranskaya, 'New Sources on the Role of Soviet Submarines in the Cuban Missile Crisis', *Journal of Strategic Studies*, 28: 2, April 2005, pp. 233–59; Thomas S. Blanton and William Burr, 'The Submarines of October: US and Soviet Naval Encounters during the Cuban Missile Crisis', National Security Archive, George Washington University, <http://www2.gwu.edu/~nsarchiv/NSAEBB/NSAEBB75/index2.htm> (last accessed 25 July 2015).
73. ExComm meeting, 25 October 1962, *FRUS 1961–1963 XI*, document 71, <https://history.state.gov/historicaldocuments/frus1961-63v11/d71> (last accessed 25 July 2015).
74. State Department to Embassy in Brazil, 26 October, *FRUS 1961–1963 XI*, document 81, <https://history.state.gov/historicaldocuments/frus1961-63v11/d81> (last accessed 25 July 2015).
75. ExComm meeting, 25 October 1962, *FRUS 1961–1963 XI*, document 73, <https://history.state.gov/historicaldocuments/frus1961-63v11/d73> (last accessed 25 July 2015).
76. Note for the Record, 19 November 1962, PREM 11/3972, TNA.
77. Kennedy, *Thirteen Days*, p. 36.
78. See Sheldon M. Stern, *The Cuban Missile Crisis in American Memory: Myths versus Reality* (Stanford, CA: Stanford University Press, 2012), pp. 68–90, for an assessment of Rusk's ExComm contributions.
79. ExComm meeting, 25 October 1962, *FRUS 1961–1963 XI*, document 73, <https://history.state.gov/historicaldocuments/frus1961-63v11/d73> (last accessed 25 July 2015).
80. May and Zelikow, *The Kennedy Tapes*, p. 414; Kennedy–Macmillan telephone conversation, 25 October 1962, *FRUS 1961–1963 XI*, document 74, <https://history.state.gov/historicaldocuments/frus1961-63v11/d74> (last accessed 25 July 2015).
81. Dobrynin to USSR Foreign Ministry, 25 October 1962, *Cold War International History Project Bulletin*, 8/9, Winter 1996–7, p. 286, <http://www.wilsoncenter.org/publication/bulletin-no-89-winter-1996> (last accessed 25 July 2015).
82. Telegram from Soviet Ambassador to Cuba Alekseev to USSR Foreign Ministry, 25 October 1962, ibid. p. 287.
83. CIA daily report, 'The Crisis USSR/Cuba', 27 October 1962, National Security Archive, George Washington University,

<http://www2.gwu.edu/~nsarchiv/nsa/cuba_mis_cri/docs.htm> (last accessed 25 July 2015); Hilsman to Rusk, 26 October 1963, recording Khrushchev's conversation with Knox on 24 October, *FRUS 1961–1963 X-XI-XII*, document 419, <http://history.state.gov/historicaldocuments/frus1961-63v10-12mSupp/d419> (last accessed 25 July 2015). Khrushchev's willingness to talk with Knox reflected his view that business interests had great influence over the US government. He did not engage in a comparable discussion with American diplomats.
84. Mission to UN to State Department, 25 October 1962, *FRUS 1961–1963 XI*, document 62, <https://history.state.gov/historicaldocuments/frus1961-63v11/d62> (last accessed 25 July 2015).
85. Protocol No. 61 Session of 25 October 1962, *Cold War International History Project Bulletin*, 17/18, Fall 2012, pp. 308–9, <http://www.wilsoncenter.org/publication/bulletin-no-17-18> (last accessed 25 July 2015).
86. Ibid. pp. 308–9.

# 5 A World Crisis, 22–28 October 1962

It cannot be said that other Governments were consulted with any intention of their advice being taken into account.

*David Ormsby-Gore*

## The United Nations

The UN provided a forum for states to consult the protagonists and each other during the missile crisis. The organisation had played a peacekeeping role in various trouble spots such as Kashmir, but had had no success in moderating the Cold War; each superpower tended to use the veto in the Security Council to frustrate any measures advocated by the other.[1] In October 1962 the United States had the backing of fellow Security Council members the United Kingdom, France and Taiwan, along with non-permanent members Ireland, Venezuela and Chile. Ghana, the other non-permanent member, supported Cuba on the grounds of respect for the UN Charter, which upheld the principle of territorial integrity and political independence.[2] The Security Council was the scene of confrontation. On 23 October, Adlai Stevenson, who had recovered his stride after the embarrassment over the Bay of Pigs in April 1961, condemned the installation of the missiles in Cuba as a profound threat to the peace.[3] Cuban representative Mario García Incháustegui maintained that Cuba had been forced to arm itself in response to US aggression. He argued that the quarantine contravened the UN Charter, which obliged members to seek to resolve disputes through peaceful negotiations.[4] In his despatch to Moscow, Inchaustegui's Soviet counterpart Valerian Zorin maintained that Stevenson's address was one of 'demagoguery and hypocrisy'.[5] Not having been briefed, Zorin neither confirmed nor denied the presence of the missiles in Cuba. On 24 October he made what British Ambassador to the UN Patrick Dean described as 'a cleverly constructed statement'. Zorin emphasised that every country was entitled to choose what weapons of defence were stationed on its soil, and that by announcing the quarantine, the United States had presented the Security Council with a fait accompli rather than seeking prior approval of its actions.[6] These points were entirely valid, and confirm that the American position was far from beyond reproach.

The following day, when Zorin demanded proof of nuclear missiles in Cuba, Stevenson gained the advantage. He replied that he had 'clear and incontrovertible evidence', asking whether the Soviet Union had 'placed and is placing medium and intermediate range missiles and sites in Cuba'. Zorin dismissed the question on the grounds that he was 'not in an American courtroom'. Stevenson, however, was prepared to wait 'until hell freezes over' for an answer. He displayed newly-declassified photographs of the missile sites, including some highly detailed, and therefore readily intelligible, images from low-level reconnaissance flights. Zorin was placed in an invidious position.[7] Britain's ambassador in Washington, David Ormsby-Gore, praised the 'care taken to produce convincing photographic evidence in the Security Council',[8] while Dean commented that Stevenson undoubtedly 'got the best of Mr Zorin'. Dean was surprised at Stevenson's forcefulness, having always found him too 'ready to seek for explanations and sometimes excuses for the behaviour of the Russians'. He explained the fresh attitude by saying that the ambassador was shocked at Soviet audacity 'in installing this large offensive base in Cuba'.[9] President Kennedy was most impressed: 'I never knew Adlai had it in him.'[10] Stevenson's performance undermined the Soviet position in world opinion,[11] and was a major coup in the history of the Security Council.

There was a tradition of the UN Secretary-General, acting on his own authority and in the face of a divided Security Council, intervening in major disputes.[12] Acting Secretary-General Sithu U Thant has been depicted as an 'unsung mediator' during the missile crisis, but his efforts to act as a go-between derived in part from external pressure – a British diplomat noted how some UN delegations tended 'to run around telling the Secretary-General to do something'.[13] After Kennedy's broadcast on 22 October, U Thant proposed that the Soviets suspend arms shipments for two or three weeks while the United States suspended the quarantine. Khrushchev was willing to accept the moratorium, telling U Thant that he had ordered Soviet ships bound for Cuba to stay away from the interception area. He added, though, that the order was temporary since he could not keep ships immobilized on the high seas indefinitely.[14] While the US government did not reject the proposal, there was concern that, as Kennedy put it, there were 'no assurances that arms won't be sent in there' and that work on the missile sites would continue. There was also the need to address the issue of verification, with the President noting that 'the missiles that are presently pointing at us should be subjected to inspection'.[15]

US officials hoped to use U Thant to provide cover for an approach that they had devised themselves. On 24 October, Rusk dictated to his friend and former assistant to U Thant, Andrew Cordier, the text of a statement for U Thant to announce. The statement requested that the governments of the United States, the Soviet Union, Cuba, Turkey and Italy accept UN observers at their missile sites and then take part in the Eighteen Nations Disarmament Committee at Geneva. Rusk strove to conceal his role. Later in the day, he decided to suspend the approach, still weighing up how the Soviets were likely to react. Around midnight on 24–5 October, President Kennedy instructed Stevenson to suggest to U Thant that he make a statement requesting Khrushchev to keep Soviet vessels out of the blockade area while appealing to Kennedy himself not to intercept the Soviet vessels until preliminary talks had begun. The President realised that it would be easier for Khrushchev to accept these terms if they appeared to come from the Secretary-General rather than from the US government. The next afternoon U Thant made a statement along the lines requested. Khrushchev soon agreed to preliminary talks and announced that he had ordered the captains of the Soviet vessels to stay out of the interception area. From that afternoon, talks involving U Thant and Soviet and American representatives were held at the UN.[16]

Dean Rusk revealed in 1987 that during the evening of 27 October, the President instructed him to telephone Andrew Cordier, to

> dictate to him a statement which would be made by U Thant ... proposing the removal of both the Jupiters and the missiles in Cuba. Mr Cordier was to put that statement in the hands of U Thant only after a further signal from us. That step was never taken and the statement I furnished to Mr Cordier has never seen the light of day. So far as I know, President Kennedy, Andrew Cordier and I were the only ones who knew of this particular step.[17]

The proposal intentionally bypassed the UN mission in New York, so that it looked like it had originated from the office of U Thant. Politically, this would have made it easier for the administration to accept a *public* deal concerning the Jupiters, although that would prove unnecessary given the Soviet willingness to accept private terms.

## The Organization of American States

Kennedy had asserted in his 22 October speech that Soviet nuclear missiles in Cuba constituted 'an explicit threat to the peace and security of all the Americas, in flagrant and deliberate defiance of the Rio Pact of 1947', as well as 'the traditions of this nation and hemisphere'. Article 6 of the Pact, a defence treaty, referred to action in the event of a 'fact or situation that might endanger the peace of America', while Article 8 specified various responses.[18] The Rio Pact was followed in 1951 by the Organization of American States (OAS), which was intended to promote political and economic cooperation within the Western Hemisphere. For OAS members, the confrontation over the missiles in Cuba was an alarming feature of a larger set of issues concerning the impact of the Cuban Revolution: US and Latin American support for counter-revolutionary intervention against Castro's government, the presence of hundreds of Cuban exiles in neighbouring countries seeking to overthrow Castro and Cuban efforts to promote regional insurrection.[19]

The US administration looked to the OAS rather than the UN to help legitimise the blockade and any military action against Cuba, feeling that the OAS was the optimal machinery for a crisis in the Western Hemisphere. It was felt imperative that OAS members lend their endorsement, even if a little arm-twisting was required. Dean Rusk instructed US ambassadors to Latin American states 'to use whatever pressure tactics you think will be the more effective in securing prompt support in Organ of Consultation [of the OAS] . . . keeping in mind strong US and governmental feelings which will exist about any country which does not support Hemispheric solidarity on this issue'.[20] On 23 October Rusk succeeded in persuading the OAS, meeting in Washington, to support the quarantine.[21] The diplomatic success strengthened the US position politically and legally. President Kennedy was, as Ormsby-Gore noted, 'heartened by the news that the OAS had voted almost unanimously in support of the United States' action'.[22] Yet American solicitude towards legal niceties never extended to admitting that the Soviets had violated no laws by placing the missiles in Cuba.

## NATO

### The NATO Council

The North Atlantic Treaty had been signed in 1949 largely to deter a Soviet assault on Western Europe, and the North Atlantic Treaty Organisation was established soon after to provide an institutional foundation for cooperation. There was a significant NATO dimension to the missile crisis: an attack on a US vessel enforcing the quarantine would, according to Article 6 of the North Atlantic Treaty, call for collective action by the alliance; there were fears of Soviet action against Berlin or Turkey; and, as Rusk noted, US policy was broadly 'directed at a potential threat to the total strategic balance endangering other NATO countries at least as much as the United States'.[23] President Kennedy wanted to ensure that if the Soviets attacked any 'NATO countries we do not want them to say that they had not been consulted about the actions we were taking in Cuba'.[24] Countries experiencing such an attack might have had more pressing concerns, but the Administration did make particular efforts to keep NATO allies informed. However, the efforts were not always well received, given how they fell short of proper consultation. Former Secretary of State Dean Acheson briefed the NATO Council just minutes before the President's speech on 22 October, a move that a US diplomat described as mere 'consent-building notification after the fact'. The Dutch representative to NATO reported that his British, West German, Italian, Canadian, Belgian and Turkish colleagues all resented the short notice. The Belgian representative 'complained strongly' to Acheson about how Supreme Allied Commander in Europe General Lauris Norstad had put NATO air forces in 'a state of alert ... without any consultation with the Alliance'.[25] Although the North Atlantic Council issued a resolution recommending the support of the United States in the UN Security Council, this was of little practical significance as the Security Council did not have anything to vote on.[26]

The US government extended special treatment to the principal NATO allies – Britain, France and West Germany – as part of the support-building exercise. A number of emissaries were dispatched to outline the American position and to justify the quarantine. Ambassador David Bruce, Dean Acheson, and Ambassador Walter C. Dowling saw Harold Macmillan in London, President Charles de Gaulle in Paris, and Chancellor Konrad Adenauer in Bonn respectively.[27] CIA officers Sherman Kent (who went to Paris with Acheson), Jack Smith (Bonn), and Chester Cooper (London) had the duty of answering questions about the incriminatory photographs, copies of which were used to dispel any reservations about US policy.[28]

### Britain

Britain, the third country after the United States and the Soviet Union to have developed nuclear weapons, hosted American nuclear-armed bombers and submarines, and jointly-operated Thor nuclear missiles. The 'special relationship' – a nexus of institutional ties and informal habits of communication and cooperation – was such that the British knew about the discovery of the Soviet missiles in Cuba well before the presidential address of 22 October. They may have learned unofficially through their intelligence sources as early as 17 October, and certainly British senior officials had the benefit of a briefing two days later from Deputy Director of the CIA Ray Cline at a conference on intelligence methodology at the CIA's headquarters.[29] These British officials were better informed than Ambassador David Bruce in London, who, according to his diary, only learned that 'something unusual was astir' on 21 October. He received instructions from Washington that he should meet a military plane at Greenham Common airport in Berkshire at midnight. There he would be briefed on what he needed to do. Following State Department instructions, he even took a revolver with him when he met the party from Washington. Fortunately, the weapon was surplus to requirements, but the bottle of whisky that he had also brought went down well.[30]

Bruce had the duty of briefing Harold Macmillan, with the help of Chester Cooper, who brought copies of the photographs of the missile sites. As Bruce had not seen the images, Cooper took the lead in the briefing, which took place at 10 Downing Street at noon on 22 October. He recalled that he 'unwrapped the pictures and pointed out the ICBM sites under various stages of construction', and that Macmillan and Bruce were 'clearly amazed at the details and clarity of the photographs. They shook their heads in disbelief at the risks the missile sites presented and at the Soviets' gall and chicanery.' However, Macmillan struck a sceptical note, pointing out that the British had lived in the shadow of the Soviet bomb for years, and so the Americans could adjust to the presence of Soviet missiles in Cuba. At the same time, he felt that if President Kennedy regarded the missiles as a threat then 'that is good enough for me'.[31]

Bruce had sought to use a copy of the President's forthcoming speech for the briefing, but was unable to obtain a copy: 'Several calls to the [State] Department obtained only the reply that things had become fouled up.' Eventually, at 'about seven o'clock . . . we had the humiliation of receiving from the British a copy of the speech, which had been promised for delivery to us before noon today'.[32] Whatever the difficulties, the support of the British, given their diplomatic experience and their status as a global power, was appreciated. Throughout the crisis Kennedy valued the chance to talk with a seasoned statesman, keeping in close touch with the Prime Minister with daily telephone calls. Kennedy favoured no other leader with so much of his time. On 25 October he asked Macmillan for his views about invading Cuba. Macmillan had favoured military action initially, but changed his mind, perhaps out of knowledge of Kennedy's personal feelings communicated to him through Ormsby-Gore. The Prime Minister suggested that 'we ought not to do anything in a hurry. We ought just to let this develop' for 'a day or two'. The next day he warned in a telegram that 'events have gone too far . . . you must try to obtain your objectives' by means other than an invasion.[33]

Ormsby-Gore saw President Kennedy four times during the course of the week of October 21, and on three of these occasions for long periods. There were also a number of telephone conversations between them. The Ambassador has been credited with encouraging the administration to reduce the radius of the blockade. On 23 October he suggested that Soviet ships 'ought to be allowed to come pretty close into Cuba as this would give the Russians a little more time to consider the situation'. The blockade area was reduced from 800 miles (the 'Walnut Line') to 500 miles (the 'Chestnut Line').[34] The Ambassador encouraged the Americans to release the incriminatory photographs to the press in London, Paris and other capitals, so that the US position over Cuba could be better understood.[35] Macmillan offered to immobilise the Thor nuclear missiles as a contribution to a settlement, although Kennedy did not take up the proposal.[36]

Britain provided intelligence material to the US from its embassy in Havana and from the monitoring of Soviet shipping.[37] British policymakers, including Foreign Secretary Alec Douglas-Home, backed American policy in representations to Soviet diplomats in London.[38] There was also a significant British intelligence contribution from the espionage of Oleg Penkovsky. From April

1961 until the autumn of 1962, Penkovsky spied from a senior position within Soviet military intelligence in a joint operation run by the CIA and Britain's Secret Intelligence Service (MI6). By the time he was arrested on 22 October, Penkovsky had provided a great deal of military intelligence. Although this did not extend to the deployments in Cuba, his information helped US photo-analysts to identify the missiles and to assess their state of readiness.[39]

However, the Anglo-American relationship had its limitations. While the Prime Minister was a welcome sounding board for Kennedy, Ambassador Ormsby-Gore stated that 'I cannot honestly think of anything said from London that changed the US action – it was chiefly reassurance.'[40] Although American officials – and indeed the President – listened carefully to his views, Ormsby-Gore was not the only influence on US thinking about the scale of the quarantine and the question of releasing the intelligence images to the media. He may therefore be regarded as only a peripheral influence on some lesser US policies. In London, the British government had reservations about the quarantine. The Foreign Office complained that 'Drastic enforcement of the blockade measures against British shipping would cause acute difficulties for us in Parliament and outside.'[41] The Lord Chancellor stated that the quarantine, given that it deprived the Soviets of freedom of the seas, was 'not in conformity with international law'.[42]

The opposition Labour Party backed American policy, but only with reservations. At least until the public release of the intelligence photographs, Leader Hugh Gaitskell speculated that 'the American reaction had really been engendered by the elections'.[43] Similarly, British newspapers challenged the authenticity of the missiles until the evidence had been released.[44] There were public demonstrations against US policy in London and other British cities. Bruce reported on 23 October that 'The Embassy sustained a massive assault this evening. About 2,000 people had gathered in Grosvenor Square, amongst them tough elements probably belonging to the Communist Party.' Bruce instructed the Marines and other Embassy personnel 'that under no circumstances' were 'they to use pistols, even if they are attacked', as the use of tear gas would be sufficient to repulse the assailants. However, he left open the possibility that if rioters were able to 'penetrate above the first floor of the building . . . we should open fire', to protect the code room.[45] The image of American Embassy personnel shooting British protestors would have been an awful development, and would have provided rich pickings for Soviet propaganda.

## France

President Charles de Gaulle of France had been a growing diplomatic challenge within the NATO alliance, with his nationalistic assertion of French interests often clashing with American policies. He had in 1959, for example, withdrawn French vessels from the NATO Mediterranean Command. One concern for the US government in the early 1960s was the independent French nuclear programme, which was at odds with American nuclear strategy and support for non-proliferation. However, on 20 October President Kennedy asked Rusk to 'reconsider the present policy of refusing to give nuclear weapons assistance to France . . . in light of present circumstances a refusal to help the French is not worthwhile'.[46] The idea was to preempt French objections to a possible deal involving US weapons in Cuba and to obviate the perception that the United States was willing to remove nuclear weapons of all kinds from Europe. Rusk, however, presented the State Department line by arguing that whether or not the French provided support depended on 'how intimately we consult with them', not 'on provision of nuclear aid . . . We would not earn [de Gaulle's] respect by changing our policy toward him when we were in trouble.'[47] After his meeting with Dean Acheson and the CIA's Sherman Kent on 22 October, the French President questioned the likely effectiveness of the quarantine, and noted pointedly that the US emissaries were on a mission of 'notification and not . . . consultation, since the decision has already been taken'. Nevertheless, he added that

for the first time, the United States are directly threatened, since the missiles . . . can only be targeting the United States. President Kennedy wants to react immediately. France cannot object, since it is normal for a country to defend itself, even with preventive measures, once it is threatened.[48]

As such, the French government gave the US its backing. Furthermore, the French embassy in Havana provided valuable information about the internal situation in Cuba.[49] The US government greatly appreciated the support from another major ally.

### The Federal Republic of Germany (FRG)

During the missile crisis, Konrad Adenauer, who had feared that the Kennedy administration might do a deal over Berlin at the FRG's expense, now questioned the wisdom of directing American efforts at Khrushchev rather than Castro. The latter was 'in the forefront. He offered his country for the missiles and thus facilitated the threat to the United States.' The US government should have 'moved earlier against Castro, and ... even now as matter of tactics we should build him up as [the] principal villain in [the] piece'. This might 'rally support among Cuban people, and at same time make it easier for Khrushchev to stand aside while we deal with the Cuban problem by military means'.[50] German as well as French diplomats rejected the US notion that Soviet policy in Cuba was connected with the Berlin crisis. At an EEC foreign ministers' meeting on 23 October Gerhard Schroeder (FRG) and Maurice Couve de Murville (France) chided the others for accepting the US view that the two affairs were connected. They maintained that 'the two questions are, in fact, very different'; Moscow was directing its policies towards the United States and Cuba, not Berlin.[51] Concerns of this nature notwithstanding, Chancellor Adenauer backed the American stance during the missile crisis, telling Ambassador Walter Dowling and the CIA's Jack Smith that 'You may tell your president that I will support him in meeting this challenge.'[52]

### Other NATO Allies

Along with Turkey, Italy hosted a fleet of Jupiter missiles, which would be vulnerable to a Soviet first strike. Italian Prime

Minister Amintore Fanfani learned of the crisis only on the evening of Kennedy's speech. As with David Bruce in London, US Ambassador Frank Reinhardt struggled to obtain a copy of the address, giving Fanfani just half of the President's forthcoming speech, plus a brief note from Kennedy himself. On the evening of 23 October Fanfani stated his government's position, expressing solidarity with the United States for seeking recourse to the UN but not for establishing the blockade.[53] The following day, 24 October, Fanfani wrote privately to Kennedy:

> Mr President, Italy understands and feels the grave concerns for the maintenance of peace ... created by the concentration of offensive nuclear weapons on the island of Cuba. However, I would be derelict to an elementary duty of friendship if I did not say ... that the measures decided upon by you cause the gravest risks of all.[54]

There was also the issue of the Jupiter missiles, which might end up part of an agreement with the Soviet Union. Ambassador Reinhardt noted that removal of the missiles would 'probably be manageable' because 'Public awareness of Jupiter installations in Italy is ... minimal.' The Italian government had accepted the missiles in the first place 'primarily because we wanted it [sic] do so'.[55] Evidence suggests that to resolve the crisis Fanfani was willing to consider a trade involving the removal of the Jupiter missiles from Italy, although in the event the Soviets only expressed interest in the missiles in Turkey.[56] However, the Italian Prime Minister was another ally with doubts about American policies.

The Netherlands was a firm member of NATO and a keen advocate of close transatlantic relations, but extended only tepid support to the United States during the missile crisis. Upon hearing of the confrontation, Foreign Minister Joseph Luns refused to abandon his holiday on the French Riviera, telling Prime Minister Jan de Quay that he opposed the American policy and would not make a declaration of support. The Dutch had extensive maritime, commercial and colonial interests in the Caribbean and beyond, and had recently criticised the American embargo against Cuba.

It was felt that supporting the US on this issue would damage the credibility of Dutch maritime transport, especially in countries associated with the Non-Aligned Movement. More importantly, in August 1962 the Netherlands had lost New Guinea, its last colony in Asia, and begrudged the lack of US support on this matter. Furthermore, Luns and some of his colleagues reasoned that Cuba was outside NATO territory and so not their concern. However, under pressure from parliamentarians who were critical of de Quay's initial, equivocal statements on the matter and concerned about the confrontation escalating, Luns returned to The Hague. He accepted that the government of the Netherlands would issue a statement of support for the US position. In his diary, Prime Minister de Quay described the mood in his cabinet as 'kind of indifferent' and indicated that he would have liked to have provided firmer backing for Kennedy.[57]

On 22 October, US Ambassador to Canada Livingston Merchant briefed Canadian Prime Minister John Diefenbaker. Although Canada backed the US embargo on trade with Cuba and provided intelligence information through its embassy in Havana, Diefenbaker was, according to Merchant, 'somewhat brusque in manner and openly skeptical in attitude concerning the missile menace'.[58] Speaking in the House of Commons soon after Kennedy's television and radio address, Diefenbaker sought an 'independent inspection' by the UN to 'provide an objective answer to what is going on in Cuba'. Only three days later did he offer his country's backing for American policy.[59] According to a Canadian official, Diefenbaker was 'seriously concerned over the future implications of the absence of genuine consultation and [about] the limited advance notice of the President's decision on Cuba announced October 22'.[60] Diefenbaker was reluctant to place the Canadian military on alert status, even though the North American defence system was highly integrated. However, Defence Minister Douglas Harkness readied the Canadian navy and air force on 23 October. Despite reservations by some leading officials, Canada therefore undertook an active military support role.[61]

David Ormsby-Gore presented a favourable verdict of the US handling of allies during the crisis, arguing that

The selection of Mr Acheson to brief the North Atlantic Council, the dispatch of members of the Central Intelligence Agency to London and Ottawa to brief the Prime Ministers of the United Kingdom and Canada ... the briefing given to Ambassadors in Washington before the President's broadcast on October 22 – all these were impressive manifestations of a carefully thought-out approach to the problem of how to mobilise all the resources of United States diplomacy to gain support for the President's case.[62]

It is clear that US policymakers were very much concerned with the NATO dimension of the missile crisis, as shown by the information campaign, the concern about what allies would think if the Soviet missiles were permitted to remain in Cuba, anxiety about Berlin, and, after 28 October, the wish for secrecy about trading US Jupiter missiles in Turkey out of concerns for allied unity.[63] However, the Kennedy administration was more interested in building consent for steps that it had already decided rather than eliciting and responding to the ideas and concerns of allies. Chester Cooper noted how European leaders were not being consulted but 'forcefully instructed how important it was for President Kennedy to have their full support over the next dangerous days and weeks'.[64] Allies were seen almost as a nuisance, an inhibition on the US freedom of action. Bundy feared 'the amount of noise we would get from our allies saying that they can live with Soviet MRBMs, why can't we?' Although Rusk expressed solicitude towards the implications of the confrontation for US alliance relationships,[65] he later testified that it would have been risky to engage in proper consultation because 'we could not be sure in advance what the response of our NATO allies would be'.[66] The US therefore made its policies unilaterally. Ormsby-Gore noted in relation to the quarantine that 'It cannot be said that other Governments were consulted with any intention of their advice being taken into account.'[67] While after 22 October numerous channels of communication were available to allies to put forward their views,[68] with the British taking particular advantage, the ExComm transcripts indicate no particular concern with allied perspectives. The view was that, according to Walt Rostow of the State Department, the missile crisis was 'an American show'.[69]

## Brazil and Other Latin American States

At the same time, the US administration encouraged efforts to mediate the dispute. Brazil was Latin America's most populated and perhaps most politically significant country. At the time of the crisis, Brazil was led by President João Goulart of the centre-left Brazilian Workers Party (PTB). After visiting Washington in April 1962, US officials hailed him as a worthy partner in the Alliance for Progress. But in subsequent months they began to fear that he might lead his country towards communism, so US officials approved covert aid to his opponents and considered deploying the CIA to overthrow him. There were concerns about Brazil's refusal to break relations with Havana, and its continued promotion of a scheme to 'neutralize' the island that would leave Fidel Castro in power. Brazil resisted US efforts to rally the OAS to approve harsh measures against Cuba, and rejected any interference in Cuba's internal affairs.

Brazilian diplomacy during the crisis had three dimensions. First, in the OAS, Brazil endorsed the quarantine but refused to approve the use of force. Second, Brazil promoted a scheme in the UN to 'denuclearise' Latin America, an idea in which the Soviet Deputy Minister for Foreign Affairs, Frol Kozlov, expressed interest during a discussion with the Brazilian ambassador in Moscow on 23 October. Brazilian ambassador in Washington Roberto Campos thought that the plan offered Cuba and the Soviet Union a chance 'to save face', thereby 'diminishing the dangerous direct confrontation'.[70] He thought that Brazil might be able to 'lead the pro-denuclearization movement', certainly in Latin America and among most neutral states. Denuclearisation could extend to NATO's nuclear installations in Turkey.[71] Brazilian diplomats pursued the idea in the UN at a time when Kennedy and his advisors were searching desperately for a way to get the Soviet missiles out of Cuba without violence. Rusk, for one, saw merit in the Brazilian initiative. However, after several weeks of discussions, the plan came to nothing due to Cuban demands that any denuclearisation scheme should also apply to US bases in Puerto Rico and the Panama Canal Zone, and should be linked to the evacuation of foreign military bases in the hemisphere, including Guantánamo.

The third Brazilian initiative involved sending an emissary to Havana to meet with Castro, in an attempt to mediate. The trip derived from a secret US appeal to Brazil. During the ExComm talks the idea of communicating with Castro emerged on more than one occasion. On 17 October Stevenson urged Kennedy to have 'your personal emissary deliver your messages' to Castro and Khrushchev. A State Department paper outlining a 'Political Path' to the resolution of the crisis suggested an approach to Castro 'through a Latin American representative in Cuba, probably the Brazilian ambassador'. On 26 October Rusk told US Ambassador to Brazil Lincoln Gordon to meet with the new Brazilian prime minister, Hermes Lima, to arrange for the Brazilian ambassador in Havana to convey a message to Castro, as if it was a Brazilian initiative. The Ambassador was to emphasise that the Soviet Union's use of Cuba as a nuclear missile base has 'placed the future of the Castro regime and the well-being of the Cuban people in great jeopardy'.[72] Prime Minister Lima would then hold out the prospect of improved relations with the United States and Latin American countries if Castro expelled the Soviets and stopped trying to promote revolution abroad. Brazilian representatives were very willing to participate in the initiative because resolving the crisis would not only end the danger but would boost their country's international standing. The missile crisis ended before the efforts could bear fruit, but they provided further evidence that the crisis created complex ripples beyond the United States, the Soviet Union and Cuba. The Brazilian denuclearisation scheme contributed to the Treaty of Tlatelolco of 1967, which banned nuclear weapons in Latin America.[73]

The Mexican government maintained relations with Cuba during the missile crisis. This was not through admiration for Castro but out of a tradition of non-interference in other countries' internal affairs. Also, President Adolfo Lopez Mateos was conscious of domestic opinion and of widespread support for Cuba within Mexico. In the OAS on 23 October the Mexican government, alongside the governments of Brazil, Bolivia and Uruguay, abstained on the question of taking military action against the missile bases. The Mexicans sought to strike a balance, on one hand between opposing interventionist policies and an invasion of Cuba, while on the other hand supporting the removal of the Soviet missiles. Having attacked the US position on Cuba for its 'paralysis and lack of foresight' before the crisis, Guatemala's far-right military president firmly endorsed Kennedy's insistence that the missiles must be removed and declared Guatemala's armed forces ready for action. A state of emergency was imposed in the Dominican Republic, while Costa Rica offered its ports and air-space to help support the blockade.[74] Argentina, the Dominican Republic and Venezuela contributed destroyers to the blockade.[75] The United States made significant commitments to some Latin American states in order to obtain their support. The agree-ment of Haiti and other nations in the Caribbean was needed to implement the quarantine, but President Duvalier exacted a price when in November he got the US government to agree to build a modern airport in his country. Furthermore, President Kennedy resumed military support for Peru against the wishes of the State Department to help ensure 'solidarity in [the] face [of the] Cuba–Soviet threat to hemispheric security'.[76]

## Non-Aligned and Neutral States

Despite efforts by the US delegation to the UN, there was little success in strengthening the American position with most non-aligned states, that is, developing countries who adopted a neutral stance in the Cold War and grouped together under the banner of non-alignment. Patrick Dean noted that throughout the crisis these states showed a 'regrettable tendency to give the benefit of any doubt to the Russians rather than to the Americans'. He considered that the American mission to the UN 'had not taken sufficient trouble to brief the uncommitted delegations in the early stages'. Later, even when those delegations were briefed about the American position, 'there were still some who for emotional reasons were unwilling to accept the evidence'.[77]

At the same time, American records indicate that the adminis-tration was heartened by the reaction of some non-aligned states during the missile confrontation. Ambassador to the West African state of Guinea William Attwood recorded that on 23 October he encountered messages indicating that the Soviets were 'planning a Moscow–Havana airlift via Conakry'. The following day the Acting Foreign Minister, Alpha Diallo, stated that 'the Russians had requested landing rights in Conakry for long-range jets' between the Soviet Union and Cuba. He also stated that he had turned down the request. Guinean President Ahmed Sékou Touré explained that 'The reason we refused to help the Russians establish military sites in Cuba is that we are against all foreign military bases everywhere,' including Guantánamo. 'But we could not agree' with Castro 'when he invited the Russians to come in with their missiles. That was in violation with non-alignment.' The Guinean version of non-alignment clearly served the Americans well, although Guinea's representative at the Afro-Asian Jurists Conference in Conakry gave way to pro-communist pressure and voted for a resolution denouncing 'American imperialism'.[78]

During the missile crisis President Tito of Yugoslavia strove to mediate a settlement. His efforts derived from his fear of nuclear conflagration, his wish to preserve a socialist regime in the Western Hemisphere, and from what he saw as a chance to strengthen the non-aligned movement, twenty-two members of which had met the previous year in Belgrade. He had in mind the reciprocal American and Soviet actions of lifting the quarantine and removing long-range missiles from Cuba with UN assistance. The participation of the latter was especially fitting in the context of non-alignment given how the UN gave a voice to Third World and non-aligned states. Tito's efforts were cordially received in Havana, with the Yugoslav ambassador enjoying privileged access – second only to that of the Soviet ambassador – to top Cuban leaders throughout the crisis.[79] As with other initiatives to resolve the crisis, the Yugoslav effort was overtaken by the Kennedy–Khrushchev deal on 28 October.

Although politically and militarily neutral, Switzerland was anti-communist and well-disposed to the United States. Through their embassy in Havana the Swiss represented US diplomatic interests in Cuba. US policymakers saw an opportunity for Swiss mediation. After the ambassadorial briefings in Washington on 22 October, Rusk approached the Swiss ambassador, August Lindt, to ask discretely about the possibility of having the Swiss

Ambassador in Cuba, Emil Stadelhofer, emphasise to Castro the danger Cuba faced and that he should consider breaking away from the Soviet Union. Rusk explained that the US would be willing to talk with Castro if Cuba detached itself from the Soviet Union. There were concerns in the Foreign Ministry in Berne that the suggested initiative could damage Swiss neutrality, but there was also an unwillingness to reject a chance of defusing the crisis. Duly, Stadelhofer managed to meet with Raúl Roa García, Cuba's Foreign Minister, but did not manage to obtain an audience with Castro. Moreover, Ambassador Lindt and the Foreign Ministry had concluded that Cuba could not be drawn away from the Soviet Union and told Stadelhofer that a meeting with Castro was no longer a priority. The missile crisis was over by 7 November when Stadelhofer was able to see Castro. Stadelhofer had worked hard to turn Rusk's suggestion into reality, and the episode demonstrates the US interest – evident also in relation to backing Brazilian efforts – in resolving the missile crisis by engaging Cuba. This was something that Chancellor Adenauer, for one, had urged, although he wanted a more public initiative than the measures the administration actually took.[80]

## The Warsaw Pact

At the time of the Berlin crisis in 1961 the Soviet government had consulted extensively with Warsaw Pact members, especially the German Democratic Republic.[81] During the missile crisis Moscow ordered Warsaw Pact forces to increase their preparedness,[82] and Soviet Deputy Foreign Minister Vasili Kuznetsov briefed the ambassadors to the Soviet Union from Poland, Czechoslovakia, Bulgaria and East Germany.[83] However, Khrushchev had not told the satellite governments about the installation of missiles in Cuba, nor did he make any attempt to consult them during the crisis. The Polish leader Władysław Gomułka reflected that during the confrontation the 'danger of war . . . became reality, a question of today, a question of the hour, it became an immediate threat, which the entire world faced. One careless step, one careless action could have pushed the world over into the abyss of war.'[84] Like most Soviet (and US) allies, Gomułka had no enthusiasm for a war over an issue thousands of miles away and about which he had not been consulted. Elsewhere behind the Iron Curtain, the Hungarian government wished to play down the confrontation out of concern that it could create anger against the Soviet Union, disturbing the pacification that had been ongoing since the Soviets had crushed the Hungarian revolution in 1956.[85]

Despite reservations, Soviet allies followed the Moscow line dutifully. In Hungary there were mass rallies expressing support for Cuba. In the GDR, the Socialist Unity Party of Germany (SED) outlined a 'mass-propaganda' campaign condemning US 'aggression' against Cuba.[86] The following day the SED agreed a directive to the effect that the US blockade was 'a crass violation of international law, a blow against freedom of the seas, and against free trade'.[87] During the crisis Khrushchev took time to deal with some of the concerns of the East German leader, Walter Ulbricht. Relations between them had suffered in recent months over economic differences. Following their meeting on 27 October, Ulbricht returned to the GDR satisfied, Khrushchev having endorsed his economic reforms. Although Khrushchev's Cuban gambit was on the verge of failure and his relationship with Castro about to undergo unprecedented strain, he could at least take steps to improve his relationship with an ally closer to home.[88]

## The Sino-Indian War

At the time of the crisis, India, a non-aligned state under the leadership of Jawaharlal Nehru, was struggling in a border war in the Himalayas with communist China; the Chinese launched their heaviest attack to date on 20 October.[89] Dean Rusk suggested that the Chinese, who had diplomats in Cuba, might have chosen their moment

> with knowledge that [a] Russian build-up was occurring in Cuba. They may also have considered that whether [or not] the missile plot succeeded or failed, [the] US would be likely to be fully occupied with

[the] Cuban crisis and thus unlikely to be able to turn [its] attention to actions in [the] Himalayas.[90]

The US administration saw the clash in the most dramatic terms. President Kennedy reflected that the conflict in South Asia could be as fateful for American interests as the missile crisis, while the State Department commented that the Sino-Indian fighting was 'second in importance only to Cuba in present global confrontation between the Free World and the Sino-Soviet Bloc'.[91] On 28 October, Kennedy tried to reassure President Ayub Khan of Pakistan, who was in contention with India over Kashmir, that the threat to India had to be seen in a global context:

> We see another instance of Communist aggression almost as close to your borders as Cuba is to ours – the Chinese Communist attack on India. It also concerns me greatly. The Chinese have moved quickly, with large forces to take territory beyond that immediately in dispute; it is no longer a border wrangle. In my judgment, the long-run significance of this move cannot be exaggerated.[92]

The war presented Moscow with a dilemma. On the one hand, Soviet officials favoured peaceful coexistence and valued their developing relationship with India, as these had helped Moscow to gain influence in other non-aligned states, but at the same time, they wanted to minimise tensions with China. The Soviets decided to extend modest support for Beijing, not least out of a desire for Chinese backing in the missile crisis. Support for the Chinese, as British Ambassador to the Soviet Union Frank Roberts suggested, came 'at the cost of jeopardizing a heavy investment in Indian friendship by abandoning their long-sustained neutrality in the Sino-Indian frontier dispute'. Yet in exchange Beijing provided only half-hearted backing for the Soviet Union during the confrontation with the United States, while extending vigorous support for Fidel Castro.[93] The fighting between India and China ended in a decisive victory for the latter within a few weeks, and soon the Americans and the British began supplying India with arms for defence against the Chinese. Although China withdrew from the border area rather than pressing its advantage, the war confirmed the Western image of Chinese expansionism and showed that the world did not stand still during the missile crisis.

## Notes

1. Although the Western effort during the Korean War of 1950–3 was carried out under the UN banner, this was only possible because the Soviet Union was boycotting the Security Council, on the grounds that the nationalist government of Chiang Kai-shek was still occupying the Chinese seat even though the communist Mao Zedong had seized power. US troops would undoubtedly have fought in Korea without UN endorsement, though.
2. Bertrand G. Ramcharan, *Preventive Diplomacy at the UN* (Bloomington: Indiana University Press, 2008), p. 109.
3. Editorial note, *Foreign Relations of the United States (FRUS) 1961–1963 XI Cuban Missile Crisis and Aftermath* (Washington, DC: USGPO, 1996), document 49, <https://history.state.gov/historical-documents/frus1961-63v11/d49> (last accessed 25 July 2015).
4. Tomas Diez Acosta, *October 1962: The 'Missile' Crisis as Seen from Cuba* (New York: Pathfinder, 2002), p. 163.
5. Zorin to USSR Foreign Ministry, 23 October 1962, *Cold War International History Project Bulletin*, 8/9, Winter 1996–7, <http://www.wilsoncenter.org/publication/bulletin-no-89-winter-1996> (last accessed 25 July 2015).
6. New York to Foreign Office, 24 October 1962, FO 371/162376, The National Archives, Kew, England (TNA); Peter Catterall, 'Modifying "a very dangerous message": Britain, the Non-aligned, and the UN during the Cuban Missile Crisis', in David Gioe, Len Scott and Christopher Andrew (eds), *An International History of the Cuban Missile Crisis: A 50-Year Retrospective* (London: Routledge, 2014), p. 81.
7. Harvard Kennedy School, Belfer Center for Science and International Affairs, Cuban Missile Crisis, <http://www.cubanmissilecrisis.org/background/original-historic-sources/videos/> (last accessed 25 July 2015); Robert F. Kennedy, *Thirteen Days: A Memoir of the Cuban Missile Crisis* (New York: Norton, 1969), pp. 75–6.
8. The administration's handling of the Cuban Crisis, 12 November 1962, CAB 21/5581, TNA.
9. The Cuban Crisis in the United Nations, 12 November 1962, CAB

21/5581, TNA; New York to Foreign Office, 7 November 1962, FO 371/162399, TNA.

10. Kenny O'Donnell and David Powers, with Joe McCarthy, *'Johnny We Hardly Knew Ye': Memories of John Fitzgerald Kennedy* (Boston: Little, Brown, 1972), p. 334.

11. Arthur M. Schlesinger, Jr., *A Thousand Days: John F. Kennedy in the White House* (New York: Houghton Mifflin, 1965), p. 705.

12. Abram Chayes, *The Cuban Missile Crisis: International Crises and the Role of Law* (New York: Oxford University Press, 1974), p. 58.

13. A. Walter Dorn and Robert Pauk, 'Unsung Mediator: U Thant and the Cuban Missile Crisis', *Diplomatic History*, 33: 2, April 2009, pp. 261–92; Catterall, 'Modifying "a very dangerous message"', p. 81; New York to Foreign Office, 31 October 1962, PREM 11/ 3691, TNA.

14. Ramacharan, *Preventive Diplomacy at the UN*, p. 111.

15. Ernest R. May and Philip D. Zelikow (eds), *The Kennedy Tapes: Inside the White House During the Cuban Missile Crisis* (Cambridge, MA: Belknap, 1997), p. 387.

16. Toshihiko Aono, 'Leading from Behind: Anglo-American Diplomacy and Third Party Mediation during the Cuban Missile Crisis', in Gioe et al. (eds), *An International History of the Cuban Missile Crisis*, p. 202.

17. Editorial note, *FRUS 1961–1963 XI*, document 99, <https://history. state.gov/historicaldocuments/frus1961-63v11/d99> (last accessed 25 July 2015).

18. Appendix I, draft memorandum of the legal adviser, 29 September 1962, in Chayes, *The Cuban Missile Crisis*, pp. 135–6.

19. Tanya Harmer, 'Mexican Diplomacy and the Cuban Missile Crisis: Documents from the Foreign Ministry Archives in Mexico City', *Cold War International History Project Bulletin*, 17/18, Fall 2012, p. 191, <http://www.wilsoncenter.org/publication/bulletin-no-17-18> (last accessed 25 July 2015).

20. Thomas Risse-Kappen, *Cooperation among Democracies: The European Influence on US Security Policy* (Princeton, NJ: Princeton University Press, 1995), pp. 150–1.

21. Editorial note, *FRUS 1961–1963 XI*, document 49, <https://history. state.gov/historicaldocuments/frus1961-63v11/d49> (last accessed 25 July 2015).

22. Washington to Foreign Office, 24 October 1962, FO 371/162386, TNA.

23. State Department to Mission to NATO, 28 October 1962, *FRUS*

*1961–1963 XI*, document 100, <https://history.state.gov/historical documents/frus1961-63v11/d100> (last accessed 25 July 2015).

24. ExComm meeting, 27 October, *FRUS 1961–1963 XI*, document 94, <https://history.state.gov/historicaldocuments/frus1961-63v11/d94> (last accessed 25 July 2015).

25. Frank Costigliola, 'Kennedy, the European Allies, and the Failure to Consult', *Political Science Quarterly*, 110: 1, Spring 1995, pp. 113–14.

26. Chayes, *The Cuban Missile Crisis*, p. 75.

27. NSC meeting, 21 October 1962, *FRUS 1961–1963 XI*, document 38, <https://history.state.gov/historicaldocuments/frus1961-63v11/d38> (last accessed 25 July 2015).

28. Chester L. Cooper, *In the Shadows of History: 50 Years Behind the Scenes of Cold War Diplomacy* (Amherst: Prometheus, 2005), p. 197.

29. L. V. Scott, *Macmillan, Kennedy and the Cuban Missile Crisis: Political, Military and Intelligence Aspects* (New York: St Martin's Press, 1999), pp. 39–48.

30. Raj Roy and John W. Young (eds), *Ambassador to Sixties London: The Diaries of David Bruce, 1961–1969* (Dordrecht: Republic of Letters, 2009), p. 78.

31. Cooper, *In the Shadows of History*, p. 199.

32. Bruce diary, in Roy and Young (eds), *Ambassador to Sixties London*, p. 79.

33. Scott, *Macmillan, Kennedy*, pp. 183–4; May and Zelikow, *Kennedy Tapes*, pp. 387, 393. See also Nigel Ashton, *Kennedy, Macmillan and the Cold War: The Irony of Interdependence* (Basingstoke: Palgrave, 2002), pp. 74–89.

34. Washington to Foreign Office, 24 October 1962, PREM 11/3690, TNA; Kennedy, *Thirteen Days*, p. 67.

35. Editorial note, *FRUS 1961–1963 XI*, document 37, <https://history.state.gov/historicaldocuments/frus1961-63v11/d37> (last accessed 25 July 2015); Michael F. Hopkins, 'David Ormsby-Gore, 1961–65', in Michael F. Hopkins, Saul Kelly and John W. Young (eds), *The Washington Embassy: British Ambassadors to the United States, 1939–77* (Basingstoke: Palgrave, 2009), pp. 137–9.

36. See Stephen Twigge and Len Scott, 'The Other Other Missiles of October: The Thor IBMs and the Cuban Missile Crisis', *Electronic Journal of International History*, 3, 30 January 2012, <http://sas-space.sas.ac.uk/3387/> (last accessed 25 July 2015).

37. Scott, *Macmillan, Kennedy*, p. 149.

38. Andrew Holt, *The Foreign Policy of the Douglas-Home Government: Britain, the United States and the End of Empire* (Basingstoke: Palgrave, 2014), p. 7.

39. See David Gioe, 'Handling HERO: Joint American Tradecraft in the Case of Oleg Penkovsy', in Gioe et al. (eds), *An International History of the Cuban Missile Crisis*, pp. 135–75; Len Scott, 'Espionage and the Cold War: Oleg Penkovsky and the Cuban Missile Crisis', *Intelligence and National Security*, 14: 3, Autumn 1999, pp. 23–47; Len Scott, 'Oleg Penkovsky, British Intelligence and the Cuban Missile Crisis', in Robert Dover and Michael S. Goodman (eds), *Learning from the Secret Past: Cases in British Intelligence History* (Washington, DC: Georgetown University Press, 2011), pp. 344–74. See also the CIA documents released under the Freedom of Information Act available at <http://www.foia.cia.gov/collection/lt-col-oleg-penkovsky-western-spy-soviet-gru> (last accessed 25 July 2015).

40. Sean Greenwood, *Britain and the Cold War, 1945–91* (Basingstoke: Palgrave Macmillan, 2000), pp. 160–1 [see also document 5, Appendix 4 in this volume for Ormsby-Gore's analysis of US unilateralism (from which the quotation at the head of this chapter derives)].

41. Foreign Office to Washington, 25 October 1962, FO 371/162375, TNA.

42. Memorandum from the Lord Chancellor, 25 October 1962, CAB 189/111, TNA.

43. Meeting at Admiralty House, 23 October 1962, PREM 11/3689, TNA.

44. George W. Ball, *The Past has Another Pattern: Memoirs* (New York: Norton, 1982), pp. 299–300.

45. Roy and Young (eds), *Ambassador to Sixties London*, pp. 80–1.

46. ExComm meeting, 20 October 1962, *FRUS 1961–1963 XI*, document 34, <https://history.state.gov/historicaldocuments/frus1961-63v11/d34> (last accessed 25 July 2015).

47. Erin R. Mahan, *Kennedy, de Gaulle, and Western Europe* (New York: Palgrave Macmillan, 2002), p. 135.

48. Meeting between General Charles de Gaulle and Dean Acheson, Paris, 22 October 1962, *Cold War International History Project Bulletin*, 17/18, Fall 2012, pp. 750–2, <http://www.wilsoncenter.org/publication/bulletin-no-17-18> (last accessed 25 July 2015).

49. Garret J. Martin, 'French Documents on the Cuban Missile Crisis', *Cold War International History Project Bulletin*, 17/18, Fall

2012, p. 750, <http://www.wilsoncenter.org/publication/bulletin-no-17-18> (last accessed 25 July 2015).

50. Memorandum of Conversation, 28 October 1962, *Cold War International History Project Bulletin*, 17/18, Fall 2012, p. 634, <http://www.wilsoncenter.org/publication/bulletin-no-17-18> (last accessed 25 July 2015); Bonn to State Department, 28 October 1962, *FRUS 1961–1963 X-XI-XII Microfiche Supplement, American Republics; Cuba 1961–1962; Cuban Missile Crisis and Aftermath*, document 440, <http://history.state.gov/historicaldocuments/frus 1961-63v10-12mSupp/d440> (last accessed 25 July 2015).

51. Mahan, *Kennedy, de Gaulle and Western Europe*, pp. 135–6.

52. Memorandum of Conversation between Adenauer and Acheson, Bonn, 23 October 1962, *Cold War International History Project Bulletin*, 17/18, Fall 2012, pp. 624–5, <http://www.wilson center.org/publication/bulletin-no-17-18> (last accessed 25 July 2015).

53. Leonardo Campus, 'Italian Political Reactions to the Cuban Missile Crisis', in Gioe et al. (eds), *An International History of the Cuban Missile Crisis*, p. 244.

54. Ibid.

55. Rome to State Department, 26 October 1961, *FRUS 1961–1963 X-XI-XII*, document 423, <http://history.state.gov/historicaldocu-ments/frus1961-63v10-12mSupp/d423> (last accessed 25 July 2015).

56. Leopoldo Nuti, 'Italy and the Cuban Missile Crisis', *Cold War International History Project Bulletin*, 17/18, Fall 2012, pp. 661–3, <http://www.wilsoncenter.org/publication/bulletin-no-17-18> (last accessed 25 July 2015).

57. Rimko van der Maar, 'The Netherlands, the Missile Crisis, and Cuban–Dutch Relations, 1962–1964: Documents from the Dutch Archives', *Cold War International History Project Bulletin*, 17/18, Fall 2012, pp. 674–5, <http://www.wilsoncenter.org/publication/bulletin-no-17-18> (last accessed 25 July 2015).

58. Merchant to Rusk and Ball, undated, *FRUS 1961–1963 Western Europe and Canada XIII* (1994), document 441, <https://history.state.gov/historicaldocuments/frus1961-63v13/d441> (last accessed 25 July 2015).

59. Asa McKercher, '"The most serious problem"? Canada–US relations and Cuba, 1962', *Cold War History*, 12: 1, February 2012, pp. 69–70.

60. Merchant to Rusk and Ball, undated, *FRUS 1961–1963 XIII*,

document 441, <https://history.state.gov/historicaldocuments/frus 1961-63v13/d441> (last accessed 25 July 2015).

61. See Asa McKercher, 'A "Half-Hearted Response"? Canada and the Cuban Missile Crisis, 1962', *International History Review*, 33: 2, June 2011, pp. 335–52.

62. The administration's handling of the Cuban Crisis, 12 November 1962, CAB 21/5581, TNA.

63. Risse-Kappen, *Cooperation among Democracies*, p. 176.

64. Cooper, *In the Shadows of History*, p. 197.

65. Meeting at the White House, 16 October 1962, *FRUS 1961–1963 XI*, document 18, <https://history.state.gov/historicaldocuments/ frus1961-63v11/d18> (last accessed 25 July 2015).

66. Costigliola, 'Kennedy, the European Allies, and the Failure to Consult', p. 114.

67. The administration's handling of the Cuban Crisis, 12 November 1962, CAB 21/5581, TNA.

68. Risse-Kappen, *Cooperation among Democracies*, p. 151.

69. Walt Rostow, 'Some Lessons from Cuba', 15 November 1962, in Laurence S. Chang and Peter Kornbluh (eds), with foreword by Robert S. McNamara, *The Cuban Missile Crisis, 1962: A National Security Archive Documents Reader* (New York: The New Press, 1992), p. 314.

70. Brazilian Embassy in Washington (Campos), 23 October 1962, *Cold War International History Project Bulletin*, 17/18, Fall 2012, pp. 237–8, <http://www.wilsoncenter.org/publication/bulletin-no-17-18> (last accessed 25 July 2015).

71. Ibid. p. 239.

72. Department of State to the Embassy in Brazil, 26 October, *FRUS 1961–1963 XI*, document 81, <https://history.state.gov/historical-documents/frus1961-63v11/d81> (last accessed 25 July 2015).

73. The account of Brazilian policies derives largely from: James G. Hershberg, 'Brazil and the Cuban Missile Crisis: Documents from the Foreign Ministry Archives in Brasília', *Cold War International History Project Bulletin*, 17/18, Fall 2012, pp. 229–31, <http://www.wilsoncenter.org/publication/bulletin-no-17-18> (last accessed 25 July 2015); William M. LeoGrande and Peter Kornbluh, *Back Channel to Cuba: The Hidden History of Negotiations between Washington and Havana* (Chapel Hill: University of North Carolina Press, 2014), pp. 53–9. See also James G. Hershberg, 'The United States, Brazil, and the Cuban Missile Crisis, 1962 (Part 1)', *Journal of Cold War Studies*, 6: 2, Spring 2004, pp. 3–20; James G.

Hershberg, 'The United States, Brazil, and the Cuban Missile Crisis, 1962 (Part 2)', *Journal of Cold War Studies*, 6: 3, Summer 2004, pp. 5–67.

74. Tanya Harmer, 'Mexican Diplomacy and the Cuban Missile Crisis: Documents from the Foreign Ministry Archives in Mexico City', *Cold War International History Project Bulletin*, 17/18, Fall 2012, pp. 191–2, <http://www.wilsoncenter.org/publication/bulletin-no-17-18> (last accessed 25 July 2015).

75. Dino Brugioni, *Eyeball to Eyeball: The Inside Story of the Cuban Missile Crisis*, edited by Robert F. McCort (New York: Random House, 1991), p. 363.

76. Stephen G. Rabe, *The Most Dangerous Area in the World: John F. Kennedy Confronts Communist Revolution in Latin America* (Chapel Hill: University of North Carolina Press, 1999), pp. 52, 121.

77. The Cuban Crisis in the United Nations, 12 November 1962, CAB 21/5581, TNA.

78. Robert B. Rakove, *Kennedy, Johnson and the Nonaligned World* (Cambridge and New York: Cambridge University Press, 2013), p. 91; William Attwood, *The Reds and the Blacks* (London: Hutchinson, 1967), pp. 109–11.

79. Svetozar Rajak, 'Yugoslavia and the Cuban Missile Crisis: Documents from the Foreign Ministry Archives in Belgrade', *Cold War International History Project Bulletin*, 17/18, Fall 2012, pp. 591–4, <http://www.wilsoncenter.org/publication/bulletin-no-17-18> (last accessed 25 July 2015).

80. Stephanie Popp, 'Switzerland and the Cuban Missile Crisis', *Cold War International History Project Bulletin*, 17/18, Fall 2012, pp. 729–31, <http://www.wilsoncenter.org/publication/bulletin-no-17-18> (last accessed 25 July 2015).

81. Csaba Békés and Melinda Kalmár, 'Hungary and the Cuban Missile Crisis', *Cold War International History Project Bulletin*, 17/18, Fall 2012, p. 411, <http://www.wilsoncenter.org/publication/bulletin-no-17-18> (last accessed 25 July 2015); Mark Kramer, 'The "Lessons" of the Cuban Missile Crisis for Warsaw Pact Nuclear Operations', *Cold War International History Project Bulletin*, 5, Spring 1995, p. 59, <http://www.wilsoncenter.org/publication/bulletin-no-5-spring-1995> (last accessed 25 July 2015).

82. Webcast of Robert S. Norris, 'The Cuban Missile Crisis: A Nuclear Order of Battle, October/November 1962', Cold War International History Project, 24 October 2012, <http://www.wilsoncenter.org/

event/cuban-missile-crisis-nuclear-order-battle> (last accessed 25 July 2015).

83. Telegram from East German Ambassador, Moscow, to East German Secretary of State Otto Winzer, 26 October 1962, *Cold War International History Project Bulletin*, 17/18, Fall 2012, pp. 618–19, <http://www.wilsoncenter.org/publication/bulletin-no-17-18> (last accessed 25 July 2015).

84. Memorandum of Conversation between Polish leader Władysław Gomułka and British journalist David Astor, 19 November 1962 (excerpt), *Cold War International History Project Bulletin*, 17/18, Fall 2012, p. 512, <http://www.wilsoncenter.org/publication/bulletin-no-17-18> (last accessed 25 July 2015). See also James G. Hershberg, 'Poland, Cuba, and the Missile Crisis, 1962: Ciphered Telegrams from the Foreign Ministry Archives in Warsaw', in ibid. pp. 462–3.

85. Békés and Kalmár, 'Hungary and the Cuban Missile Crisis', pp. 411–12.

86. Socialist Unity Party of Germany (SED) Central Committee Politburo meeting, 23 October 1962, *Cold War International History Project Bulletin*, 17/18, Fall 2012, p. 616, <http://www.wilsoncenter.org/publication/bulletin-no-17-18> (last accessed 25 July 2015). See also Mark Kramer's introduction: 'East German Reactions to the Cuban Missile Crisis', ibid. p. 615.

87. Annex number 1 for record 46 of 23 October 1962, *Cold War International History Project Bulletin*, 17/18, Fall 2012, p. 616, <http://www.wilsoncenter.org/publication/bulletin-no-17-18> (last accessed 25 July 2015).

88. Aleksandr Fursenko and Timothy Naftali, *Khrushchev's Cold War: The Inside Story of an American Adversary* (New York: Norton, 2006), p. 491.

89. For the origins of the conflict and US policy responses, see Kaysen to Kennedy, attaching a joint CIA/State Department analysis, 3 November 1962, *FRUS 1961–1963 XIX South Asia* (1996), document 190, <https://history.state.gov/historicaldocuments/frus1961-63v19/d190> (last accessed 25 July 2015); Neville Maxwell, 'Forty Years of Folly: What Caused the Sino-Indian Border War and Why the Dispute is Unresolved', *Critical Asian Studies*, 35: 1, March 2003, pp. 99–112.

90. Embassy in India to Department of State, 4 May 1963, *FRUS 1961–1963 XIX*, document 289, <https://history.state.gov/historicaldocuments/frus1961-63v19/d289> (last accessed 25 July 2015).

91. Paul M. McGarr, *The Cold War in Asia: Britain, the United States and the Indian Subcontinent, 1945–1965* (Cambridge and New York: Cambridge University Press, 2013), p. 155.
92. Kennedy to Ayub Khan, 28 October 1962, *FRUS 1961–1963 XIX*, document 186, <https://history.state.gov/historicaldocuments/frus 1961-63v19/d186> (last accessed 25 July 2015).
93. The Cuba Crisis: Its Course as Seen from Moscow, 7 November 1962, FO 371/162405, TNA; Lorenz M. Luthi, *The Sino-Soviet Split: Cold War in the Communist World* (Princeton, NJ: Princeton University Press, 2008), p. 228.

# 6  Nadir and Resolution, 26–28 October 1962

We are not struggling against imperialism in order to die.

*Nikita Khrushchev*

## The Scali–Feklisov Channel

There were different layers of communication during the missile crisis, from the direct Kennedy–Khrushchev dialogue to some informal and almost surreptitious channels. On 23 October, for example, Robert Kennedy had dispatched the journalist Charles Bartlett to relay to Georgi Bolshakov (a Soviet military intelligence officer and Embassy press attaché) the administration's anger over Khrushchev's duplicity over the missile deployment in Cuba, and to stress the desire to bring the crisis to a peaceful end.[1] During a lunchtime meeting at the Occidental Restaurant in Washington on 26 October, ABC correspondent John Scali met with Alexander Feklisov (alias Fomin), whose official role was the Soviet embassy's public affairs counsellor but who was also known to be the KGB station chief. Feklisov and Scali had met infrequently since the end of 1961.[2] According to Scali, Feklisov asked if the US government would be interested in a settlement in which the missile bases would be 'dismantled under United Nations supervision and Castro would pledge not to accept offensive weapons of any kind, in return for [a] US pledge not to invade Cuba'.[3] These terms would, of course, be the same as those that settled the confrontation, alongside the removal of Jupiter missiles from Turkey. Dean Rusk saw the offer as showing that Khrushchev was willing to compromise. That evening Scali told

Feklisov that the US government 'sees real possibilities in this', and that it could be worked out between Soviet and American representatives at the UN.[4]

The significance of Feklisov's contact with the administration is uncertain, as historians have noted. It is possible that the Kremlin or the KGB may have been using him as a disposable, deniable source to test the water on the question of a deal, or he may have been working independently.[5] The latter seems more likely. Although statements in his cable to Moscow of 26 October suggest that he was the passive recipient of an offer from the Kennedy administration, American records do not shed much light on this possibility. More significantly, no evidence has emerged of the Presidium, the Foreign Ministry or the KGB in Moscow authorising Feklisov to seek a diplomatic settlement. The handling of the report he prepared after seeing Scali provides further confirmation that Feklisov's efforts at the Occidental were unauthorised. The chain of command meant that to reach Khrushchev, or a member of the Presidium, he needed the agreement of Ambassador Dobrynin. After pondering Feklisov's report for a couple of hours, Dobrynin refused to provide a signature on the grounds that that the Foreign Ministry had 'not authorised the embassy to conduct this type of negotiation'. Dobrynin had his own channel to Robert Kennedy and disdained KGB initiatives.[6] Feklisov resorted to sending his cable to KGB head Vladimir Semichastny, where it languished for four hours before reaching Andrei Gromyko. If the Presidium had asked the KGB to probe Kennedy, then the cable would no doubt have been handled more expediently.[7] Feklisov was probably engaging in a self-initiated, unauthorised probe to explore Washington's conditions for ending the confrontation, born of his personal hopes that he could resolve the crisis.

## Communications from Khrushchev

On Friday 26 October at 6:00 p.m. the latest letter arrived from Khrushchev, expressing the idea of a trade to end the confrontation. The letter was powerful and impassioned, arguing that 'you ought not now to pull on the ends of the rope in which you have tied the knot of war, because the more the two of us pull, the tighter that knot will be tied'. It would become 'necessary to cut that knot. And what that would mean is not for me to explain to you, because you yourself understand perfectly of what terrible forces our countries dispose.'[8] Khrushchev offered to remove the missiles in return for a pledge not to invade Cuba:

> You would declare that the United States will not invade Cuba with its forces and will not support any sort of forces which might intend to carry out an invasion of Cuba. Then the necessity for the presence of our military specialists in Cuba would disappear.[9]

Arthur Schlesinger commented that the letter was 'not, as subsequently described, hysterical. Though it pulsated with a passion to avoid nuclear war and gave the impression of having been written in deep emotion, why not?'[10] Dean Rusk suggested that the communication 'seemed to offer real hope' for a solution involving the supervised withdrawal of the missiles in exchange for a commitment by United States not to invade.[11] But on Saturday 27 October, Khrushchev was in touch again, with his communication also broadcast over Radio Moscow. The Soviet leader now demanded a pledge to withdraw the Jupiter missiles from Turkey along with the conditions outlined in the letter of 26 October: 'Do you consider, then, that you have the right to demand security for your own country and the removal of the weapons you call offensive, but do not accord the same right to us? You have placed destructive missile weapons, which you call offensive, in Turkey, literally next to us.'[12]

Various theories have been put forward to explain why Khrushchev had toughened his stance by adding the Jupiter missiles to his demands. One theory was that the 27 October proposal was intended to pressure the United States into accepting the 26 October proposal, and that the removal of the Jupiters was not vital to Khrushchev. The second theory was that the 26 October proposal was from Khrushchev personally and the next one from hard-line colleagues who had overruled him. The third theory was that the Soviet leader was responding to apparent hints from the

US government – through, in particular, a 25 October newspaper column by Walter Lippman – that a deal involving the Jupiter missiles would be acceptable and that he decided to expand his terms accordingly. The fourth theory was that Khrushchev had simply changed his mind. Recent research has provided a different line of understanding, namely, that the tougher letter was drafted on 25 October, with Khrushchev then deciding to present the more moderate terms in the light of his belief that an attack on Cuba was imminent. After receiving contrary indications, he put forward the Jupiter demand.[13] Recent interpretations have emphasised the role of Lippman's column in particular in highlighting the potential of the Jupiters as an element in a possible deal.[14] Khrushchev had upped the ante in line with how his fears of invasion had receded, at least momentarily, but his 27 October message still involved substantial concessions. First, there was an admission that nuclear missiles were present in Cuba. Second, there was a proposal for their removal under the aegis of the UN, as Kennedy had demanded in his 22 October speech.[15] The letter of 27 October would not impede a settlement.

## Proposing Nuclear War

Although Khrushchev had not consulted him, Fidel Castro thought that adding the Jupiters to the proposed settlement showed 'great diplomatic skill'. He predicted that it would have 'a huge influence on global public opinion' as it placed 'the USA government in a difficult position, and exposes the illegality of its actions'.[16] There was at least a sense of reason and proportion in these ideas, but Castro's position even extended – horrifyingly – to proposing a preemptive nuclear strike on the United States in the event of an invasion of Cuba. In a letter dictated in Spanish to Ambassador Alekseev, who translated it into Russian,[17] Castro told Khrushchev on 26 October that if the United States invaded then the Soviet Union should undertake an 'act of clear legitimate defense, however harsh and terrible the solution would be'.[18] Khrushchev would not entertain the prospect of a nuclear attack even momentarily, telling Castro four days later that a first strike on the United States 'would have been the start of a thermonuclear world war . . . we are not struggling against imperialism in order to die'.[19] He told a member of the Czech Communist Party that upon hearing Castro's demand, 'We were completely aghast. Castro clearly has no idea what a thermonuclear war is. After all, if a war started, it would primarily be Cuba that would vanish from the face of the earth.' Only someone 'who has no idea what nuclear war means, or who has been so blinded, for instance, like Castro, by revolutionary passion, can talk like that'.[20]

Later, the Cuban leader maintained that his arguments had been lost in translation. He 'did not suggest being the first in delivering a blow against the adversary territory during the crisis', only if 'there were an aggression against Cuba and Soviet people would be perishing together with the Cubans'.[21] The letter was intended merely to bolster Khrushchev's resolve to act firmly in the event of an American attack, not to start a nuclear war.[22] There is reason, though, to think that Castro did propose a preemptive nuclear strike – motivated by a blend of nihilistic passion and, as Khrushchev suggested, sheer ignorance about nuclear war. The Cuban leader thought that the confrontation would go nuclear: he stated later that he was 'ready to use nuclear weapons . . . we took it for granted' that if there was an American invasion 'there would have been a nuclear war anyway'.[23] The letter gave Khrushchev an impression of Castro's utter irresponsibility and recklessness, and provided a justification for not consulting him about the settlement.

## Escalating Danger

While Kennedy and Khrushchev were anxious not to take any steps that might exacerbate the confrontation, they could not control everything. Evidence has emerged of American command and control difficulties, including a false nuclear war alarm at a military base in Wisconsin at around midnight on 25 October. The following day there was a test launch of an ICBM from a base in California, which might have been interpreted by Soviet base watchers as portending an attack on the Soviet Union. Another missile was tested on the same day from a location near Cape Canaveral in Florida, and was briefly misidentified by US radar personnel.[24] The continued testing of missiles confirmed the need for tight command and control measures, but such measures were absent. The danger was especially evident in connection with another incident. On the night of 26–7 October a U-2 aircraft piloted by Captain Chuck Maultsby from Eielson Air Force Base in Alaska was on a mission over the Arctic collecting air samples to monitor Soviet nuclear tests. However, Maultsby was navigating by the stars, became confused by the Northern Lights and drifted into Soviet territory.[25] When Soviet MiGs scrambled to intercept the U-2, F-102 interceptors took off to the rescue. These planes were on alert status so had nuclear-tipped air-to-air missiles.[26] US authorities guided Maultsby back to his base safely. Kennedy complained of the misadventure that 'There is always some son of a bitch who doesn't get the word.'[27] However, no-one had thought to cancel the U-2 missions. Khrushchev was greatly shaken and distressed by the incident. He complained on 28 October that 'an intruding American plane could be easily taken for a nuclear bomber, which might push us to a fateful step'.[28] This was a fair appraisal of the danger.[29]

Far less is known about Soviet command and control, although there is some evidence available. Only Moscow could make the decision to fire nuclear weapons at the American mainland. Lieutenant General Nikolai Beloborodov, head of the Soviet nuclear arsenal in Cuba, reflected that

> The presence of nuclear weapons in the operation was intended to exclude the possibility of military action, therefore the military objectives were to ensure nuclear safety, [ensure] strictly restricted access to nuclear warheads to eliminate the possibility of unsanctioned actions, and to ensure operational, engineering and technical camouflage.[30]

To reassure Kennedy, Khrushchev told the US businessman William E. Knox on 24 October that

> all sophisticated equipment were [sic] under direct, 100% Soviet control. They would never be fired except in defense of Cuba and then

only on [his] personal instructions . . . as Commander-in-Chief of the Armed Forces.[31]

It does appear from other evidence that Soviet commanders in Cuba could not launch the weapons without codes sent from the Centre.[32] So far as the use of the tactical nuclear weapons is concerned, on 8 September Defence Minister Rodion Malinovsky and Chief of the General Staff Matvei Zakharov gave local commanders discretion concerning the use of the weapons, using them 'as instruments of local warfare . . . to achieve the complete destruction of the invaders on the Cuban territory and to defend the Republic of Cuba'.[33] Similarly, in the Presidium session on 22–3 October (see Chapter 3) Khrushchev stated that 'the tactical atomic weaponry' could be used against an American assault, but Anastas Mikoyan moderated the willingness to use the tactical nuclear weapons. It was decided that the missiles would only be used with conventional warheads.[34] Yet Khrushchev told William Knox on 24 October that the Guantánamo naval base would 'disappear the first day' after a US invasion of Cuba.[35] On the night of 26–7 October Soviet forces in Cuba moved the FKR cruise missiles armed with nuclear warheads to a launch position 15 miles from Guantánamo naval base. Once at the launch position local commanders would prepare to 'destroy the target' upon receipt of orders from the general staff in Moscow.[36] Whether the move was entirely a local initiative or stemmed from an order from Moscow is not known, but it does suggest a willingness at some level to use tactical nuclear weapons.

Although the Soviet Union held back from challenging the blockade, there was still scope for confrontation at sea. A carrier and five destroyers began pursuing one of the four Soviet submarines – vessel B-59 – that had been deployed for the defence of Cuba. Efforts were made to signal the vessel to surface. Finally, on 29 October B-59 submerged and managed to escape the American vessels. Soviet submarines B-130 and B-36 had to surface on 28 and 31 October respectively. The former, its engines defective, had to be towed back to Murmansk by a Soviet tugboat, while the other, after charging its accumulators, took evasive measures and disappeared. The last of the four Soviet submarines, B-4, remained undiscovered. Soviet submarines largely ignored the sonar and depth charge signals from the US ships, surfacing only because they needed to replenish air and batteries, or because of mechanical problems. The signalling explosions were interpreted not as harmless signals but as acts of aggression, with the submarine captains fearing that war had started while they were submerged and cut off from communications with Moscow. The commanders were permitted to use the nuclear-tipped torpedoes only on instruction from Moscow, but there were no permissive action links (PALs) to prevent the unauthorised use of the weapons. If the captains had used the torpedoes, they would probably have faced a US response with nuclear depth charges. Even an initial nuclear exchange of limited scope could have precipitated an escalation, especially aggravated by the ignorance of the US command about the presence of nuclear torpedoes on the submarines.[37] The issue of the Soviet submarines was an especially perilous – and less-publicised – aspect of the Cuban Missile Crisis.

There were further sources of danger. In a meeting with his general staff on 26 October, Fidel Castro drafted a communiqué for the Secretary-General of the UN: 'any warplane that invades Cuban airspace does so at the risk of meeting our defensive fire'.[38] American intelligence flights, especially those at low altitude, caused him great concern. He told Khrushchev that earlier overflights of Cuba were carried out 'without a determined military purpose or without a real danger stemming', but now he feared 'a surprise attack on certain military installations'.[39] As he had ordered at the beginning of the crisis, Cuban anti-aircraft troops fired at low-level US reconnaissance aircraft with anti-aircraft guns and small arms.[40] The Soviets made a contribution of greater impact. The deputy commander of Soviet forces on Cuba, General Leonid Garbuz, and the commander of Soviet anti-aircraft forces, General Stepan Grechko, decided on their own initiative to use a surface-to-air missile. Garbuz recollected that he was concerned that 'all our missile starting positions had been uncovered, and we must not allow the secret information to fall into the hands of the Pentagon'.[41]

The result was the destruction of a U-2 piloted by Major Rudolf Anderson, one of the two pilots who had first photographed the missile sites. The stricken aircraft landed on Cuba. A CIA informer indicated that Anderson's body was taken 'for embalming and is presently in the custody of the Russian forces deployed in the vicinity of the city'. The pilot was described as 'being about 27 and was wearing a flight jacket with an emblem denoting service in Korea. Photographs of his three children were in among his effects as well as a set of dog tags'.[42] Initially Khrushchev blamed Cuban forces for destroying the U-2. He admonished Castro that the 'Pentagon militarists' would use the episode as an excuse to wage an attack and prevent a peaceful resolution of the crisis.[43] As Khrushchev had feared, the U-2 incident could have led to a dangerous escalation, because Kennedy and his advisers had decided that in the event of the destruction of an American aircraft over Cuba they would order an attack on the surface-to-air missile site responsible. They believed that the Kremlin had authorised the attack to escalate the crisis.[44] Maxwell Taylor, for one, pushed hard for a strike on the site in question. Yet the wisdom of this course of action was debatable. Dean Acheson has suggested that attacking the SAM site

> would have achieved the worst of both courses. It would have pre-
> cipitated violence without accomplishing more than the destruction of
> the surface-to-air missiles, which had shot down the U-2. It would not
> have touched the source of the trouble, the nuclear missiles.[45]

As well as stimulating a desire to destroy the SAM site responsible, the destruction of the U-2 fostered a general sense that military action was inevitable and imminent. Robert McNamara 'felt that we must now look to the major airstrike to be followed by an invasion of Cuba . . . we would need to call up the reserves now'.[46] Dean Rusk stated that although the United States had combined 'reasonable diplomatic offers and military pressure in even balance', the development of the missile bases continued and more missiles were thought to be becoming operational. Although the Soviets had yet to challenge the quarantine, some vessels were sailing towards the exclusion area. All this meant, according to Rusk, that the US government might soon have decided 'in its own interest and that of its fellow nations in the Western

Hemisphere to take . . . military action . . . to remove this growing threat to the Hemisphere'.[47]

## Trading the Missiles in Turkey

The idea of sacrificing the Turkish missiles – put forward in Khrushchev's communication of 27 October – presented difficulties for the administration, as the views of officials make clear. Even though early accounts of the missile crisis tended to present him as being all too ready to strike a deal with the Soviets, Adlai Stevenson maintained that the

> effect of Khrushchev's Turkey proposal was that, as a result of his own clandestine intrusion into the Western Hemisphere, he gets a guarantee of Cuban integrity and the removal of the Turkey base, whereas all we get is removal of an intrusion which he should not have made anyway.[48]

Dean Rusk, although a consistent advocate of a diplomatic settlement, maintained that 'the question of US missiles in Turkey . . . must be kept separate from Soviet missiles in Cuba. The Turkish missile problem should be dealt with in the context of NATO vs. Warsaw Pact.'[49] Robert F. Kennedy, McGeorge Bundy, US Ambassador to NATO Thomas Finletter, Paul Nitze, NATO commander Lauris Norstad and John McCone expressed similar concerns, fearing reactions in Turkey, NATO and in the 'free world' generally if the US government surrendered the Jupiters.[50] At the same time, it was appreciated that eliminating the weapons would not represent a significant military sacrifice. Robert McNamara argued that they were 'a pile of junk' – they were deployed above ground in unprotected sites, took fifteen minutes to prepare for firing and were difficult to move to new launch positions.[51] Vice-President Lyndon B. Johnson was uncharacteristically quiet in the ExComm meetings, but had wavered between military action and a negotiated solution. Now, taking his cue from McNamara, he suggested that as the military equivalent of a Model T Ford the Jupiter missiles were 'not worth a damn'.[52] Despite political

reservations about the merits of a Jupiter deal, Dean Rusk recognised that technologically the weapons had their limitations:
'we joked about which way those missiles would go if they were
fired'.[53] McGeorge Bundy believed that the missiles could be dispensed with as part of a trade so long as it was suitably finessed.[54]

There are firm indications that from the beginning of the crisis
President Kennedy was willing to withdraw the Jupiters. As noted
in Chapter 3, he had ordered a study in August about how to
bring about the removal of the missiles, given their limited military value, without upsetting the Turks.[55] He raised the idea of a
Cuba–Turkey exchange in ExComm on 18 October, and on 21
October he mentioned to David Ormsby-Gore the prospect of a
deal that might involve 'the reciprocal closing of bases'.[56] Six days
later the President noted

> that over a year ago we wanted to get the Jupiter missiles out of
> Turkey because they had become obsolete and of little military
> value. If the missiles in Cuba added 50% to Soviet nuclear capabil-
> ity, then to trade these missiles for those in Turkey would be of
> great military value. But we are now in the position of risking war
> in Cuba and in Berlin over missiles in Turkey which are of little
> military value.[57]

Recognising that the Jupiters could be dispensed with but concerned about how it might appear to Ankara and other allies, the
President 'considered a draft message . . . to persuade the Turks
to suggest to us that we withdraw our missiles'.[58] Evidence suggests that the idea was not so far-fetched. The Turkish Foreign
Minister, Salim Sarper, had told Dean Rusk in April 1961 that
although it would have been politically embarrassing for the
missiles to be withdrawn at that stage given that the Turkish
Parliament had only just agreed the appropriations, it would
be much easier once Polaris nuclear submarines were available
in the Mediterranean.[59] The submarines were now coming into
service, and they would more than compensate militarily for
the Jupiters. Although in a telegram of 24 October Ambassador
Raymond Hare in Ankara maintained that withdrawing the missiles would pose 'acute difficulties' for the US relationship with

Turkey, he also stated – in classic diplomatic fashion – that 'if proper means could be found, [a] good case could be made for removal of missiles from Turkey as [a] counter for [the] removal of Soviet missiles from Cuba', subject to finding 'proper means'.[60] On 25 October a senior figure in the Turkish Foreign Ministry told a Canadian official that the government could probably accept the decommissioning of the Jupiters. It is likely that some Kennedy administration officials had obtained this information by 27 October, before Robert F. Kennedy left for the secret meeting with Dobrynin that would resolve the crisis.[61] However, intimations that sacrificing the Jupiters might be acceptable in Turkey were tentative and few, and did not mean that it was time to celebrate a Jupiter deal.

## The Agreement

There remained the question of how to respond to Khrushchev's communications of 26 and 27 October, with the latter presenting tougher terms than the former. There was no time for delay. President Kennedy noted that 'the Russians were making various proposals so fast, one after the other, that they were creating a kind of shield behind which work on the missile sites in Cuba continued'.[62] Robert F. Kennedy's memoir *Thirteen Days* records that

> I suggested, and was supported by Ted Sorensen and others, that we ignore the latest Khrushchev letter and respond to his earlier letter's proposal ... that the Soviet missiles would be removed from Cuba under UN inspection and verification if, on its side the United States would agree with the rest of the Western hemisphere not to invade Cuba.[63]

The tactic of ignoring the most recent letter in favour of the previous one has been referred to as the 'Trollope Ploy', a reference to a plot device used by the nineteenth-century novelist Anthony Trollope. The idea that RFK made this suggestion, and that it was implemented fully, has appeared even in some very recent accounts of the missile crisis. It has been seen as an example of diplomatic ingenuity that led to a breakthrough.[64] In reality the ploy was largely a later fabrication by Kennedy officials, with its plausibility resting on the false perception that Khrushchev's suggested deal involving American missiles in Turkey was completely rejected. In fact, it was difficult for President Kennedy to ignore the Saturday message precisely because it was public. Therefore his eventual message to Khrushchev – despatched at 20:05 on 27 October – did not ignore the proposal about Turkey. Instead, it was stated – with studied imprecision – that resolving the confrontation over Cuba would 'enable us to work toward a more general arrangement regarding "other armaments"'. The phrase 'other armaments' left scope for a deal relating to Turkey, without raising the point explicitly.[65]

It was still necessary to address the issue of the missiles in Turkey with greater exactitude than merely referring to 'other armaments'. Early in the evening of 27 October, soon after an ExComm meeting, President Kennedy met secretly with McGeorge Bundy, Dean Rusk, Robert McNamara, Robert F. Kennedy, George Ball, Theodore Sorensen, Roswell Gilpatric and Llewellyn Thompson. The President knew that outright rejection of an agreement involving the Jupiters was too much of a luxury, and he had confidence that whatever their reservations the eight advisers he had assembled could be trusted to maintain their discretion. Although ExComm had guided and helped Kennedy to refine his thinking,[66] he now felt it right to abandon corporate decision-making, in what amounted to a decisive expression of presidential leadership. The meeting of the select few – a mini ExComm, or perhaps ExExComm – lasted just twenty minutes.[67] Robert F. Kennedy then saw Ambassador Dobrynin in the Justice Department at about 19:45, outlining the deal that Kennedy and the inner circle had agreed to put forward. In his own account, RFK told the ambassador forcefully that

> those missile bases have to go and they have to go right away. We had to have a commitment by at least tomorrow that those bases were removed. This was not an ultimatum, but just a statement of fact. He should understand that if they did not remove those bases then we

would remove them. His country might take retaliatory action but he should understand that if they did not remove those bases then we should remove them.[68]

Dobrynin's record of the meeting covers the same ground substantively, although the Attorney General is presented as being more fearful than assertive. RFK described the pressure on the President from the military to attack the bases, with the result that:

> A real war will begin, in which millions of Americans and Russians will die. We wish to avoid that any way we can, I'm sure that the government of the USSR has the same wish. However, taking time to find a way out [of the situation] is very risky ... The situation might get out of control, with irreversible consequences.[69]

Kennedy junior then outlined the terms: the removal of the missiles from Cuba, in return for a public agreement to 'keep the peace in the Caribbean' and a secret concession that the missiles would be removed from Turkey within five months.[70]

Historians remain divided about whether Robert F. Kennedy had delivered an *offer* or an *ultimatum* to the Soviets. His version of the meeting presents him as behaving forcefully, something that is less evident in Dobrynin's account. Nikita Khrushchev even maintained in his memoirs that the President and his brother were pleading for Soviet help:

> ... the president didn't know how to get out of this situation, that the military men were putting heavy pressure on him, insisting that he take military action against Cuba, and that a very difficult situation had arisen for the president. '... the president is asking that you help solve the problem.' ... In a state of great nervous tension, he kept repeatedly appealing for prudence and good sense, asking us to help the president get out of this situation.[71]

Ultimatum or not, the secret use of the RFK–Dobrynin channel on 27 October had a successful precedent with the Berlin tank stand-off in which RFK had communicated with Khrushchev through the Soviet Embassy almost exactly a year earlier. The Checkpoint

Charlie deal and the Jupiter element of the missile crisis agreement both aimed to defuse dangerous confrontations, involved mutual force agreements, used informal channels, and relied on oral rather than written pledges. Both were secret, too. Although one cannot be sure that the earlier agreement served as a template for the 1962 accord, the Kennedy brothers could scarcely have missed the parallel.[72]

ExComm had on 27 October discussed demanding an end to Cuban revolutionary activities in Latin America in return for the removal of the missiles. Robert F. Kennedy presented the terms in his talk with Dobrynin, but did not raise the issue again.[73] As US Secretary of State for Inter-American Affairs Edwin M. Martin noted later, there were problems with the demand, given the difficulty of defining 'subversion', the difficulty of tracing the sponsors of subversive activities, and because an agreement about the issue would limit the opportunity for the US government to subvert the Castro regime.[74] So, by the evening of 27 October the administration had presented an offer combining Khrushchev's proposals: the Soviet Union would withdraw the missiles from Cuba under UN supervision, while the United States would 'give assurances against an invasion of Cuba'.[75] Privately, the administration had pledged that the Jupiter missiles would be removed from Turkey, but as noted in Chapter 5, the administration's reaching out to Andrew Cordier and U Thant on 27 October indicated a willingness to accept a *public* deal concerning the Jupiters. Clearly the Cordier initiative went no further, as the crisis was ended by direct communication between US and Soviet officials, but the fact that President Kennedy pursued this fall-back position meant that he would have gone even further to resolve the crisis.

## Khrushchev's Retreat

Around midday on 28 October (it was early in the morning in Washington), after hearing from Dobrynin, Khrushchev met with the entire Presidium at a dacha in the Moscow suburbs. He strove to persuade his colleagues to reach a decision:

There was a time, when we advanced, like in October 1917, but in March 1918 we had to retreat, having signed the Brest–Litovsk agreement with the Germans. Our interests dictated this decision – we had to save Soviet power. Now we found ourselves face to face with the danger of war and of nuclear catastrophe, with the possible result of destroying the human race. In order to save the world, we must retreat. I called you together to consult and debate whether you are in agreement with this kind of decision.[76]

After presenting his case for a tactical withdrawal, Khrushchev was able to proceed with the deal with the administration that Robert F. Kennedy had outlined to Dobrynin. Why then did he yield? A Western diplomat suggested that Khrushchev had realised that

an American air strike against the bases in Cuba, with the consequent loss of Soviet lives, or an American landing, with the overthrowing of Castro's regime, would have left them with no other choice between a nuclear war – which they are not willing to face – and accepting a defeat much worse than the withdrawal of the missiles.[77]

This is a fair verdict, one indicating that Khrushchev faced a choice between a conflagration and an honourable retreat in the face of superior American power. Especially critical in bringing Khrushchev to the firm realisation that retaining nuclear missiles was not worth the risk of war were intimations from Castro that the United States was poised to invade. In his letter to Khrushchev on 26 October advocating a preemptive nuclear attack, Castro had stated that 'from reports in our possession I consider that the aggression is almost imminent within the next 24 or 72 hours'.[78] Khrushchev explained later to Castro that 'because you had made the categorical statement that you had incontrovertible proof that an invasion was about to happen, we were forced to take immediate steps [agreeing to withdraw the missiles] so as to rule out the possibility of invasion'.[79] While urging nuclear war, Castro's letter had, paradoxically, played a part in ending the confrontation peacefully. As with his decision to accept the nuclear missiles, Castro was in this sense an actor and not merely acted upon or overlooked during the crisis of October 1962. Furthermore, Castro's intimations that the Americans were poised to invade fitted in alarmingly with Robert F. Kennedy's offer to Dobrynin, in which he stated that a response was required 'by at least tomorrow'.[80]

By this stage, too, Khrushchev had seen clearly how matters might escalate, with destruction of the American spy plane and the accidental US penetration of Soviet airspace. Having neglected to consider that the US administration might discover the missiles early and failing to anticipate the response, Khrushchev seems now to have felt that enough was enough. In fact, research indicates that he was ready to settle even without the Jupiter deal, despite his 27 October letter to the US government. This means that the Kennedy administration conceded more than was required. When Khrushchev learned that the US government had made the additional concession he was delighted, because it implied a parallel between Soviet missiles in Cuba and American missiles in Turkey. As such, it justified, in his mind at least, his longstanding complaints about the Jupiters and his initiative to station missiles in Cuba.[81] Yet withdrawing the missiles was still a setback for Soviet policy, as there is, as was noted in Chapter 2, no indication that Khrushchev had planned to install the missiles simply to withdraw them as part of an arrangement with the United States. He had intended that the weapons were to remain in Cuba indefinitely. For David Ormsby-Gore – who did not know about the Jupiter deal – Khrushchev had 'decided on virtually a complete climb-down over the Cuban missile bases'.[82] Early on Sunday morning Washington time, Radio Moscow broadcast Khrushchev's acceptance of the US offer, which also reached the President through normal diplomatic channels.[83] The missile crisis – or at least its most dangerous phase – had ended.

What would Kennedy have done had Khrushchev not conceded? Although Robert F. Kennedy had suggested to Dobrynin that military attacks against Cuba could not be held off for long, it is likely that the President would have stalled before stepping over that threshold. Kennedy stated on 27 October that 'tomorrow we could consider increasing the pressure by adding POL (petrol, oil, lubricants) to the list of prohibited goods'.[84] Robert McNamara stated emphatically that Kennedy 'did not want to invade Cuba. He didn't want to invade it on Sunday 28th, he didn't want to invade it on Monday 29th, he didn't want to invade it ever, if he could avoid it.' Instead of invading, the President would have authorised a tightening of the quarantine, by adding 'POL to the embargo list . . . this would have strangled Cuba economically'.[85] Kennedy's desire to postpone military action meant that Khrushchev was too fearful of an invasion, and conceded too readily; had he held out, he could have gained a public commitment to withdraw the Jupiter missiles from Turkey. This means that, paradoxically, both leaders had conceded too much, but both had recognised that matters could escalate to the extent that no-one would prevail in any meaningful sense. In any event, the settlement of 28 October left much to be ironed out. President Kennedy, for one, was 'under no illusion that that the problem of Soviet missiles in Cuba is solved'.[86]

## Notes

1. Aleksandr Fursenko and Timothy Naftali, '*One Hell of a Gamble*': *Khrushchev, Castro, and Kennedy, 1958–64* (New York: Norton, 1997), pp. 249–51.
2. Aleksandr Fursenko and Timothy Naftali, 'Soviet Intelligence and the Cuban Missile Crisis', in James G. Blight and David A. Welch (eds), *Intelligence and the Cuban Missile Crisis* (Abingdon: Frank Cass, 1998), p. 80.
3. Scali to Hilsman, undated, *Foreign Relations of the United States (FRUS) 1961–1963 XI Cuban Missile Crisis and Aftermath* (Washington, DC: USGPO, 1996), document 80, <https://history.state.gov/historicaldocuments/frus1961-63v11/d80> (last accessed 25 July 2015).
4. Editorial note, 26 October, *Foreign Relations of the United States (FRUS) 1961–1963 XI Cuban Missile Crisis and Aftermath* (Washington, DC: USGPO, 1996), document 84, <https://history.state.gov/historicaldocuments/frus1961-63v11/d84> (last accessed 25 July 2015) [document 7, Appendix 4 in this volume].
5. Raymond L. Garthoff, *Reflections on the Cuban Missile Crisis* (Washington, DC: Brookings, 1987), p. 50.

6. Michael M. Dobbs, *One Minute to Midnight: Kennedy, Khrushchev and Castro on the Brink of Nuclear War* (New York: Knopf, 2008), p. 168.
7. Fursenko and Naftali, 'Soviet Intelligence', pp. 80–3.
8. Khrushchev to Kennedy, 26 October 1962, *FRUS 1961–1963 XI*, document 84, <https://history.state.gov/historicaldocuments/frus 1961-63v11/d84> (last accessed 25 July 2015).
9. Ibid.
10. Arthur M. Schlesinger, Jr., *A Thousand Days: John F. Kennedy in the White House* (New York: Houghton Mifflin, 1965), p. 707.
11. State Department to Mission to NATO, 28 October 1962, *FRUS 1961–1963 XI*, document 100, <https://history.state.gov/historical documents/frus1961-63v11/d100> (last accessed 25 July 2015).
12. Khrushchev to Kennedy, 27 October 1962, *FRUS 1961–1963 XI*, document 91, <https://history.state.gov/historicaldocuments/ frus1961-63v11/d91> (last accessed 25 July 2015) [document 8, Appendix 4 in this volume].
13. Don Munton, 'Hits and Myths: The *Essence*, the Puzzles and the Missile Crisis', *International Relations*, 26: 3, September 2012, p. 316; Aleksandr Fursenko and Timothy Naftali, *Khrushchev's Cold War: The Inside Story of an American Adversary* (New York: Norton, 2006), p. 488.
14. David R. Gibson, *Talk at the Brink: Deliberation and Decision during the Cuban Missile Crisis* (Princeton, NJ: Princeton University Press, 2012), p. 139; Dobbs, *One Minute to Midnight*, pp. 198–9. See also Fursenko and Naftali, *Khrushchev's Cold War*, p. 489. For the Lippman article see *Washington Post*, 25 October 1962, p. A-25, column 1.
15. Current Intelligence Memorandum, 27 October, *FRUS 1961–1963 XI*, document 98, <https://history.state.gov/historicaldocuments/ frus1961-63v11/d98> (last accessed 25 July 2015).
16. Alekseev to USSR Foreign Ministry, 27 October 1962, *Cold War International History Project Bulletin*, 8/9, Winter 1996–7, p. 291, <http://www.wilsoncenter.org/publication/bulletin-no-89-win ter-1996> (last accessed 25 July 2015).
17. Laurence Chang and Peter Kornbluh (eds), with foreword by Robert S. McNamara, *The Cuban Missile Crisis, 1962: A National Security Archive Documents Reader* (New York: The New Press, 1992), p. 375.
18. Castro to Khrushchev, 26 October 1962, National Security Archive, George Washington University, <http://www2.gwu.edu/~nsarchiv/

nsa/cuba_mis_cri/docs.htm> (last accessed 25 July 2015) [document 10, Appendix 4 in this volume].

19. Khrushchev to Castro, 30 October 1962, National Security Archive, George Washington University, <http://www2.gwu.edu/~nsarchiv/nsa/cuba_mis_cri/docs.htm> (last accessed 25 July 2015).

20. Conversation between the delegations of the CPCz and the CPSU, 30 October 1962, *Cold War International History Project Bulletin*, 17/18, Fall 2012, p. 401, <http://www.wilsoncenter.org/publication/bulletin-no-17-18> (last accessed 25 July 2015) [document 12, Appendix 4 in this volume].

21. Alekseev to USSR Foreign Ministry, 31 October 1962, *Cold War International History Project Bulletin*, 8/9, Winter 1996–7, p. 306, <http://www.wilsoncenter.org/publication/bulletin-no-89-winter-1996> (last accessed 25 July 2015).

22. James G. Blight, Bruce J. Allyn and David A. Welch (eds), with foreword by Jorge I. Dominguez, *Cuba on the Brink: Castro, the Missile Crisis, and the Soviet Collapse* (New York: Pantheon, 1993), pp. 109–10.

23. Ibid. p. 252.

24. Scott D. Sagan, *The Limits of Safety* (Princeton, NJ: Princeton University Press, 1993), pp. 78–80, 98–100, 122–30. See also Campbell Craig, 'Testing Organisation Man: The Cuban Missile Crisis and *The Limits of Safety*', *International Relations*, 26: 3, September 2012, pp. 291–303.

25. Kennedy to Khrushchev, 28 October 1962, *FRUS 1961–1963 XI*, document 104, <https://history.state.gov/historicaldocuments/frus1961-63v11/d104> (last accessed 25 July 2015).

26. Len Scott, 'Eyeball to Eyeball: Blinking and Winking, Spyplanes and Secrets', *International Relations*, 26: 3, September 2012, p. 355.

27. Anatoli I. Gribkov and William Y. Smith, *Operation Anadyr: US and Soviet Generals Recount the Cuban Missile Crisis* (Chicago: Edition Q, 1994), p. 144.

28. Khrushchev to Kennedy, 28 October 1962, *FRUS 1961–1963 XI*, document 102, <https://history.state.gov/historicaldocuments/frus1961-63v11/d102> (last accessed 25 July 2015).

29. Sagan, *Limits of Safety*, pp. 138–42. The U-2 incident came to light publicly in Roger Hilsman, *To Move a Nation: The Politics of Foreign Policy in the Administration of John F. Kennedy* (Garden City, NY: Doubleday, 1967), p. 221.

30. 'The War was Averted (Soviet nuclear weapons in Cuba, 1962): Report of Lieutenant General Nikolai Beloborodov, head of

the Soviet nuclear arsenal in Cuba', undated, National Security Archive, George Washington University, <http://www2.gwu.edu/ ~nsarchiv/NSAEBB/NSAEBB449/docs/Doc%202%20Nikolai% 20Beloborodov%20Memoir.pdf> (last accessed 15 January 2015).

31. Hilsman to Rusk, 26 October 1963, recording Khrushchev's conversation with Knox on 24 October, *FRUS 1961–1963 X-XI-XII Microfiche Supplement, American Republics; Cuba 1961–1962; Cuban Missile Crisis and Aftermath*, document 419, <http://history. state.gov/historicaldocuments/frus1961-63v10-12mSupp/d419> (last accessed 25 July 2015).

32. Svetlana Savranskaya and Thomas Blanton (eds), with Anna Melyakova, 'Last Nuclear Weapons Left Cuba in December 1962: Soviet Military Documents Provide Detailed Account of Cuban Missile Crisis Deployment and Withdrawal', National Security Archive, George Washington University, <http://www2.gwu.edu/~ nsarchiv/NSAEBB/NSAEBB449/> (last accessed 25 July 2015).

33. Malinovsky and Zakharov to Pliyev, 8 September 1962, National Security Archive, George Washington University, <http://www2. gwu.edu/~nsarchiv/NSAEBB/NSAEBB449/docs/Doc%207% 201962.09.08%20Memorandum%20from%20Malinovsky% 20and%20Zakharov%20Informing%20of%20Decision%20to% 20Provide%20IL-28s%20and%20Luna%20Missiles%20&% 20Pre-delegation%20of%20Launch%20Authority%20to% 20Pliyev.pdf> (last accessed 25 July 2015).

34. Protocol No. 60 Session of 22–23 October 1962, *Cold War International History Project Bulletin*, 17/18, Fall 2012, p. 306, <http://www.wilsoncenter.org/publication/bulletin-no-17-18> (last accessed 25 July 2015); Fursenko and Naftali, *Khrushchev's Cold War*, pp. 471–2.

35. Hilsman to Rusk, 26 October 1963, recording Khrushchev's conversation with Knox on 24 October, *FRUS 1961–1963 X-XI-XII*, document 419, <http://history.state.gov/historicaldocuments/frus 1961-63v10-12mSupp/d419> (last accessed 25 July 2015). For an assessment of Guantánamo's military vulnerability, see Blaine L. Pardoe, *The Fires of October: The Planned Invasion of Cuba during the Missile Crisis of 1962* (Stroud: Fonthill, 2012), pp. 62–4.

36. Michael Dobbs, 'The Soviet Plan to Destroy Guantánamo Naval Base', National Security Archive, George Washington University, <http://www2.gwu.edu/~nsarchiv/nsa/cuba_mis_cri/dobbs/gitmo. htm> (last accessed 25 July 2015); Dobbs, *One Minute to Midnight*, pp. 178–81.

37. Svetlana V. Savranskaya, 'New Sources on the Role of Soviet Submarines in the Cuban Missile Crisis', *Journal of Strategic Studies*, 28: 2, April 2005, pp. 233–59. See also Peter Huchthausen, *October Fury* (New York: John Wiley, 2002), and William Burr and Thomas Blanton, 'The Submarines of October: US and Soviet Naval Encounters during the Cuban Missile Crisis', National Security Archive, George Washington University, National Security Archive, George Washington University, <http://www2.gwu.edu/~nsarchiv/NSAEBB/NSAEBB75/> (last accessed 25 July 2015).
38. Dobbs, *One Minute to Midnight*, p. 159.
39. Castro to Khrushchev, 28 October 1962, National Security Archive, George Washington University, <http://www2.gwu.edu/~nsarchiv/nsa/cuba_mis_cri/docs.htm> (last accessed 25 July 2015).
40. Chang and Kornbluh (eds), *The Cuban Missile Crisis*, p. 377. For the 'Blue Moon' low-level reconnaissance programme see William Ecker and Kenneth Jack, with introduction by Michael Dobbs, *Blue Moon over Cuba: Aerial Reconnaissance during the Cuban Missile Crisis* (Oxford: Osprey, 2012).
41. Michael Dobbs, 'The Shootdown of Major Anderson', National Security Archive, George Washington University, <http://www2.gwu.edu/~nsarchiv/nsa/cuba_mis_cri/dobbs/anderson.htm> (last accessed 25 July 2015). See also Blight et al., *Cuba on the Brink*, pp. 105, 113–14, 120.
42. Michael Dobbs, 'The Shootdown of Major Anderson', National Security Archive, George Washington University, <http://www2.gwu.edu/~nsarchiv/nsa/cuba_mis_cri/dobbs/anderson.htm> (last accessed 25 July 2015).
43. Gribkov and Smith, *Operation Anadyr*, p. 67.
44. ExComm meeting, 23 October 1962, *FRUS 1961–1963 XI*, document 47, <https://history.state.gov/historicaldocuments/frus1961-63v11/d47> (last accessed 25 July 2015); Chang and Kornbluh (eds), *The Cuban Missile Crisis*, p. 376.
45. Dean Acheson, 'Homage to Plain Dumb Luck', in Robert A. Divine (ed.), *The Cuban Missile Crisis* (New York: Wiener, 1988), p. 195.
46. ExComm meeting, 27 October 1962, *FRUS 1961–1963 XI*, document 94, <https://history.state.gov/historicaldocuments/frus1961-63v11/d94> (last accessed 25 July 2015).
47. State Department to Mission to NATO, 28 October 1962, *FRUS 1961–1963 XI*, document 100, <https://history.state.gov/historical-documents/frus1961-63v11/d100> (last accessed 25 July 2015).
48. Mission to United Nations to State Department, 27 October, *FRUS*

*1961–1963 XI*, document 92, <https://history.state.gov/historical documents/frus1961-63v11/d92> (last accessed 25 July 2015).

49. Dino Brugioni, *Eyeball to Eyeball: The Inside Story of the Cuban Missile Crisis*, edited by Robert F. McCort (New York: Random House, 1991), p. 468; ExComm meeting, 27 October, *FRUS 1961–1963 XI*, document 90, <https://history.state.gov/historicaldocu ments/frus1961-63v11/d90> (last accessed 25 July 2015).

50. Embassy in France to Department of State, 25 October 1962, *FRUS 1961–1963 XI* (all the following references are from this volume), document 75, <https://history.state.gov/historicaldocu ments/frus1961-63v11/d75>; ExComm meeting, 26 October 1962, document 79, <https://history.state.gov/historicaldocuments/frus 1961-63v11/d79>; ExComm meeting, 27 October, document 90, <https://history.state.gov/historicaldocuments/frus1961-63v11/ d90>; ExComm meeting, 27 October 1962, document 94, <https:// history.state.gov/historicaldocuments/frus1961-63v11/d94> (docu ments last accessed 25 July 2015).

51. Philip Nash, *The Other Missiles of October: Eisenhower, Kennedy, and the Jupiters, 1957–1963* (Chapel Hill: University of North Carolina Press, 1997), p. 3.

52. Ernest R. May and Philip D. Zelikow (eds), *The Kennedy Tapes: Inside the White House During the Cuban Missile Crisis* (Cambridge, MA: Belknap, 1997), p. 591. On Johnson's role see Sheldon M. Stern, *The Cuban Missile Crisis in American Memory: Myths versus Reality* (Stanford, CA: Stanford University Press, 2012), pp. 148–53.

53. James Blight and David A. Welch, *On the Brink: Americans and Soviets Reexamine the Cuban Missile Crisis* (New York: Noonday, 1989), p. 172.

54. ExComm meeting, 27 October, *FRUS 1961–1963 XI*, document 90, <https://history.state.gov/historicaldocuments/frus1961-63v11/ d90> (last accessed 25 July 2015).

55. NSAM 181, 23 August1962, *FRUS 1961–1963 X*, document 386, <https://history.state.gov/historicaldocuments/frus1961-63v10/ d386> (last accessed 25 July 2015).

56. Don Munton, 'The Fourth Question: Why Did John F. Kennedy Offer up the Jupiters in Turkey?', in David Gioe, Len Scott and Christopher Andrew (eds), *An International History of the Cuban Missile Crisis: A 50-Year Retrospective* (London: Routledge, 2014), pp. 265–6; Ankara to State Department, 26 October 1962, *FRUS 1961–1962 X-XI-XII*, document 425, <http://history.state.

gov/historicaldocuments/frus1961-63v10-12mSupp/d425> (last accessed 25 July 2015).

57. ExComm meeting, 27 October, *FRUS 1961–1963 XI*, document 90, <https://history.state.gov/historicaldocuments/frus1961-63v11/d90> (last accessed 25 July 2015).

58. ExComm meeting, 27 October, *FRUS 1961–1963 XI*, document 94, <https://history.state.gov/historicaldocuments/frus1961-63v11/d94> (last accessed 25 July 2015).

59. Blight and Welch, *On the Brink*, p. 173.

60. Munton, 'The Fourth Question', p. 271.

61. Munton, 'Hits and Myths', pp. 314–15.

62. ExComm meeting, 27 October, *FRUS 1961–1963 XI*, document 90, <https://history.state.gov/historicaldocuments/frus1961-63v11/d90> (last accessed 25 July 2015).

63. Robert F. Kennedy, *Thirteen Days: A Memoir of the Cuban Missile Crisis* (New York: Norton, 1969), pp. 101–2.

64. See Stern, *The Cuban Missile Crisis*, pp. 134–47, for a demolition of the fable.

65. Kennedy to Khrushchev, 27 October 1962, *FRUS 1961–1963 XI*, document 95, <https://history.state.gov/historicaldocuments/frus1961-63v11/d95> (last accessed 25 July 2015) [document 11, Appendix 4 in this volume].

66. Gibson, *Talk at the Brink*, p. 6.

67. Stern, *The Cuban Missile Crisis*, p. 146.

68. Robert F. Kennedy to Rusk, 30 October 1962, *FRUS 1961–1963 XI*, document 96, <https://history.state.gov/historicaldocuments/frus1961-63v11/d96> (last accessed 25 July 2015).

69. Dobrynin report of meeting with Robert Kennedy, 27 October 1962, National Security Archive, George Washington University, <http://www2.gwu.edu/~nsarchiv/nsa/cuba_mis_cri/docs.htm> (last accessed 25 July 2015).

70. Ibid.

71. Nikita Khrushchev, *Memoirs of Nikita Khrushchev. Volume 3: Statesman, 1953–1964*, edited by Sergei Khrushchev and translated by George Shriver (University Park, PA: Pennsylvania State University Press, 2007), p. 339.

72. Munton, 'Hits and Myths', p. 315; Munton, 'The Fourth Question', pp. 270–1; Raymond L. Garthoff, 'The US–Soviet Tank Confrontation at Checkpoint Charlie', in Stephen J. Cimbala (ed.), *Mysteries of the Cold War* (Aldershot: Ashgate, 1999), pp. 73–87.

73. May and Zelikow, *The Kennedy Tapes*, p. 608, note 6.

74. Martin to Rusk, 30 October 1962, *FRUS 1961–1963 X-XI-XII*, document 463, <http://history.state.gov/historicaldocuments/frus 1961-63v10-12mSupp/d463> (last accessed 25 July 2015).

75. Kennedy to Khrushchev, 27 October 1962, *FRUS 1961–1963 XI*, document 95, <https://history.state.gov/historicaldocuments/frus 1961-63v11/d95> (last accessed 25 July 2015).

76. Fursenko and Naftali, *'One Hell of a Gamble'*, p. 284.

77. Italian Foreign Ministry on the causes and consequences of the Cuban Missile Crisis, December 1962, *Cold War International History Project Bulletin*, 17/18, Fall 2012, p. 671, <http://www. wilsoncenter.org/publication/bulletin-no-17-18> (last accessed 25 July 2015).

78. Castro to Khrushchev, 26 October 1962, National Security Archive, George Washington University, <http://www2.gwu.edu/~nsarchiv/ nsa/cuba_mis_cri/docs.htm> (last accessed 25 July 2015).

79. Khrushchev, *Memoirs*, p. 345.

80. Blight et al., *Cuba on the Brink*, p. 113.

81. Fursenko and Naftali, *Khrushchev's Cold War*, p. 490.

82. Washington to Foreign Office, 28 October 1962, FO 371/162382, TNA.

83. Khrushchev to Kennedy, 28 October 1962, *FRUS 1961–1963 XI*, document 102, <https://history.state.gov/historicaldocuments/frus 1961-63v11/d102> (last accessed 25 July 2015).

84. ExComm meeting, 27 October 1962, *FRUS 1961–1963 XI*, document 97, <https://history.state.gov/historicaldocuments/frus1961- 63v11/d97> (last accessed 25 July 2015).

85. Blight and Welch, *On the Brink*, p. 25.

86. ExComm meeting, 28 October 1962, *FRUS 1961–1963 XI*, document 103, <https://history.state.gov/historicaldocuments/frus1961- 63v11/d103> (last accessed 25 July 2015).

# 7 Aftermath I, November–December 1962

Castro: We have to be vigilant.
Mikoyan: Of course, they are bastards.
Castro: More than that . . . they are sons of bitches.

## The American 'Victory'

The Soviet agreement to withdraw the missiles from Cuba appeared to boost President Kennedy's status domestically, with his approval ratings rising from 63 per cent to 74 per cent.[1] He avoided gloating publicly about Khrushchev's climb-down, but privately he revelled in the outcome, telling friends that 'I cut his balls off.' There was some deft management of the press to ensure, in the approach to the congressional elections, that the American people were clear about who had triumphed in the confrontation. Kennedy showed journalist Walter Lippman some flattering excerpts from the crisis communications with Khrushchev, while presidential background conversations with prominent correspondents combined with skilful leaks from White House staff helped to ensure that there was no doubt about who had 'won'.[2] The Democratic position after the November congressional elections remained much the same as before. There was a net gain of four seats in the Senate and a net loss of two seats in the House. Polls indicated that domestic issues were of much greater significance in the elections than were foreign affairs.[3] Kennedy's handling of the missile crisis appeared not to have influenced the voting significantly.

The US victory won fulsome praise in the 'Free World', in part due to ignorance about the Jupiter deal. BBC Washington correspondent Christopher Serpell explained that the Kennedy administration had rejected Khrushchev's demand about the Jupiters on the grounds that no-one should 'do business with a stick-up man'.[4] Harold Macmillan, who thought that conceding the Jupiters would have done 'great injury to NATO' and wondered why Khrushchev 'suddenly abandon[ed] the Cuba–Turkey deal', considered that President Kennedy had 'conducted his affair with great skill, energy, resourcefulness and courage'.[5] The Belgian Foreign Minister Paul Henri-Spaak felt that American policy had been 'a spectacular success . . . acting with firmness but restraint had greatly strengthened the free world'.[6] There was public criticism in Canada of the Ottawa government's foot-dragging about supporting the United States during the missile crisis.[7] In Latin America, President Morales of Honduras commented that the 'efforts leading to the withdrawal of Soviet missiles . . . were magnificent'.[8] Further afield, President Khan of Pakistan 'expressed great admiration for the manner in which President Kennedy handled the Cuban question'.[9] Egypt's President Gamal Nasser credited the administration as having acted 'in a manner devoid of aggressive incitement'.[10] US diplomat William Attwood stated that in the non-aligned African state of Guinea, 'the people . . . seemed pleased with the outcome' of the missile crisis.[11]

Success in the missile crisis benefited US standing in the UN. Secretary of State Dean Rusk noted in December 1962 how the 'normal Soviet stridency' in the Security Council had since the crisis been 'muted', and the Soviet delegation left 'in disarray'. The revelation of nuclear missiles in Cuba had done 'pervasive' damage to Soviet credibility, and had boosted confidence in 'the words and actions of the United States'. The Latin American caucus in the General Assembly had 'coalesced into a more effective political grouping after the demonstration of unanimity in the OAS vote of 23 October on Cuba'. Overall, 'free world' members of the Assembly were much more willing to 'stand up and be counted', with more references to Soviet colonialism and imperialism, and 'fewer communist rebuttals and less neutralist yawning, than in recent years'. Rusk concluded that 'the drama of that Security Council confrontation' between Adlai Stevenson and

Zorin on 25 October had been especially important in enhancing American prestige in the UN.[12]

Yet Kennedy faced criticism from Congress in the wake of the missile crisis, including from Senators Barry Goldwater (Republican, Arizona), Kenneth Keating (Republican, New York), and Strom Thurmond (Democrat, South Carolina), along with Representative Donald Bruce (Republican, Indiana). Goldwater charged that the pledge 'locked Castro and communism into Latin America' and had 'thrown away the key to their removal',[13] while Senator Keating maintained that there were up to 40,000 Soviet troops in Cuba; that the Soviets had sent eighty medium-range missiles, of which forty remained; and that radioactive material was continuing to arrive in Cuba.[14] Keating's estimate of Soviet troops was remarkably accurate, but it was only guesswork. His other charges were without foundation.

The Joint Chiefs of Staff, who had advocated the use of force consistently, doubted the sincerity of the Soviet retreat. Led by Curtis LeMay, they wrote to Kennedy on 28 October recommending executing the planned air strikes and invasion the following day unless there was 'irrefutable evidence' of immediate Soviet action to remove the missile sites. They warned that the Soviets might be using a delaying tactic while the missile build-up progressed. Naturally, Kennedy could not concede to such demands. Soon after the confrontation he met with the Chiefs as a formality, to thank them for their counsel. The President was shocked when Admiral George W. Anderson called the settlement 'the greatest defeat in our history', and urged an invasion forthwith. According to McNamara, Kennedy was left 'absolutely shocked' and 'stuttering in reply'.[15] Anderson was, however, in a minority even among military leaders, and even Dean Acheson, a strong advocate of attacking Cuba, congratulated Kennedy after the resolution of the crisis.[16]

Although Latin American states now appeared more willing to back the US in the UN, the OAS demanded more leadership from Washington in order to prevent regional communist 'subversion'. Many Latin American governments opposed President Kennedy's promise not to invade Cuba and were aggrieved at the continued presence of thousands of Soviet troops on the island. The

Argentine representative to the OAS wanted to know what proposals for action the US government had in mind; the Venezuelan representative asked what was being done to address the fact that Cuba remained 'ferociously' armed; and the El Salvadorian representative wanted to know if there had been any secret Soviet–US deals that the Latin Americans should know about. The crisis had amplified already powerful fears about Cuba and strengthened those demanding continued anti-Castro measures.[17]

The Cuban opposition to Castro rued the outcome of the crisis. Anti-Castro activist José Miró Cardona, head of the Cuban Revolutionary Council, resigned from his position, arguing in a bitter resignation letter that the US government had been 'the victim of a masterful Russian game'. Khrushchev had

> achieved his immediate objectives: a) to retain his barracks for attack and subversion in the Caribbean; b) strengthen the military capabilities of Fidel Castro to destroy the first attempt at insurrection; and c) consolidate the Communist Regime in [Latin] America, [through] the first step for peaceful coexistence, the immobilization of the United States and with the United States the rest of the Continent, [which is] as disappointed as the Cuban patriots and as bewildered as them with respect to the future.[18]

The views of Cardona and other Kennedy critics showed that the perception of victory or defeat in the missile crisis was very much in the eye of the beholder.

## A 'cold shower' for the 'infinitely electrified masses'

Khrushchev presented his policies as a success, telling representatives of the Czech Communist Party, for example, that

> We agreed to dismantle the missiles . . . because their presence in Cuba is essentially of little military importance to us. The missiles were meant to protect Cuba from attack; they helped us to wrench out of the imperialists the statement that they would not attack Cuba, and they thus served their main purpose.[19]

In his memoirs he put the case still more strongly: 'The Caribbean crisis was a bright ornament that brilliantly set off our foreign policy, and in relations with the west: in that I include my policy as a member of the collective that decided policy and achieved a brilliant success in behalf of Cuba without firing a single shot.'[20] However, the Soviet military was far less impressed. Khrushchev explained later that when he had 'asked the military advisors if they could assure me that holding fast would not result in the death of five hundred million human beings, they looked at me as though I was out of my mind, or, what was worse, a traitor'.[21] The Cuban government was even less satisfied than was the Soviet military. As seen in the previous chapter, Khrushchev had not bothered to consult Havana about settling the confrontation. In his view, Cuban involvement would only have complicated matters, not least because feelings were running high. Had

> we ... allowed ourselves to be carried away by certain passionate sectors of the population [in Cuba] and refused to come to a reasonable agreement with the US government, then a war could have broken out, in the course of which millions of people would have died and the survivors would have pinned the blame on the leaders for not having taken all the necessary measures to prevent that war of annihilation.[22]

Arguments such as these did not go far. President Osvaldo Dorticós complained that the Cuban and Latin American peoples would see the decision to dismantle the missiles as a defeat for the Soviet government. Even though Kennedy had pledged that the United States would not sponsor an invasion, Cuba could not 'weaken its vigilance'. Removing the missiles was – in a striking metaphor – a 'cold shower' for the 'infinitely electrified masses'.[23] Castro was especially aggrieved. He complained effusively to Anastas Mikoyan, who had been sent to Cuba to mend fences. The main concern was that instead of simply striking a deal bilaterally with the Americans, the Soviets could have said that they were willing to remove the missiles only after 'discussion with the Cuban government ... instead of immediately giving orders to evacuate the strategic weapons'. Moscow should then have demanded the liquidation of the American naval base at

Guantánamo. Cuba had been left in an invidious position: the Americans 'seek to determine what weapons we can possess', and continued to violate Cuban airspace with photo reconnaissance missions. Furthermore, Castro suspected (correctly, in relation to the Jupiter missiles) that elements of the negotiations with the United States had been concealed from him.[24]

The Cuban leader's disgruntlement with the Soviet Union was clear during Mikoyan's three-week visit when he disappeared without word for two days.[25] Castro was the most irate member of the Cuban leadership. Once, after an especially sharp comment from Castro, Mikoyan noticed that Che Guevara, Dorticós and Carlos Rodriguez wanted 'to erase what happened; they don't want us to take Fidel's outburst seriously'.[26] Mikoyan, whose steadfast dedication to duty was clear when he remained in Cuba despite the death of his wife at home, emphasised that the absolute priority was to prevent an attack against Cuba: 'We did everything so that Cuba would not be destroyed.'[27] Castro at least respected Mikoyan's emollient efforts, telling him that 'We are thankful for your desire to explain all these developments to us and for all your efforts in this regard.'[28] The underlying Cuban–Soviet solidarity remained in place. Castro and Mikoyan were united in their hostility to the Americans, shown by their condemnation of them as 'sons of bitches' and 'bastards'.[29] At dinner Mikoyan once told his hosts that they 'would not find better friends than us', to which they – including Castro – 'nodded their assent' and 'warmly smiled'.[30] Years later Castro would describe Mikoyan warmly,[31] but his ill-feeling about Soviet conduct – especially that of Khrushchev – during the missile crisis never disappeared entirely.

## No Inspection Regime

Ending the quarantine was a sensitive matter for President Kennedy given that he had, as Adlai Stevenson noted, 'announced to the nation' on 22 October that this action was 'dependent on UN observation and upon receipt of adequate assurance against reintroduction of weapons'.[32] There was a belief, given the deception shrouding the emplacement of the missiles, that the Soviets simply could not be trusted. Dean Rusk feared a situation in which 'bargains are fudged, secrecy prevents verification, agreements are reinterpreted, and by one means or another the Soviet Government seeks to sustain and advance the very policy which it has apparently undertaken to give up'.[33] The CIA noted that increased knowledge of American intelligence methods and sources in relation to Cuba enabled the Soviet military to adopt improved measures of concealment and deception.[34] Pressure from Congress and from Cuban émigrés made verifying the removal of the missiles all the more sensitive. On 1 November, Press Secretary Pierre Salinger explained to Grigory K. Zhukov of the Soviet mission to the UN that 'We must . . . no matter what, publish evidence that the missiles have been dismantled and taken away.' Any form of verification would do: 'Let it be representatives of the UN or of the Red Cross, let it be observation photos taken from the air, it is all the same to us.'[35]

The Soviets dismantled and withdrew the missiles promptly, as confirmed by US photographic intelligence and shipping analysis. Stevenson told Mikoyan on 1 November that he was 'very favorably impressed' by the progress.[36] However, the fact that the Soviets cooperated so readily should not have been a surprise. The CIA noted that there were no military grounds why the Soviet Union would secrete nuclear missiles in Cuba after the confrontation, as doing so would raise the possibility of

a second Cuban crisis . . . which would be unlikely to leave the Castro regime intact. A renewed crisis would find the Soviets in an even more disadvantageous position than before to protect their interests and avoid humiliation.[37]

There remained the formality of establishing a suitable inspection regime in Cuba. In his public address of 22 October and his communications to Khrushchev, Kennedy had not referred specifically to ground-level inspections, but clearly this was what he had in mind. The Soviets, fearing the loss of their technological secrets, had refused to permit on-site inspection until the missiles were removed,[38] but were willing to help establish such facilities to reassure the US government that the weapons had been removed permanently. However, Castro was unyielding from the outset, displaying great sensitivity on the issue. On 28 October he put forward 'five points' that in his view provided grounds for a settlement. He demanded an end to the American economic blockade of Cuba; US-sponsored subversion and sabotage on the island; attacks by Cuban émigrés; the American violation of Cuban airspace and territorial waters; and the US presence at Guantánamo.[39] Castro used the 'five points' to assert his country's pride and independence. The British Ambassador in Havana noted that they were 'nailed to the mast to the accompaniment of a massive propaganda exercise with meetings, resolutions, pamphlets, posters and full orchestration by press and radio'.[40]

Moscow backed Castro's demands, but without enthusiasm, as they had not been part of the deal with the Americans. The Cuban leader had no means of enforcing his terms. Doubting the sincerity of the non-invasion pledge, he complained later that 'we have still not achieved acceptance of the five points. We made concessions. It did not give us anything other than the lifting of the blockade.'[41] Castro's national pride and a desire to uphold Cuban sovereignty led him to oppose ground inspections in Cuba. When U Thant visited Havana to facilitate the settlement of the missile crisis, Castro told him that 'Cuba is a sovereign and independent state and it would not allow any external organization – be it the UN or anything else – to interfere'.[42] Castro did express a willingness to permit UN inspection in Cuba in return for reciprocal inspections of Florida and Puerto Rico, to prevent the Americans from preparing an invasion, but this was more about demonstrating the legal equality of both sides than making a viable proposition.[43] He also suggested inspections 'carried out outside of the territorial waters of Cuba',[44] but what went on there was by definition beyond Cuban jurisdiction.

The Soviets encouraged Castro to accept an inspection regime, as this had been agreed with the Americans. Mikoyan tried to persuade him that 'it was not a question of any permanent or general inspection . . . representatives of neutral countries would carry out verification only once'. This did not involve 'hurting Cuba's sovereignty'.[45] There was no progress on this issue, and President

Kennedy and his colleagues soon wearied of the prospect of continued talks about inspection. A concession was in order. On 12 November, Robert F. Kennedy told Ambassador Dobrynin that 'we are not insisting on [ground inspections] as an unalterable and fundamental condition' of lifting the quarantine.[46] The Americans never succeeded in obtaining a system of ground level verification, so there was a continued reliance on aerial surveillance. Castro complained bitterly about reconnaissance aircraft 'flying at 100 meters over our military bases and units. This is bad for the morale of our people and makes them resentful ... Now our enemy knows everything.'[47] There was the danger of the Cubans shooting down another American plane, creating what Dobrynin described as a 'new and highly undesirable chain reaction of events in the Cuban affair'.[48] Fortunately, no further aircraft were shot down, and aerial surveillance satisfied American wishes.

As American intelligence was never certain about the presence of the nuclear warheads for the missiles, it was difficult to press the Soviets to cooperate in verifying their withdrawal. If the US government expressed ignorance about the presence or otherwise of the warheads, then Moscow might decide to leave them in Cuba, knowing that they would not be detected. However, the warheads, like the missiles, were soon withdrawn. US intelligence received indications that they were removed from Cuba on the vessel *Aleksandrovsk* on 5 November.[49] On 20 November, Khrushchev assured Kennedy that 'All the nuclear weapons have been taken away from Cuba.'[50] The US government took this on trust, but the statement was premature, as tactical nuclear weapons remained. The Soviets maintained a discreet silence about their presence – which, as noted in Chapter 3, the Americans had strongly suspected but never confirmed – on the fair assumption that openness would only complicate an already fraught situation. Castro was keen that his country's armed forces should have the use of the weapons. Soviet Defence Minister Rodion Malinovsky favoured leaving them behind for Cuban use, but this was a minority view among Soviet officials. Mikoyan made it clear that Cuba could not readily be controlled, and as such it was decided to remove the weapons. The position, as the

Presidium confirmed, was that 'these weapons belong to us, and are to be kept in our hands only; we have never transferred them to anyone, and we do not intend to transfer them to anyone'.[51] Cuba retained some Luna and FKR missiles armed with conventional warheads. The presence of tactical nuclear weapons in Cuba was not confirmed publicly until after the Cold War.

## Soviet Bombers

The US and Soviet governments argued about IL-28 bombers in Cuba. At the beginning of November, President Kennedy insisted to Khrushchev that 'our exchange of letters' during the confrontation 'covers the IL-28s, since your undertaking was to remove the weapons we described as offensive'. Kennedy categorised the bombers as offensive because they could 'carry nuclear weapons for long distances' and so could strike the United States and 'other Western Hemispheric countries'.[52] Here he was following the counsel of the Chiefs of Staff, who argued that the continued presence of the bombers in Cuba posed a long-term threat to American security.[53] There was public pressure, too. Robert F. Kennedy told Anatoly Dobrynin that 'for domestic policy considerations, it was very important to receive . . . firm agreement to the removal of the IL-28 planes'.[54] However, Khrushchev noted correctly that there was no mention of bombers in the communications during the crisis, and so contended that the agreement related only to missiles and rejected the view that the bombers were 'offensive'.[55] Andrei Gromyko told US officials that when first produced fifteen years earlier, the IL-28 was 'the first Soviet plane with a turboreactive engine'. Since then, technology had moved on, and now these bombers were fit for little more than use as 'training machines . . . and to some extent as defensive means – for the coastal defense of a territory with the [support] of anti-aircraft machines'. The use of the IL-28s for offensive purposes would mean 'sending people to certain death'.[56]

The Cuban stance strengthened Soviet resistance to removing the bombers. Suspecting that the Soviets were about to yield, Castro complained to Mikoyan that 'The same thing happened with the missiles – first you made a commitment, then you started to remove them.' He would accept the removal of the aircraft only in return for US concessions such as ending violations of Cuban airspace as well as the naval blockade.[57] Patrick Dean noted that Vasili Kuznetsov, who was discussing the details of the settlement in the UN with John McCloy and Adlai Stevenson, was 'typically Soviet' in refusing to yield about the bombers. Dean thought that Kuznetsov intended to 'spread the discussions over a long period in order to wear down Stevenson's resistance'. Even with McCloy's robust backing, Stevenson would 'need great stamina if he is to succeed in getting satisfaction from the Russians on the Iluyshins 28'.[58]

President Kennedy did not wish to push the issue too far. While he could tighten the blockade to renew the pressure on the Soviets, he was reluctant, as he put it, to create 'a crisis fever again'. The bombers were 'just one more hazard of life. They don't have the impact that the missiles had.'[59] Khrushchev ended up conceding the aircraft anyway, acknowledging that Kennedy had 'made certain statements and therefore the question of removal of IL-28 planes assumed a certain significance and probably created certain difficulties'.[60] He may also have recognised that the obsolescence of the aircraft was just as much a reason for removing them from Cuba as for leaving them there. Khrushchev agreed on 20 November that the IL-28s would be removed within a month,[61] and so that day Kennedy announced the lifting of the quarantine and the end of the US military alert.[62] The Warsaw Pact countries ended their alerts, too, so ending the military confrontation. On 7 December, the Soviet Union's Minister of the Merchant Fleet, V. Bakaev, told his superiors that the IL-28 planes had been removed from Cuba. The *Okhotsk*, which carried twelve of the forty-two aircraft, had spotted American aircraft 'flying back and forth over the ship, taking photos'. The boxes containing the IL-28s were opened for the US aircraft to photograph. The other two Soviet vessels carrying IL-28s were subject to similar monitoring and surveillance procedures.[63] Castro had to accept that the Soviets had surrendered the bombers, just as he had to accept that the agreement ending the confrontation was made without his consent.

## The Evasive Non-invasion Pledge

The Soviet government doubted that the US administration would make a firm commitment never to invade Cuba. On 30 October, Vasili Kuznetsov and Valerian Zorin at the UN told Moscow that 'Kennedy's statement about the USA government's readiness to "give assurances that there will be no invasion of Cuba" will be interpreted by the Americans in the narrow sense, as saying that the USA and the Latin American countries will not attack Cuba with their own armed forces.'[64] This would leave an opening for another Washington-supported invasion by Cuban émigrés. Mikoyan told Stevenson and McCloy that the Soviet government wanted a formal agreement enforced and approved by the Security Council. There would be 'guarantees of non-intervention . . . on the part of other countries of the Western Hemisphere, recognition of the sovereignty and territorial integrity of the Cuban Republic, observation of its territorial inviolability, [and] non-interference into its domestic affairs'.[65]

However, the administration sought to preserve its room for manoeuvre on the issue. At the 20 November press conference in which he announced the end of the quarantine, President Kennedy stated that 'peace in the Caribbean' depended not only on the removal of 'all offensive weapons' but on 'adequate verification and safeguards, and if Cuba is not used for the export of aggressive Communist purposes'.[66] The following day Kennedy told ExComm that he wanted 'to preserve our right to invade Cuba in the event of civil war, if there were guerrilla activities in other Latin American countries or if offensive weapons were reintroduced into Cuba'. He was also concerned that that a comprehensive no-invasion guarantee would strengthen Castro.[67] In December 1962 the President rebuffed a request from Khrushchev for a formal non-invasion pledge because there was no ground inspection regime, and because Cuba was engaged in subversive activities in the Western Hemisphere.[68] Khrushchev was in no position to force the White House to comply, not least because the rapid dismantlement of the missile sites in Cuba had weakened his position.[69] Furthermore, by treating the pledge as anything less than decisive he would have had nothing to show publicly for having placed missiles in Cuba, so negating his claim of victory.[70] The ambiguity of the non-invasion pledge indicates that the Cuban Missile Crisis was not settled in a watertight fashion; the US commitment might be described as a 'non-non-invasion' or an 'evasive non-invasion' pledge.

## The Jupiter Deceit

Dobrynin noted that on 28 October Robert F. Kennedy urged strict secrecy about the assurance to remove the Jupiter missiles from Turkey: 'Especially so that the correspondents don't find out. At our place for the time being even [Press officer Pierre] Salinger does not know about it'.[71] The administration strove to keep the matter very tightly held, and proved capable of out-right deceit. Robert McNamara told the Joint Chiefs of Staff on 29 October that there was 'no Cuba–Turkey deal', but soon the 'problem of removing Jupiters from Turkey ... on [the] grounds of obsolescence' would require attention.[72] Dean Rusk told Ambassador David Ormsby-Gore that 'there had been no "cozy deals" in connection with the change in the Soviet position'.[73] Perhaps suspecting a trade involving the Jupiters and wanting to put US officials in an awkward position, the Turkish ambassador in Washington lavished deep gratitude for President Kennedy's apparent refusal to surrender the missiles.[74] Within the US government, a suspicious Lauris Norstad, NATO's Supreme Allied Commander in Europe, established himself as the chief guardian of the Jupiters. He wrote to the President on 29 October that raising the question of the missiles in Turkey once more 'would seem to deny the soundness of your position on the Soviet missiles in Cuba', and would weaken NATO. Kennedy avoided the issue altogether in his reply, but word that the missiles were to be removed spread throughout the administration. William Tyler of the State Department's Office of European Affairs told Rusk that although the Jupiters were becoming obsolescent they remained a 'significant military asset for NATO'. The US government should not associate itself with any withdrawal effort 'in the near future'. Other officials expressed similar concerns, but

President Kennedy succeeded in neutralising any representations that reached his desk.[75]

In a cynical episode, Kennedy used Adlai Stevenson in a way that suggested that a Jupiter trade had been rejected. In an account of the missile crisis by journalists Charles Bartlett and Stewart Alsop in December 1962, an official source charged that 'Adlai wanted a Munich', in the form of trading 'the Turkish, Italian, and British missile bases for the Cuban bases'. The article also presented Stevenson as the lone peace-at-any price advocate in ExComm and indicated that the President listened 'politely' before rejecting his 'Munich' proposal. It has been suggested Kennedy himself was the official who had spoken to the journalists.[76] In a memo to the President, Arthur Schlesinger condemned the Bartlett and Alsop story as being 'wrong in almost every particular'. The 'Adlai wanted a Munich' assertion was entirely false because Stevenson had stated, in the words of Schlesinger, that 'Turkey and Italy should not be included in the initial offer. Their inclusion would divert attention from the Cuban threat to the general problem of foreign bases.' Stevenson did not even mention the British bases.[77] But the President showed no inclination to repair Stevenson's reputation. Although during the crisis Kennedy was inclined to a 'dovish' position, he wanted his public image to remain one of toughness and resolution.[78]

The White House rejected Soviet requests for written confirmation that the Jupiter missiles would be withdrawn. Robert F. Kennedy told Ambassador Dobrynin on 30 October that he was 'not prepared to formulate such an understanding in … even the most confidential letters … who knows where and when such letters can surface or be somehow published'.[79] The Soviets did not push the matter, nor did they breach the confidentiality that had been agreed. Khrushchev remained discreet because that is what had been decided with Kennedy, and perhaps more significantly because he did not want to antagonise Castro any further. Khrushchev and his top associates even hid the deal from some senior Soviet diplomats. On 29 October the Soviet chargé d'affaires at the Washington embassy asked a US official when the American government was going to respond to Khrushchev's offer of 27 October, in which the issue of the missiles in Turkey had been raised publicly. Even though he had been sent to New York to discuss the settlement with Adlai Stevenson and John McCloy in the UN, Vasili Kuznetsov appeared not to know about the Jupiter settlement. President Kennedy told his negotiators – who were as ignorant as Kuznetsov – to keep the Jupiter question out of the talks.[80]

In December, Dean Rusk and Robert McNamara presented a cover story explaining the pending withdrawal of the missiles from Turkey in terms of the need to 'modernize Alliance missile capability [by] removing a highly vulnerable system which, during the Cuban crisis, provided [an] inviting target to the Soviets should [the] US have been forced to undertake military action against Cuba'.[81] The Jupiters were indeed 'highly vulnerable', but the timing of the withdrawal stemmed mainly from the secret assurance to Khrushchev. In February 1963 there were efforts to mislead Congress, as was evident in this exchange:

> Senator Stennis: [Withdrawal of the Jupiters] has nothing to do with the Cuban situation or anything like that.
> McNamara: Absolutely not ... the Soviet government did raise the issue [but the] President absolutely refused even to discuss it. He wouldn't even reply other than that he would not discuss the issue at all.[82]

Rusk also made a contribution of equal dishonesty:

> Senator Hickenlooper: The removal of the missiles from Turkey ... was in no way, shape or form, directly or indirectly, connected with the settlement, the discussions or the manipulation of the Cuban situation?
> Rusk: That is correct, sir.[83]

It was decided to use the withdrawal of Jupiters from Italy as a further method of misdirection. This approach went back to the missile crisis, during which President Kennedy conceded that at a suitable time, and upon Soviet request, the US should agree to remove missiles from both Italy and Turkey. On 27 October 1962, Robert McNamara suggested withdrawing the missiles from Italy in order to encourage the Turks to agree to a similar move. Although Khrushchev had only sought the removal of the missiles from Turkey, the missiles in Italy ended up part of the measures that resolved the missile crisis. In December McNamara proposed to Defence Minister Giulio Andreotti that the missiles would be dismantled by 1 April and replaced by nuclear-armed Polaris submarines in the Mediterranean. In January McNamara formally proposed the removal of the weapons from Italy. The US government denied any connection between the dual withdrawals, although early in 1963 the foreign policy consultant Henry Kissinger reported of his visit to Rome that practically all of the leading Italian politicians he met 'suspected that withdrawal might be the result of US agreement with Russians'. The Italian President, Antonio Segni, even complained 'that [the] US decision on withdrawal had apparently been made during Cuban crisis and Italy [had] only [been] informed three months later'.[84]

Although, as was seen in Chapter 6, there had been subtle intimations that a trade-off might be acceptable to Ankara, Turkish assent to the removal of the Jupiter missiles came at a price. At the beginning of February Foreign Minister Feridun Erkin told Ambassador Raymond Hare that the government of Turkey had accepted the replacement of Jupiters by Polaris but sought compensatory military aid. Soon Major General Robert Wood, representing McNamara, worked out the details with Ankara. The package included F104G aircraft and other conventional weapons. The removal of the Jupiters was subject to the formal approval of the North Atlantic Council (NAC), but this did not pose an obstacle. The NAC met in February but concluded that as the removal of the Jupiters was already under way the issue of approval was redundant.[85] The US government had presented a fait accompli, so the withdrawals proceeded without NATO discussion. The removal of the missiles began on 1 April. Robert McNamara told the President three weeks later, 'The last Jupiter missile in Turkey came down yesterday,' and that the final warhead would be out in a few days.[86]

The first of the substitutes for the Jupiters, a Polaris submarine equipped with sixteen nuclear missiles, was on station in the Mediterranean at the end of March, and the second in April. With a range of 1,500 miles, the Polaris missiles were more accurate and safer from attack than the Jupiters, not least because the submarines could remain submerged for two months. However, both the Turks and Italians resented how major decisions were taken with no meaningful consultation. US diplomat Robert Dillon recorded that the former were 'very upset because they recognized for the first time that we were quite capable of making a deal with the Soviets behind their backs on matters of direct interest to them'.[87] Both Kennedy and Khrushchev had made an agreement behind the backs of their allies – the former in relation to Turkey and NATO, the latter, Cuba.[88] Public knowledge about the deal over Turkey emerged only gradually. Arthur Schlesinger's *A Thousand Days* (1965) and Elie Abel's *The Cuban Missile Crisis* (1966) both indicated that Kennedy had rejected the idea of a trade over the missiles.[89] Theodore Sorensen admitted in 1989 that he had edited Robert F. Kennedy's *Thirteen Days* (1969) to eliminate the indication that President Kennedy had offered to remove the missiles from Turkey. However, the book was not entirely misleading because it states: 'President Kennedy had been anxious to remove those missiles from Turkey and Italy for a long period of time . . . it was our judgment that, within a short time after this crisis was over, those missiles will be gone.'[90] There were further intimations in the 1960s and in the 1970s that a deal had been struck, but Sorensen's confession and the growing availability of documentary evidence embedded full knowledge of the deal in the literature.[91] By this stage, the matter was no longer so sensitive – indeed, Kennedy's concession was seen as expedient and sensible, if tainted by dishonesty.

## Notes

1. David Coleman, 'Presidential Approval Ratings', The Fourteenth Day: JFK in the Aftermath of the Cuban Missile Crisis, <http://jfk-14thday.com/jfk-presidential-approval-ratings/> (last accessed 25 July 2015).
2. Michael R. Beschloss, *The Crisis Years: Kennedy and Khrushchev, 1960–1963* (New York: Harper Collins, 1991), p. 548.

3. Ibid. p. 557; Thomas G. Paterson and William J. Brophy, 'October Missiles and November Elections: The Cuban Missile Crisis and American Politics, 1962', *The Journal of American History*, 73: 1, June 1986, pp. 87–119.
4. Jean Seaton and Rosaleen Hughes, 'The BBC and the Cuban Missile Crisis: Private Worlds and Public Service', in David Gioe, Len Scott and Christopher Andrew (eds), *An International History of the Cuban Missile Crisis: A 50-Year Retrospective* (London: Routledge, 2014), p. 66.
5. Harold Macmillan, *The Macmillan Diaries, Vol II – Prime Minister and After*, edited by Peter Catterall (London: Pan, 2012), pp. 516–17; Peter Catterall, 'At the End of the Day: Macmillan's Account of the Cuban Missile Crisis', *International Relations*, 26: 3, September 2012, p. 275.
6. Conversation between Rusk, Spaak et al., 27 November 1962, *Foreign Relations of the United States (FRUS) 1961–1963 Western Europe and Canada XIII* (1994), document 54, <https://history.state.gov/historicaldocuments/frus1961-63v13/d54> (last accessed 25 July 2015).
7. Don Munton and David A. Welch, The Cuban Missile Crisis: A Concise History, 2nd edn (Oxford and New York: Oxford University Press, 2012), p. 93.
8. Memorandum of conversation, 30 November 1962, *FRUS 1961–1963 XII American Republics* (1996), document 158, <https://history.state.gov/historicaldocuments/frus1961-63v12/d158> (last accessed 25 July 2015).
9. Memorandum of conversation, 28 November 1962, *FRUS 1961–1963 XIX South Asia* (1996), document 212, <https://history.state.gov/historicaldocuments/frus1961-63v19/d212> (last accessed 25 July 2015).
10. William Attwood, *The Reds and the Blacks* (London: Hutchinson, 1967), pp. 109–11; Robert B. Rakove, *Kennedy, Johnson and the Nonaligned World* (Cambridge and New York: Cambridge University Press, 2013), p. 91.
11. Attwood, *The Reds and the Blacks*, p. 111.
12. Rusk to Kennedy, undated, *FRUS 1961–1963 XXV Organization of Foreign Policy, Information Policy, United Nations, Scientific Matters* (2001), document 232, <https://history.state.gov/historicaldocuments/frus1961-63v25/d232> (last accessed 25 July 2015).
13. Beschloss, *The Crisis Years*, p. 556.

14. David Coleman, *The Fourteenth Day: JFK and the Aftermath of the Cuban Missile Crisis* (New York: Norton, 2012), pp. 197–8.
15. Beschloss, *The Crisis Years*, p. 544.
16. Arthur M. Schlesinger, Jr., *Robert Kennedy and His Times* (New York: Ballantine Books, 1979), p. 524.
17. Tanya Harmer, 'Mexican Diplomacy and the Cuban Missile Crisis: Documents from the Foreign Ministry Archives in Mexico City', *Cold War International History Project Bulletin*, 17/18, Fall 2012, pp. 191–2, <http://www.wilsoncenter.org/publication/bulletin-no-17-18> (last accessed 25 July 2015).
18. José Miró Cardona to the Revolutionary Council of Cuba, 9 April 1963, ibid. p. 225.
19. Conversation between the delegations of the CPCz and the CPSU, 30 October 1962, ibid. p. 401.
20. Nikita Khrushchev, *Memoirs of Nikita Khrushchev. Volume 3: Statesman, 1953–1964*, edited by Sergei Khrushchev and translated by George Shriver (University Park, PA: Pennsylvania State University Press, 2007), pp. 328–9.
21. Richard Ned Lebow and Janice Gross Stein, *We All Lost the Cold War* (Princeton, NJ: Princeton University Press, 1994), p. 141.
22. Khrushchev to Castro, 30 October 1962, National Security Archive, George Washington University, <http://www2.gwu.edu/~nsarchiv/nsa/cuba_mis_cri/docs.htm> (last accessed 25 July 2015).
23. Alekseev to Soviet Ministry of Foreign Affairs, 28 October 1962, *Cold War International History Project Bulletin*, 8/9, Winter 1996–7, pp. 293–4, <http://www.wilsoncenter.org/sites/default/files/CWIHP_Bulletin_8-9.pdf> (last accessed 25 July 2015).
24. Sergo Mikoyan, *The Soviet Cuban Missile Crisis: Castro, Mikoyan, Kennedy, Khrushchev and the Missiles of November*, edited by Svetlana Savranskaya (Stanford, CA: Stanford University Press, 2012), p. 203; conversation between Castro and Mikoyan, 4 November 1962, in ibid. p. 311; conversation between Mikoyan and Castro, 3 November 1962, *Cold War International History Project Bulletin*, 5, Spring 1995, pp. 93–4, <http://www.wilsoncenter.org/publication/bulletin-no-5-spring-1995> (last accessed 25 July 2015); Mikoyan to CC CPSU, 6 November 1962, National Security Archive, George Washington University, <http://www2.gwu.edu/~nsarchiv/nsa/cuba_mis_cri/docs.htm> (last accessed 25 July 2015) [see also document 13, Appendix 4 in this volume for Cuban attitudes].
25. Mikoyan, *The Soviet Cuban Missile Crisis*, pp. 218–20.

26. Mikoyan to CC CPSU, 6 November 1962, National Security Archive, George Washington University, <http://www2.gwu.edu/~nsarchiv/nsa/cuba_mis_cri/docs.htm> (last accessed 25 July 2015).

27. Conversation between Mikoyan and Cuban leaders, 5 November 1962, National Security Archive, George Washington University, <http://www2.gwu.edu/~nsarchiv/nsa/cuba_mis_cri/docs.ht> (last accessed 25 July 2015).

28. Mikoyan to CC CPSU, 6 November 1962, National Security Archive, George Washington University, <http://www2.gwu.edu/~nsarchiv/nsa/cuba_mis_cri/docs.htm> (last accessed 25 July 2015).

29. Conversation between Mikoyan, Castro and others, 19 November 1962, in Mikoyan, *The Soviet Cuban Missile Crisis*, p. 448 [see also document 15, Appendix 4 in this volume for a statement of Havana's attitudes to the United States].

30. Mikoyan to CC CPSU, 17 November 1962, in ibid. p. 439.

31. James G. Blight, Bruce J. Allyn and David A. Welch (eds), with foreword by Jorge I. Dominguez, *Cuba on the Brink: Castro, the Missile Crisis, and the Soviet Collapse* (New York: Pantheon, 1993), p. 92.

32. Mission to the UN to Department of State, 19 November 1962, *FRUS 1961–1963 XI*, document 191, <https://history.state.gov/historicaldocuments/frus1961-63v11/d191> (last accessed 25 July 2015).

33. State Department to Mission to UN, 3 November 1962, *FRUS 1961–1963 XI*, document 141, <https://history.state.gov/historicaldocuments/frus1961-63v11/d141> (last accessed 25 July 2015).

34. National Intelligence Estimate, 14 June 1963, *FRUS 1961–1963 XI*, document 347, <https://history.state.gov/historicaldocuments/frus1961-63v11/d347> (last accessed 25 July 2015).

35. Dobrynin to Foreign Ministry, forwarding telegram from G. A. Zhukov, 1 November 1962, *Cold War International History Project Bulletin*, 8/9, Winter 1996–7, pp. 307–8, <http://www.wilsoncenter.org/sites/default/files/CWIHP_Bulletin_8-9.pdf> (last accessed 25 July 2015).

36. Conversation between Mikoyan, McCloy and Stevenson, 1 November 1962, ibid. pp. 315–20.

37. CIA memorandum, 'Deployment and Withdrawal of Soviet Missiles and other Significant Weapons in Cuba', 29 November 1962, in Mary S. McAuliffe (ed.), *CIA Documents on the Cuban Missile Crisis* (Washington, DC: CIA History Staff, 1992), pp. 357–60.

38. ExComm meeting, 29 October 1962, *FRUS 1961–1963 XI*, document 111, <https://history.state.gov/historicaldocuments/frus1961-63v11/d111> (last accessed 25 July 2015).

39. Laurence Chang and Peter Kornbluh (eds), with foreword by Robert S. McNamara, *The Cuban Missile Crisis, 1962: A National Security Archive Documents Reader* (New York: The New Press, 1992), pp. 241–2.

40. The Cuban Crisis, 10 November 1962, FO 371/162408, The National Archives, Kew, England (TNA).

41. Conversation between Mikoyan, Castro and others, 22 November 1962, in Mikoyan, *The Soviet Cuban Missile Crisis*, p. 485.

42. Kennedy to Khrushchev, 15 November 1962, *FRUS 1961–1963 XI*, document 181, <https://history.state.gov/historicaldocuments/frus1961-63v11/d181> (last accessed 25 July 2015).

43. Mikoyan, *The Soviet Cuban Missile Crisis*, p. 197; U Thant, *View from the UN: The Memoirs of U Thant* (Newton Abbot: David and Charles, 1978), pp. 188, 192.

44. Conversation between Mikoyan and U Thant, 2 November 1962, *Cold War International History Project Bulletin*, 8/9, Winter 1996–7, pp. 311–13, <http://www.wilsoncenter.org/sites/default/files/CWIHP_Bulletin_8-9.pdf> (last accessed 25 July 2015).

45. Conversation between Castro and Mikoyan, 4 November 1962, in Mikoyan, *The Soviet Cuban Missile Crisis*, pp. 311–12.

46. Dobrynin to USSR Foreign Ministry, 12 November 1962, *Cold War International History Project Bulletin*, 8/9, Winter 1996–7, pp. 331–3, <http://www.wilsoncenter.org/sites/default/files/CWIHP_Bulletin_8-9.pdf> (last accessed 25 July 2015).

47. Conversation between Castro and Mikoyan, 13 November 1962, in Mikoyan, *The Soviet Cuban Missile Crisis*, p. 397.

48. Dobrynin to USSR Foreign Ministry, 1 November 1962, *Cold War International History Project Bulletin*, 8/9, Winter 1996–7, p. 309, <http://www.wilsoncenter.org/sites/default/files/CWIHP_Bulletin_8-9.pdf> (last accessed 25 July 2015).

49. Raymond L. Garthoff, 'US Intelligence in the Cuban Missile Crisis', in James G. Blight and David A. Welch (eds), *Intelligence and the Cuban Missile Crisis* (Abingdon: Frank Cass, 1998), pp. 34–5.

50. Khrushchev to Kennedy, 20 November 1962, *FRUS XI*, document 196, <https://history.state.gov/historicaldocuments/frus1961-63v11/d196> (last accessed 25 July 2015).

51. CPSU instruction to Mikoyan, 22 November 1962, National Security

Archive, George Washington University, <http://www2.gwu.edu/~nsarchiv/nsa/cuba_mis_cri/621122%20CPSU%20Instructions%20to%20Mikoyan.pdf> (last accessed 25 July 2015).

52. Kennedy to Khrushchev, 6 November 1962, *FRUS 1961–1963 XI*, document 155, <https://history.state.gov/historicaldocuments/frus 1961-63v11/d155> (last accessed 25 July 2015).

53. Taylor, 'Talking Paper for Meeting with the President', 16 November 1962, *FRUS 1961–1963 XI*, document 187, <https://history.state.gov/historicaldocuments/frus1961-63v11/d187> (last accessed 25 July 2015).

54. Dobrynin to USSR Foreign Ministry, 12 November 1962, *Cold War International History Project Bulletin*, 8/9, Winter 1996–7, p. 331, <http://www.wilsoncenter.org/sites/default/files/CWIHP_Bulletin_8-9.pdf> (last accessed 25 July 2015).

55. Khrushchev to Kennedy, 14 November 1962, *FRUS 1961–1963 XI*, document 176, <https://history.state.gov/historicaldocuments/frus1961-63v11/d176> (last accessed 25 July 2015).

56. Gromyko to Kuznetsov and Zorin, 5 November 1962, *Cold War International History Project Bulletin*, 8/9, Winter 1996–7, p. 334, <http://www.wilsoncenter.org/sites/default/files/CWIHP_Bulletin_8-9.pdf> (last accessed 25 July 2015).

57. Conversation between Castro and Mikoyan, 13 November 1962, in Mikoyan, *The Soviet Cuban Missile Crisis*, p. 397.

58. New York to Foreign Office, 7 November 1962, FO 371/162399, TNA.

59. Coleman, *The Fourteenth Day*, p. 147.

60. Khrushchev to Kennedy, 20 November 1962, *FRUS 1961–1963 XI*, document 196, <https://history.state.gov/historicaldocuments/frus1961-63v11/d196> (last accessed 25 July 2015).

61. Kennedy to Khrushchev, 21 November 1962, *FRUS 1961–1963 XI*, document 202, <https://history.state.gov/historicaldocuments/frus1961-63v11/d202> (last accessed 25 July 2015).

62. Joint Chiefs of Staff to McNamara, 28 November 1962, *FRUS 1961–1963 XI*, document 215, <https://history.state.gov/historical documents/frus1961-63v11/d215> (last accessed 25 July 2015).

63. Bakaev to CC CPSU, 7 December 1962, *Cold War International History Project Bulletin*, 8/9, Winter 1996–7, p. 337, <http://www.wilsoncenter.org/sites/default/files/CWIHP_Bulletin_8-9.pdf> (last accessed 25 July 2015).

64. Kuznetsov and Zorin to USSR Foreign Ministry, 30 October 1962, *Cold War International History Project Bulletin*, 8/9, Winter

1996–7, p. 302, <http://www.wilsoncenter.org/sites/default/files/
CWIHP_Bulletin_8-9.pdf> (last accessed 25 July 2015).

65. Conversation between Mikoyan, McCloy and Stevenson, 1
November 1962, ibid. pp. 315–20.

66. Henry A. Kissinger, *The White House Years* (London: Weidenfeld
and Nicolson and Michael Joseph, 1979), p. 646.

67. ExComm meeting, 21 November 1962, *FRUS 1961–1963 XI*,
document 201, <https://history.state.gov/historicaldocuments/frus
1961-63v11/d201> (last accessed 25 July 2015).

68. Kennedy to Khrushchev, 14 December 1962, *FRUS 1961–1963 XI*,
document 247, <https://history.state.gov/historicaldocuments/frus
1961-63v11/d247> (last accessed 25 July 2015).

69. Mikoyan, *The Soviet Cuban Missile Crisis*, p. 199.

70. Arnold Horelick, 'The Cuban Missile Crisis: An Analysis of Soviet
Calculations and Behavior', Memorandum RM-3779-PR, The Rand
Corporation, September 1963, pp. 6–7 <http://www.rand.org/
pubs/research_memoranda/RM3779.html> (last accessed 25 July
2015).

71. Dobrynin to USSR MFA, 28 October 1962, *Cold War International
History Project Bulletin*, 5, Spring 1995, p. 76, <http://www.wil
soncenter.org/publication/bulletin-no-5-spring-1995> (last accessed
25 July 2015).

72. JCS meeting, 29 October 1962, *FRUS 1961–1963 X-XI-XII
Microfiche Supplement, American Republics; Cuba 1961–1962;
Cuban Missile Crisis and Aftermath*, document 453, <http://history.
state.gov/historicaldocuments/frus1961-63v10-12mSupp/d453>
(last accessed 25 July 2015).

73. Memorandum of conversation, 28 October 1962, *FRUS 1961–
1963 XI*, document 106, <https://history.state.gov/historicaldocu-
ments/frus1961-63v11/d106> (last accessed 25 July 2015).

74. Memorandum of conversation, 29 October 1962, *FRUS 1961–
1963 XI*, document 110, <https://history.state.gov/historicaldocu
ments/frus1961-63v11/d110> (last accessed 25 July 2015).

75. Philip Nash, *The Other Missiles of October: Eisenhower, Kennedy,
and the Jupiters, 1957–1963* (Chapel Hill: University of North
Carolina Press, 1997), pp. 153–5.

76. Ibid. p. 158.

77. Schlesinger to Kennedy, 2 December 1962, *FRUS 1961–1963 X-XI-
XII*, document 561, <http://history.state.gov/historicaldocuments/
frus1961-63v10-12mSupp/d561> (last accessed 25 July 2015).

78. Lawrence Freedman, *Kennedy's Wars: Berlin, Cuba, Laos, and*

*Vietnam* (Oxford and New York: Oxford University Press, 2000), p. 220.

79. Dobrynin to the USSR Foreign Ministry, 30 October 1962, *Cold War International History Project Bulletin*, 8/9, Winter 1996–7, p. 304, <http://www.wilsoncenter.org/sites/default/files/CWIHP_Bulletin_8-9.pdf> (last accessed 25 July 2015).

80. Nash, *The Other Missiles*, pp. 155–6.

81. State Department to Embassy in Italy, 18 December 1962, *FRUS 1961–1963 XIII*, document 160, <https://history.state.gov/historicaldocuments/frus1961-63v13/d160> (last accessed 25 July 2015).

82. Nash, *The Other Missiles*, p. 157.

83. Ibid. p. 157.

84. Ibid. pp. 161–2; Leonardo Campus, 'Italian Political Reactions to the Cuban Missile Crisis', in Gioe et al. (eds), *An International History of the Cuban Missile Crisis*, pp. 237–8.

85. Nash, *The Other Missiles*, pp. 163–4.

86. Don Munton, 'The Fourth Question: Why Did John F. Kennedy Offer Up the Jupiters in Turkey?', in Gioe et al. (eds), *An International History of the Cuban Missile Crisis*, p. 258.

87. Robert S. Dillon interviewed by Charles Stuart Kennedy, 17 May 1990, Association for Diplomatic Studies and Training, Foreign Affairs Oral History Program, Arlington, VA, <http://www.adst.org> (last accessed 25 July 2015).

88. Nash, *The Other Missiles*, p. 147.

89. Elie Abel, *The Missiles of October: The Cuban Missile Crisis, 1962* (London: MacGibbon and Kee, 1969), pp. 175–6; Arthur M. Schlesinger, Jr., *A Thousand Days: John F. Kennedy in the White House* (New York: Houghton Mifflin, 1965), p. 707.

90. Robert F. Kennedy, *Thirteen Days: A Memoir of the Cuban Missile Crisis* (New York: Norton, 1969), pp. 108–9.

91. Munton, 'The Fourth Question', pp. 260–2; Nash, *The Other Missiles*, pp. 151–71.

# 8 Aftermath II, 1963–70

This is a more subtle and difficult environment than the eyeball-to-eyeball world of 1961–62.

*Walt Rostow*

## Superpower Relations under Kennedy

The US administration grew concerned after the missile crisis about Soviet troops in Cuba, realising that they were better organised, better armed and more numerous than had previously been appreciated – although the highest American estimate, at 17,000, fell well short of the real number, 42,000.[1] US officials complained frequently to the Soviets about the troops, without indicating how many would have been acceptable and even though the issue had not featured in the settlement of the missile crisis. In April 1963 Nikita Khrushchev bemoaned 'the continued pressure' from Washington for the removal of Soviet personnel. He claimed that his country had 'already withdrawn twice as many troops as the largest number that had appeared in the newspapers here in the United States'.[2] Yet the reductions did not satisfy President Kennedy. In the summer of 1963, plans were devised to obtain an OAS resolution based on the so-called 'Kennedy Doctrine': the 'extension ... of the political domination or military presence of Communist powers within this hemisphere is hostile to the basic principles of the life of the Americas'.[3] There was little progress on the matter, not least because the moment for such a resolution had passed. Gordon Chase of the National Security Council thought that there was 'no sense in passing a resolution unless the OAS is prepared to act on it . . . we have let Cuba cool down considerably; at this point, many Latin Americans feel that the US is not really interested in doing much about Cuba'.[4] The troop issue remained unresolved. Dean Rusk complained to Ambassador Dobrynin in 1964 that there were 'too many' Soviet military personnel in Cuba,[5] but there was little that could be done but complain.

Republican politicians believed that the Kennedy administration had exploited and manipulated the issue of Soviet missiles in Cuba with a view to political gain in the United States. Even after the congressional elections of November 1962, there were accusations that the Soviets had not withdrawn the weapons. To assuage the critics, on 6 February the following year Robert McNamara and John Hughes of the Defense Intelligence Agency gave a televised briefing in which they used dozens of surveillance photographs to show that the Soviet missiles had gone.[6] The administration succeeded in silencing the criticisms and making it clear that there was no longer any military threat from Cuba, although there were spurious reports from agents in the country that nuclear missiles remained there.[7]

Although at the conclusion of the missile crisis Kennedy and Khrushchev had agreed to work towards an East–West *détente*, neither were zealots on the matter. Two weeks after speaking at the American University (where he advocated détente – see below), Kennedy condemned communism and the division of Germany passionately in his 'Ich bin ein Berliner' speech in West Berlin.[8] His tough line on the German question was hardly compatible with a sustained improvement in relations with the Soviet Union. He told Konrad Adenauer that 'we are dealing still with a government which had recently posed threats to the freedom of West Berlin and which, as late as October last year, undertook a peculiarly dangerous and reckless act of duplicity in Cuba'.[9] In the speech that he was to deliver in Dallas on the day of his assassination on 22 November 1963, the President intended to highlight US military superiority, and to emphasise the need to prevent an international 'Communist breakthrough'.[10] Kennedy could not forget the memory of Soviet nuclear encroachment into Cuba, and he knew that too great an enthusiasm towards improved relations with the Soviet Union would generate suspicion among allies abroad and conservatives at home.

For his part, Khrushchev had concerns about communist Chinese condemnation of his policy of peaceful coexistence with the West, and feared that agreements on arms control with the United States would exacerbate Beijing's criticisms.[11] He felt that he had been short-changed about the Cuba deal: he had 'made concessions whereas President Kennedy had not'.[12] In the run-up to the Limited Nuclear Test Ban Treaty of August 1963 (see below), he asserted in a 'talking paper' to Robert F. Kennedy (ostensibly from Dobrynin) that the US government 'had better learn that the Soviet Union was as strong as the United States and did not enjoy being treated as a second-class power.' RFK returned the paper because 'it was so insulting and rude'.[13]

Nonetheless, there were examples of improved attitudes on both sides, and of instances of concrete progress in East–West relations after the missile crisis. The confrontation made President Kennedy especially aware of the dangers of mutual misperception: 'no-one seems to be able really to read the Soviets', while the Kremlin 'would never have thought that we would react the way we did or else they would not have placed missiles in Cuba . . . both sides are to some extent blind'.[14] (He had pondered Khrushchev's reference to 'blind moles' in the letter of 26 October.)[15] In an address in December 1962, he said 'that man can and must live in peace with his neighbors and that it is the peacemakers who are truly blessed'.[16] At American University the following June, Kennedy called for a moderation of the Cold War and acknowledged that the United States and the Soviet Union had much in common, including a 'deep interest in a just and genuine peace and in halting the arms race'.[17]

In March 1963, the CIA suggested that Khrushchev had become more subdued towards superpower relations since the Cuba debacle. While previously he seemed almost to relish confrontations with the United States, in the Congo, in Laos, Berlin and Cuba, now he seemed 'sobered by the thought that the US was on the verge of attacking Soviet forces in Cuba, and appalled at the options of having to counterattack or accept humiliation'.[18] On a visit to East Berlin he said that the construction of the Berlin Wall had been 'a most important step' in strengthening East German sovereignty, and that a peace treaty was 'no longer the problem it was before the protective measures' in Berlin were taken. Khrushchev had learned to tolerate the Western presence, which he once described as 'the bone in his throat'.[19] He greeted Kennedy's American University address warmly, describing it as 'the greatest speech by any American president since Roosevelt'.[20]

In 1963 Washington and Moscow established a direct teletype link (the 'hot-line') between the Kremlin and the Pentagon to facilitate crisis communications. The idea was a US initiative stemming from the Berlin crisis in 1961 as a way of helping to prevent miscalculation and escalation, but delays in communication during the missile crisis caused by the translation, ciphering, deciphering and typing of messages gave the idea further momentum.[21] The first substantive use of the hot-line took place during the 'Six Day War' between Israel and the Soviet-backed United Arab Republic in June 1967, when Premier Alexei Kosygin used it to outline the Soviet position.[22]

Perhaps more significant for superpower relations was the Limited Nuclear Test Ban Treaty of August 1963, signed by the United States, the Soviet Union and Great Britain, and prohibiting nuclear tests in outer space, in the atmosphere and underwater.[23] Negotiations for a treaty banning the testing of nuclear weapons had begun in 1958, to ease the arms competition and to end radioactive pollution of the atmosphere, but the issues of inspections and of detection systems to monitor underground testing had proved controversial. In August 1962, during negotiations in Geneva, the Western powers had proposed a Comprehensive Test Ban Treaty and a Limited Test Ban Treaty, both of which the Soviet Union rejected. Both Kennedy and Khrushchev had mentioned arms control measures in connection with settling the missile crisis. The 1962 Treaty was not, as is often thought, the first arms control agreement of the Cold War; there were arms control elements in the Antarctic Treaty of 1961; and there was the private Cuba–Turkey missiles deal of 28 October 1962.[24] The Treaty did not prevent subterranean testing, and it did not stop the new nuclear powers, China and France, from atmospheric testing, as they were not party to the accord. Yet it was still a positive step, as it paved the way for further measures. How far the post-missile-crisis *détente* might have developed had Kennedy not been assassinated can only be speculated. Khrushchev, incidentally, was saddened by the murder, telling President Johnson that the 'villainous assassination of . . . John F. Kennedy is a . . . very grievous loss'.[25] Although they had clashed dangerously, there had been a genuine mutual respect between the two leaders.

## Superpower Relations under Johnson

Khrushchev was deposed in 1964. Although in the short term he had escaped fairly unscathed from his capitulation over the missiles in Cuba, British Ambassador in Moscow Frank Roberts had suggested presciently that over the longer run his

> authority will have been impaired. The general public may well accept the image, now being projected, of Khrushchev the peace-maker, the leader who compromised to save the world from war and also extracted from the United States an undertaking to respect Cuban integrity; but the general public hardly counts, and there are undoubtedly hard-headed Party functionaries who remember Stalin, who have access to Western appraisals of political developments and who know what Peking's judgment is; and there will at the least be a leaven of Khrushchev doubters and conceivably a potential nucleus of opposition to their present leader.[26]

Anatoly Dobrynin noted that when in October 1964 the plenary meeting of the Central Committee was agreeing Khrushchev's dismissal from office, 'many delegates strongly criticized his personal role in creating the Cuban crisis'.[27] These included Dmitri Polyanski, who mocked Khrushchev's claim that the Soviet Union had achieved a successful 'penetration' of Latin America and that the missile crisis had ended with a Soviet victory: 'we were forced to accept all the demands dictated by the US, including humiliating inspections of our ships'. The Cuban debacle 'damaged the international prestige of our country, our party, and our armed forces, while . . . helping to strengthen US prestige'.[28] There were

other factors behind Khrushchev's overthrow, including economic problems and the rift with China,[29] but the missile crisis
had tarnished him considerably. Leonid Brezhnev and Alexei
Kosygin emerged as the chief figures in domestic and foreign
policy respectively.

The Soviets were already increasing their nuclear arsenal prior
to the confrontation of October 1962, with defence spend-
ing rising by 40 per cent in 1960–2.[30] However, as Dobrynin
recorded, the Soviet 'military establishment' used the retreat over
the missiles in Cuba to accelerate the nuclear programme so
that the Soviet Union could deal with the United States from a
position of strength.[31] The Limited Nuclear Test Ban Treaty of
1963 did not preclude continued efforts to expand the arsenal.
The State Department noted in 1967 that 'the Soviets have substantially increased their ability to damage the US in a nuclear
exchange'. It was anticipated that they would soon have superiority in submarines which could launch nuclear missiles,[32] which
would provide even more destructive power than had the missiles
in Cuba. Building on his inheritance from Kennedy, President
Lyndon B. Johnson sought to initiate arms limitation (not merely
arms control) talks at a summit with Alexei Kosygin at Glassboro,
New Jersey, in June 1967. Kosygin declined to engage with the
issue until the Soviet Union had made further progress developing
its nuclear arsenal.[33]

Nonetheless, there was some progress in arms *control* in 1967.
The Outer Space Treaty, prohibiting placing weapons of mass
destruction in space, built on the Limited Nuclear Test Ban Treaty
of 1963. It was signed by the United States, the Soviet Union and
the United Kingdom.[34] In 1968 the same countries along with
fifty-three others signed the Treaty on Nuclear Non-Proliferation.
Nations without nuclear weapons agreed not to develop them;
and nuclear powers agreed to work towards arms control and
disarmament.[35] There was momentum in 1968 towards a Soviet–
American agreement limiting strategic weapons. According to the
CIA, the Soviets had developed a 'confidence in their possession
of an assured destruction capability' and wanted to end American
competition in this field.[36] Kosygin proposed to Johnson that
Strategic Arms Limitation Talks begin in Geneva.[37] After delay

caused by Soviet intervention in Czechoslovakia in 1968, SALT finally got under way with the Richard Nixon administration in 1969. In the next few years there was an array of arms control measures, along with agreements on the European borders and on the status of Berlin. Superpower relations remained, at least until the early 1980s, less confrontational than they had been in the rough period of 1958–62, when Berlin and Cuba were at centre stage. The missile crisis contributed to this state of affairs. General Andrew Goodpaster, Supreme Allied Commander Europe, suggested in 1970 that 'Since the Cuban missile crisis, [the Soviets] have a much more sobered view of the risks to them of a high-intensity provocation of the US.'[38] Moscow probably mirrored such views.

## Cuban–Soviet Relations

As was seen in the previous chapter, the lack of Soviet consultation with Havana during the missile crisis had greatly distressed Fidel Castro, with him feeling snubbed as the superpowers made an agreement over his head involving the removal of missiles that were supposed to protect his country. To make matters worse, during a visit to Moscow in May 1963 Castro learned of the secret Soviet–American arrangement over the Jupiter missiles in Turkey. Khrushchev happened to be reading out correspondence and memoranda about the missile crisis when he let slip that there had been an agreement over the removal of the Jupiters. In Castro's own account, he

> looked at him and said: 'Nikita, would you please read that part again about the missiles in Turkey and Italy?' He laughed that mischievous laugh of his. He laughed, but that was it. I was sure that they were not going to repeat it again because it was like that old phrase about bringing up the issue of the noose in the home of the man who was hung.[39]

The Jupiter missiles had nothing to do with the defence of Cuba, which meant that Khrushchev had used the country as a 'bargaining chip' to gain a self-interested concession.[40] Despite the difficulties, there was no rupture in Cuban–Soviet relations, whatever the temptations that Castro may have faced. He recognised that 'we had very close economic relations with the Soviets. The entire life of the country, the energy of the country, depended on the Soviets … The USSR supplied the oil, they supplied the weapons.'[41] Although Cuba had striven to develop its economic ties with the Chinese, they were not able to provide the same level of support as were the Soviets.[42] The CIA suggested in June 1963 that 'After a period marked by bitterness on Castro's part and by restraint on the part of the Soviets, the two parties now appear to have agreed to emphasize the consolidation of the Castro regime.'[43]

However, it would not be plain sailing, not least because of different views about Cuban efforts to spread revolution. These efforts had intensified after the missile crisis, out of a sense that after the Soviets had let Cuba down it was all the more necessary to secure other allies.[44] US records indicate that in 1963 some 4,600 Latin Americans visited Cuba to undergo what the CIA described as 'formal indoctrination', and that 'several hundred of these probably received training in the techniques of guerrilla warfare and urban terrorism'.[45] By the following year over a hundred members of the Armed Forces for National Liberation (FALN) terrorist organisation in Venezuela had received paramilitary training in Cuba and elsewhere in the communist bloc.[46] After Khrushchev's demise in 1964, the Kremlin was less willing to support the 'triumphant march of socialism' across the ocean, given how it could lead to the cost and risk of another Cuba.[47] When Kosygin visited Havana after the Glassboro summit of 1967, he told Castro firmly to back away from supporting armed struggle in Latin America and Africa. Castro accused him of leading a country that had 'turned its back upon its own revolutionary tradition'.[48] Later that year, Castro suspected that the Bolivian Communist Party – which was closely aligned with Moscow – had sabotaged Che Guevara's revolutionary activities in Bolivia, resulting in Guevara's death at the hands of Bolivian troops.[49] However, relations between the Soviet Union and Cuba began to improve from 1968 because of Castro's backing for the Soviet invasion of Czechoslovakia, and due to his awareness of the importance of Soviet economic and technological support.[50] The renewed Soviet commitment to Cuba would set the stage for a further Soviet confrontation with the US government over weapons on the island, as will be seen.

## Cuban–American Relations

Alongside providing only an 'evasive non-invasion' pledge, the Kennedy administration sustained its efforts to undermine and harass the regime in Cuba. In April 1963, President Kennedy endorsed the use of propaganda encouraging the locals to provoke and attack Soviet troops on the island, and to sabotage Cuban vessels.[51] Plans were made to exploit various developments, including the shooting down of a U-2, a revolt in Cuba, instances of Cuban intervention in Latin America and incidents at Guantánamo, in order to weaken the Castro regime.[52] In June, the President approved a CIA programme of sabotage operations in Cuba.[53] There were procedures to support an anti-Castro revolt, including the use of airdrops, air strikes and, inevitably, the launching of an invasion force.[54] Regardless of – or perhaps because of – the continued American hostility, Fidel Castro tried again to improve his relationship with Washington. In April he told US lawyer James Donovan, who had negotiated the release of US citizens from Cuban jails in December 1962, that relations with the United States should be 'developed'. Contacts between Donovan and Castro helped bring about the release of the prisoners captured during the Bay of Pigs invasion.[55] Some US officials, including McGeorge Bundy and Dean Rusk, were inclined to reach out for Castro's olive branch. Bundy felt that

> In strictly economic terms, both the United States and Cuba have much to gain from reestablishment of relations. A Titoist Castro is not inconceivable, and a full diplomatic revolution would not be the most extraordinary event in the twentieth century.[56]

However, the State Department's Bureau of Inter-American Affairs was less favourable, arguing that an accommodation with

Cuba would 'completely dry up investment' in Latin America, damaging the Alliance for Progress.[57]

There is some evidence that President Kennedy was inclined towards flexibility, with him believing that so long as Cuba ended its subversion in Latin America there could be an improved Cuban–American relationship; it was not essential that Cuba cut its ties with the Soviet Union. In October 1963 he told the French journalist Jean Daniel, who was due to meet with Castro, that the United States had turned pre-revolutionary Cuba into a 'whorehouse'.[58] In Miami in November, in his last public speech on inter-American affairs, he stated that if Cuba ended its efforts 'dictated by external powers' to promote subversion in Latin America then 'everything is possible' in Cuban–American relations. Generally, though, Kennedy remained very cautious. In his Miami speech he criticised Fidel Castro and affirmed the so-called Kennedy Doctrine that had been conceived some months earlier: 'The American States must be ready to come to the aid of any government requesting aid to prevent a take-over linked to the policies of foreign communism rather than to an internal desire for change.'[59] As with Soviet–American relations, how matters might have turned out had Kennedy not been assassinated can only be speculated. Castro, who 'voiced deep regret' at the news of the murder,[60] felt that 'because of the boost in his authority that he got after the October crisis' Kennedy 'might have been one of the presidents – or perhaps the president best able – to rectify American policy toward Cuba'.[61]

President Johnson was less zealously hostile to the regime in Cuba than had been the Kennedy administration. He certainly loathed the prospect of invading the island, telling J. William Fulbright late in 1963: 'I'm not getting into any Bay of Pigs deal.'[62] Johnson thought that covert action against Cuba was both ineffectual and morally questionable: there was the sheer 'hypocrisy of our seeking peace and talking peace and conducting this sort of activity on the side'.[63] Yet the advent of a new administration did not mark a clear break with the Kennedy era; little changed, as Johnson found the continued presence of a communist government close to the US coast an embarrassment and a political liability. There was a reluctance to adopt a more positive approach to Cuba due to concerns that Latin American allies and Cuba itself might conclude that there had been 'a switch of US policy from one of discreet encouragement and support of aggressive action against the Castro regime to one of "coexistence" and eventual accommodation with a Castro/Communist Cuba'.[64]Although Operation Mongoose ended formally early in 1963,[65] there were continued efforts under Johnson to weaken the regime in Havana. From June 1963 to April 1964 there were more than eighty acts of internal sabotage and sixty armed clashes between Cuban security forces and insurgents.[66] Much of this activity was US-sponsored. There were even attempts to do away with Castro, although these efforts were modest compared with what had gone on under Kennedy. Johnson ordered them wound up as soon as he found out.[67]

There was a direct confrontation between Cuba and the United States early in 1964, over the capture of four Cuban fishing boats near the American coast in the Florida Keys. Thirty-six Cuban fishermen were turned over to the authorities in Florida for possible prosecution under state law, while two others gained political asylum. The President concluded that the Soviet Union was using Castro to test his mettle. Johnson told his advisers to 'get ahold of Khrushchev and tell him that [Castro]'s playing a mighty dangerous game with his marbles'.[68] However, there is no evidence that Khrushchev had a hand in what was going on, which shows how Johnson overrated the Soviet desire for another confrontation in the Western Hemisphere, and did not appreciate that Castro could act independently. The presence of the vessels close to the American coast was inadvertent. The Cuban government cut off the water supply to the American naval base at Guantánamo, in retaliation for the seizure of the fishing vessels and crews,[69] and Johnson ordered the dismissal of the 3,000 Cubans who worked at the base.[70]

However, the crisis soon blew over. Castro took a generally restrained stance during the quarrel, as he had not abandoned his hopes of a rapprochement. He told journalist Lisa Howard that Cuban and American officials could 'sit down in an atmosphere of goodwill . . . and negotiate our differences'.[71] The improvement in relations did not develop, in part because of Johnson's desire to be seen as a tough anti-communist, and seemingly because his lack of confidence in foreign affairs did not dispose him towards bold initiatives. US policy towards Cuba still relied on isolating and undermining the regime in Havana.[72] This was evident in how, in response to Cuban subversion activities, the US government orchestrated OAS sanctions against the country in 1964.[73]

## NATO

The previous chapter noted the Kennedy administration's subterfuge and dissimulation concerning the removal of the Jupiter missiles from Turkey. The issue of consultation during the missile crisis remained one of sensitivity. According to Ambassador David Ormsby-Gore, some 'activists' in the US administration had concluded from the missile crisis that consultation with allies was 'wearisome' and 'repugnant'.[74] Earlier in 1962 the Kennedy administration had agreed to sell Britain 'Skybolt' nuclear missiles, helping to keep the British in the nuclear club. However, in December the decision of the US administration to cancel the development of Skybolt was communicated insensitively, seemingly reflecting the view that Britain was but one of many allies in a world in which only the superpowers counted. At a conference in Nassau in the Bahamas, President Kennedy agreed to provide Britain with Polaris-armed submarines, helping to overcome the rift between the United States and Britain.[75]

Scant consultation during the missile crisis, alongside the general perception of a reduced Soviet threat, weakened the NATO alliance. The FRG's Chancellor Konrad Adenauer had, as seen previously, supported Washington during the crisis, and under the so-called Hallstein Doctrine in January 1963 he ended diplomatic ties with Cuba when the latter extended diplomatic recognition to the German Democratic Republic. However, he considered that the failure to foresee the Soviet missiles initiative in Cuba confirmed the President's weakness towards the Soviet Union.[76] While backing the American position during the confrontation, President Charles de Gaulle of France had also concluded that 'the US had given greater priority to matters affecting its own immediate security than for example the defense of Europe'.[77] Early in 1963 de Gaulle vetoed the British application to join the European Economic Community on the grounds that the British would be a 'Trojan horse' for American influence.[78] This was a setback both for the British, who sought economic rehabilitation, and the Americans, whose 'Grand Design' policy encouraged European integration.[79]

In 1966 de Gaulle withdrew France from NATO's integrated command structure, dismissing US forces from the country and weakening the structural integrity of the alliance. Despite pressure from some advisers to punish de Gaulle, the memory of French solidarity in October 1962 led President Johnson to adopt a conciliatory stance.[80] Franco-American estrangement had already been under way by 1962, but as Arthur Schlesinger suggested, the missile crisis encouraged de Gaulle to 'come into the open' in pursuit of his own ends in Europe.[81] Walt Rostow of the State Department's Policy Planning Council saw such developments as evidence that 'we are now facing the consequences of our success last year' in the 'nuclear tests of will over Berlin and Cuba'. It was now necessary to accept 'the diffusion of effective power' away from Washington.[82] The burgeoning US commitment in Vietnam in 1964–5 (see below) also brought divisions between the United States and its transatlantic partners, with European states resisting American pressure to send combat troops, doubting that the war could be won and questioning its morality.[83]

The lack of US consultation with fellow NATO members during the crisis underscored the question of dialogue about nuclear strategy. The Eisenhower administration had proposed a supranational fleet of ships and submarines armed with nuclear weapons (the 'Multilateral Force' – MLF) to address the question of giving non-nuclear members of NATO (especially the Federal Republic of Germany) greater influence in the alliance's nuclear affairs.[84] By the time of Kennedy's death the project was floundering because the West Germans were the only real enthusiasts. Instead of a hardware solution to the alliance's nuclear problems, the Nuclear Planning Group (NPG) was established in 1966 as a forum for discussion. In 1968 the NPG agreed to the formal abandonment of the avowed Eisenhower–John Foster Dulles strategy of 'massive retaliation', in favour of 'flexible response'. Kennedy had criticised 'massive retaliation' on the grounds that it would encourage the communists to advance 'through those techniques which they deemed not sufficiently offensive to induce us to risk atomic warfare'. At least in the eyes of its admirers, 'flexible response' was more nuanced because it placed greater emphasis on the use of conventional forces and provided more room for negotiation in the event of a crisis.[85] Furthermore, the Soviet invasion of Czechoslovakia in August 1968 had a galvanising effect on NATO, helping to ease recent divisions.[86]

Flexible response was associated in the United States with the rise of the doctrine known as Mutual Assured Destruction (MAD). The missile crisis undermined the idea that in a severe crisis or war, a nuclear first strike was a valid option, in favour of the view that the Soviet Union would be deterred from a first strike as long as the United States had an effective second-strike capability. MAD would help to ensure that crises did not escalate to the unthinkable. Robert McNamara opposed the construction of anti-ballistic missile (ABM) defence systems because US development of an ABM system would encourage the Soviets to strengthen their own ABM efforts, and so would undermine the stabilising impact of MAD. Soviet–American agreements during *détente* in the 1970s limited ABM development.[87]

## The Communist World

The Brazilian ambassador in Moscow suggested in November 1962 that the missile crisis had 'created a state of disorientation in the community of socialist countries and that the great challenge of Khrushchev will be to accommodate this state of affairs'.[88] The crisis influenced relations between the Soviet Union and its partners in the Warsaw Pact. As was seen in Chapter 5, Moscow had not consulted any of the satellites about stationing missiles in Cuba, or about how to resolve the confrontation. Frank Roberts wrote that Communist Party members outside the Soviet Union were well 'aware of the dangerous situation into which [Khrushchev] led the Warsaw Treaty powers in particular and the world as a whole; and of the loss of prestige he suffered in climbing down'.[89] The missile confrontation bolstered at least one satellite's quest for greater autonomy. At the UN in late 1963, Romanian Foreign Minister Cornelieu Manescu told Dean Rusk that his country had not been party to Khrushchev's decision to station missiles in Cuba, and affirmed that there were no Soviet nuclear weapons on Romanian soil. Romania soon weakened its ties with the Warsaw Pact, and from 1969, the country no longer participated in Pact military exercises.[90] Furthermore, as the Romanians moved away from Moscow they re-orientated themselves more towards Beijing.[91] The leadership in Poland, already resentful at not being consulted during the missile crisis, objected to Moscow's lack of discussion with Warsaw Pact members about the Limited Nuclear Test Ban Treaty, especially since they were obliged to endorse it when it was opened for signature by countries other than the principals.[92]

The missile crisis influenced Sino-Soviet relations. The Mao Zedong regime asserted contradictorily that Moscow had been guilty of 'adventurism' for sending the missiles and 'capitulationism' for withdrawing them. Cuba was 'Khrushchev's Munich'.[93] An Eastern bloc diplomat observed that Cuban leaders, with their sense of abandonment caused by Khrushchev's retreat, were influenced by China's proclamations of support for them. This contributed to Anastas Mikoyan's difficulties when he sought to persuade Castro and his colleagues to accept a UN inspection regime.[94] There was a war of words between Moscow and Beijing, with Khrushchev reminding the Chinese in response to the 'Munich' taunt that they had done nothing to follow up threats they had made to the British presence in Hong Kong and to the Portuguese presence in Macao.[95] Six years later Soviet and Chinese troops clashed on the borders between the two countries, showing clearly how the Sino-Soviet relationship had degenerated.[96]

North Korea concluded from the Soviet retreat in October 1962 that Khrushchev was more concerned with peaceful coexistence with the West than he was with aiding smaller socialist countries. Later, North Korean Vice Premier Kim Il told Alexei Kosygin that as a result of the Soviet removal of the nuclear missiles from

Cuba, Pyongyang doubted that it could rely on Moscow to 'keep the obligations related to the defense of Korea it assumed in the Treaty of Friendship, Cooperation and Mutual Assistance', which had been signed in 1961. North Korea sided publicly with the Chinese in the Sino-Soviet split. Both Pyongyang and Beijing endorsed a much more militant anti-imperialist stance, although the rift between North Korea and the Soviet Union began to close after 1964.[97] For Walt Rostow, the post-missile-crisis intensification of the Sino-Soviet dispute and its effects elsewhere showed that power was moving away from Moscow as well as Washington.[98]

## The Cuban Missile Crisis and Vietnam

The United States had backed anti-communist forces in Vietnam since soon after the Second World War. The American government helped to fund France's colonial war, and after the French defeat and the division of the peninsula in 1954, propped up South Vietnam in the face of an intensifying insurgency supported by the communist North. When Kennedy entered office in 1961 there were around 600 US advisers in Vietnam, but he increased the number to 16,000 in the face of the intensifying insurgency. After the missile crisis there was a sense that Khrushchev would encourage North Vietnam to challenge the United States in Vietnam, as 'a way to humiliate us and placate' the communist China.[99] Yet there was no great enthusiasm in Moscow for the war, which the Soviets saw as a complication in a region in which traditionally they had little interest.[100]

At the same time, new research has indicated that the American victory in the missile crisis encouraged North Vietnam to increase its efforts in the South, as the outcome discredited Khrushchev's idea of peaceful coexistence with the West and boosted the allure of the Chinese national liberation doctrine. There was growing pressure in North Vietnam and an escalation of the insurgency in the South. Soon, on a visit to Hanoi, Yuri Andropov, a Soviet official responsible for liaison with communist parties in socialist countries, urged caution on the North Vietnamese government, pointing out that the missile crisis had been resolved peacefully. By the end of 1963, though, hardliners in Hanoi sanctioned all-out war in the South.[101] The missile crisis was not the only reason behind the communist escalation – there was in late 1963, for example, a desire to take advantage of the overthrow of South Vietnam's President Ngo Dinh Diem. However, the outcome of the crisis played a part. In the spring and summer of 1965 President Johnson began the bombing of North Vietnam and sent US combat troops to fight in the South, thus Americanising the war. By 1968, there were some 500,000 US military personnel in Vietnam, with no victory in sight. The last US troops were withdrawn in 1973, after nearly 60,000 US deaths, untold Vietnamese casualties and incalculable damage to the landscape and ecology. The communists seized the entire Vietnamese peninsula two years later.[102]

According to Clark Clifford, Secretary of Defense 1968–9, the advocates of the expanded US commitment in Vietnam in the 1960s were 'deeply influenced by the lessons of the Cuban Missile Crisis'. They thought that concepts like 'flexible response' and 'controlled escalation' had helped Kennedy prevail over Khrushchev.[103] The concept, which was also known as 'graduated response', developed out of the sense in the nuclear field that 'massive retaliation' was so destructive that it was unusable. According to its advocates, graduated response was used successfully as a means of deterrence during the Berlin crisis, and above all during the missile crisis. Roger Hilsman suggested that during the missile crisis Kennedy saw the quarantine as the first step 'up the ladder of coercion'.[104] Walt Rostow, who became Johnson's National Security Adviser in 1966 and was the chief architect of the bombing campaign in Vietnam, concluded from the Soviet climb-down in October 1962 that 'the communists do not escalate in response to our actions'.[105] American power, it was assumed, could surmount any challenge, whatever the circumstances or wherever the location. However, State Department analyst Paul Kattenburg suggested that 'the refined sophistication of graduated pressure or escalation seemed to elude' the communist leaders in Vietnam 'completely'.[106] Contrary to what Rostow and others might have believed, the American approach did not move the communists to stand down. Graduated response may even have benefited them by providing time to adjust to increasing military pressure.

Ideas about flexible response may have influenced *how* the United States expanded its role in Vietnam, but it did not influence *whether* it did so. Kennedy had not concluded from the missile crisis that the United States was infallible in all theatres, and he resisted pressure to engage American soldiers directly in the fighting. Direct US combat involvement in Vietnam took place three years after the missile confrontation, and even the most unreflective 'hawk' would have recognised that Vietnam in 1965 was a different proposition to Cuba in 1962 – not least because the Hanoi regime did not have to contemplate the threat of nuclear war, as had the Soviet government in October 1962. It has been suggested that President Johnson, not knowing of the secret deal that ended the missile crisis, had concluded that toughness was the key to foreign policy success, making him readier to wage war in Vietnam.[107] However, he undertook a direct military role in Vietnam only with the utmost reluctance, after having taken advice from a wide range of sources both inside and outside the administration. Some of the counsel he received used the example of the missile crisis to *oppose* escalation in Vietnam. Senator Richard Russell (Democrat, Georgia) complained that

> we have undoubtedly selected the worst possible place to fight ... I earnestly and vigorously fought to kick communism, Castro, and the missiles out of Cuba instead of temporizing with the Russians. This was ninety miles from home, whereas Vietnam is about 9,000.[108]

## The Cuban Missile Crisis: Round Three

The vagueness of the terms that had ended the missile confrontation in October 1962 led to 'round three' of the dispute over Soviet armaments in Cuba. Although Soviet and Cuban accounts are few, the outlines of what went on are clear from US records. In November 1969, the Soviet Minister of Defense, Stepan Grechko, paid a well-publicised visit to the island, accompanied by the

Deputy Chief of the Soviet Naval Staff. In the summer of 1970, American intelligence detected increased Soviet naval activity in and around Cuba. Cuba was a touchy issue for President Nixon, as it had featured in the television debates with Kennedy during the 1960 presidential election campaign, and in 1962, when he was running (unsuccessfully) for the governorship of California, he thought that the administration had exploited the presence of Soviet missiles in Cuba for domestic political gain. Now, in 1970, the approaching mid-term elections reactivated Nixon's sensitivities.[109]

In September, U-2 flights revealed the construction in Cienfuegos Bay in Cuba of what appeared to be a submarine base. National Security Adviser Henry Kissinger wondered why the Soviets had embarked 'on a venture that they should know has a low flashpoint in terms of American sensitivity'.[110] He believed that after the confrontation of 1962 there had been 'an implicit understanding that we would agree to give assurances against an invasion of Cuba if the Soviet Union would remove its offensive missiles from Cuba under UN observation and would undertake, with suitable safeguards, to halt the re-introduction of such weapons systems into Cuba'. He pointed out that the negotiations between John McCloy, Adlai Stevenson and Vasili Kuznetzov in the UN in November 1962 were intended 'to work out a satisfactory means of formalizing the Kennedy–Khrushchev "understanding"', but the talks 'eventually just fizzled out' over the failure to agree on a verification system.[111] U. Alexis Johnson of the State Department commented that

> there was never an 'agreement' in 1962. There was an exchange of letters some of which crossed each other. In essence, the discussion then concentrated on UN inspection. The only thing we focussed on were land-based missiles and IL 28's. There was really nothing else, and no 'agreement' in the conventional sense.[112]

The Joint Chiefs of Staff felt that it was essential to challenge the presence of the submarine base, believing that its military impact amounted to 'one-third of the size of the Soviet Ballistic Missile Submarine . . . force'. The Chiefs argued that acquiescence might be taken for 'weakness', with the Soviets being 'encouraged to develop other bases in this Hemisphere'.[113]

The Soviet development in Cuba came to public attention, with Senate Majority Leader Mike Mansfield (Democrat, Montana) stating that the presence of the base 'raises the most serious question in light of President John F. Kennedy's statement after the . . . Cuban Missile Crisis that offensive weapons must be kept out of the Western Hemisphere to assure "peace in the Caribbean"'. However, unlike the episode in October 1962, the incipient submarine base 'crisis' was contained rapidly by immediate dialogue. Kissinger warned Ambassador Dobrynin that the United States would 'view the establishment of a strategic base in the Caribbean with the utmost seriousness . . . whatever the phraseology of the 1962 understanding, its intent could not have been to replace land-based with sea-based missiles'. Alexander Haig of the NSC weighed in on another occasion, telling Dobrynin bluntly that the Soviets should 'either remove the base at Cienfuegos or the United States would do it for them'. There appears to have been little argument. The Soviet government affirmed that it did not wish to contradict the understanding of 1962, and the construction ended. The settlement of that year had been clarified and refined, and the third round of the confrontation over Soviet offensive armaments in Cuba was over.[114]

Why did the Nixon White House act immediately to prevent the potential 'crisis' over the Soviet base in Cuba from developing into a military confrontation? After all, the instinct of the Kennedy administration in October 1962 had been to choose a public stand-off rather than private diplomacy. For one, President Nixon and his advisers were preoccupied by two other foreign crises: the invasion of Jordan by Soviet-backed Syria, and the election in Chile of the left-wing Salvador Allende (clearly, the capacity of top US policymakers to deal with more than one challenge at once had its limits). Perhaps more significantly, the experience of 1962 showed that the Soviets would not resist American power in the Western hemisphere, and that dialogue was immensely preferable to military mobilisation and sabre-rattling. Both sides had learned the merit of eyeball-to-eyeball talking rather than eyeball-to-eyeball armed confrontation. Soviet motives for constructing the base are not apparent. Moscow may simply have been probing American power, seeking in particular to strengthen the Soviet position in the SALT process, but withdrew to avoid another dangerous confrontation and derailing SALT. Finally, as was the case in October 1962, Castro had no place in the negotiations, showing the predominance of the superpowers in a matter of importance to all three countries.[115]

## Notes

1. David Coleman, *The Fourteenth Day: JFK and the Aftermath of the Cuban Missile Crisis* (New York: Norton, 2012), p. 129.
2. Editorial note, *Foreign Relations of the United States (FRUS) 1961–1963 V Soviet Union* (Washington, DC: USGPO, 1998), document 314, <https://history.state.gov/historicaldocuments/frus1961-63v05/d314> (last accessed 25 July 2015).
3. Note 2, *FRUS 1961–1963 XII American Republics* (1996), document 167, <https://history.state.gov/historicaldocuments/frus1961-63v12/d167> (last accessed 25 July 2015).
4. Chase to Bundy, 6 June 1963, *FRUS 1961–1963 XII*, document 168, <https://history.state.gov/historicaldocuments/frus1961-63v12/d168> (last accessed 25 July 2015).
5. Conversation between Rusk and Dobrynin, 18 November 1964, *FRUS 1964–1968 XIV Soviet Union* (2001), document 72, <https://history.state.gov/historicaldocuments/frus1964-68v14/d72> (last accessed 25 July 2015).
6. Coleman, *The Fourteenth Day*, pp. 192–207; Michael B. Petersen, 'A Trial by Fire: Military Intelligence Reform and the Cuban Missile Crisis', in David Gioe, Len Scott and Christopher Andrew (eds), *An International History of the Cuban Missile Crisis: A 50-Year Retrospective* (London: Routledge, 2014), p. 127. The briefing is available at <http://jfk14thday.com/special-cuba-briefing-department-of-defense/> (last accessed 25 July 2015).
7. CIA memorandum, 'Deployment and Withdrawal of Soviet Missiles and other Significant Weapons in Cuba', 29 November 1962, in Mary S. McAuliffe (ed.), *CIA Documents on the Cuban Missile Crisis* (Washington, DC: CIA History Staff, 1992), pp. 357–60.
8. John F. Kennedy Presidential Library, Remarks at the Rudolph

Wilde Platz, Berlin <http://www.jfklibrary.org/Asset-Viewer/oEX 2uqSQGEGIdTYgd_JL_Q.aspx> (last accessed 25 July 2015).

9. Kennedy to Adenauer, 6 August 1963, *FRUS 1961–1963 XV Berlin Crisis, November 1962–January 1963* (1994), document 205, <https://history.state.gov/historicaldocuments/frus1961-63v 15/d205> (last accessed 25 July 2015).

10. President Kennedy's undelivered remarks at the Trade Mart in Dallas, 22 November 1963, in Stephen Rabe, *John F. Kennedy: World Leader* (Washington, DC: Potomac Books, 2010), pp. 215–18.

11. Embassy in the Soviet Union to the Department of State, 16 March 1963, *FRUS 1961–1963 V*, document 304, <https://history.state.gov/historicaldocuments/frus1961-63v05/d304> (last accessed 25 July 2015).

12. Moscow to State Department, 11 March 1963, *FRUS 1961–1963 X-XI-XII, Microfiche Supplement, American Republics; Cuba 1961–1962; Cuban Missile Crisis and Aftermath* (Washington, DC: USGPO), document 630, <http://history.state.gov/historical documents/frus1961-63v10-12mSupp/d630> (last accessed 25 July 2015).

13. Editorial note, *FRUS 1961–1963 V*, document 314, <https:// history.state.gov/historicaldocuments/frus1961-63v05/d314> (last accessed 25 July 2015).

14. Kennedy–Adenauer conversation, 14 November 1962, *FRUS 1961–1963 XV*, document 153, <https://history.state.gov/histori caldocuments/frus1961-63v15/d153> (last accessed 25 July 2015).

15. Khrushchev to Kennedy, 26 October 1962, *FRUS 1961–1963 XI Cuban Missile Crisis and Aftermath* (1996), document 84, <https://history.state.gov/historicaldocuments/frus1961-63v11/ d84> (last accessed 25 July 2015).

16. Kennedy's remarks at the Pageant of Peace ceremonies, 17 December 1962, The American Presidency Project, <http://www. presidency.ucsb.edu/ws/?pid=9059> (last accessed 25 July 2015).

17. Commencement address at the American University in Washington, 10 June 1963, *Public Papers of the Presidents of the United States: John F. Kennedy, January 1–November 22 1963* (Washington, DC: USGPO, 1964), pp. 459–64.

18. CIA memorandum, 18 March 1963, *FRUS 1961–1963 V*, docu-ment 305, <https://history.state.gov/historicaldocuments/frus1961-63v05/d305> (last accessed 25 July 2015).

19. Current Intelligence Review, 18 January 1963, *FRUS 1961–1963 V*, document 280, <https://history.state.gov/historicaldocuments/frus1961-63v05/d280> (last accessed 25 July 2015); Arthur M. Schlesinger, Jr., *A Thousand Days: John F. Kennedy in the White House* (New York: Houghton Mifflin, 1965), p. 760.
20. Schlesinger, *A Thousand Days*, p. 772.
21. McGhee to Kohler, 21 June 1961, *FRUS 1961–1963 V*, document 99, <https://history.state.gov/historicaldocuments/frus1961-63v05/d99> (last accessed 25 July 2015); Embassy Moscow to State Department, 24 January 1963, *FRUS 1961–1963 V*, document 283, <https://history.state.gov/historicaldocuments/frus1961-63v05/d283> (last accessed 25 July 2015).
22. Editorial note, *FRUS 1964–1968 XIV*, document 217, <https://history.state.gov/historicaldocuments/frus1964-68v14/d217> (last accessed 25 July 2015).
23. Susanna Schrafstetter and Stephen Twigge, *Avoiding Armageddon: Europe, the United States, and the Struggle for Nuclear Nonproliferation, 1945–1970* (Westport and London: Praeger, 2004), pp. 114–16.
24. Don Munton, 'Hits and Myths: The *Essence*, the Puzzles and the Missile Crisis', *International Relations*, 26: 3, September 2012, p. 315.
25. Khrushchev to Johnson, 24 November 1963, *FRUS 1961–1963 VI Kennedy–Khrushchev Exchanges* (1996), document 119, <https://history.state.gov/historicaldocuments/frus1961-63v06/d119> (last accessed 25 July 2015). For sensible accounts of the Kennedy assassination see Alice L. George, *The Assassination of John F. Kennedy: Political Trauma and American Memory* (New York and London: Routledge, 2013); William D. Rubinstein, *Shadow Pasts: History's Mysteries* (Harlow: Longman, 2008), pp. 13–41.
26. The Cuba Crisis: Its Course as Seen from Moscow, 7 November 1962, FO 371/162405, The National Archives, Kew, England (TNA).
27. Anatoly Dobrynin, *In Confidence: Moscow's Ambassador to America's Six Cold War Presidents, 1962–1986*, revised edn (Seattle: University of Washington Press, 2001), p. 93.
28. The Polyansky report on Khrushchev's mistakes in foreign policy, October 1964, *Cold War International History Project Bulletin*, 17/18, Fall 2012, p. 324, <http://www.wilsoncenter.org/publication/bulletin-no-17-18> (last accessed 25 July 2015).
29. CIA memorandum, 22 October 1964, *FRUS 1964–1968 XIV*,

document 62, <https://history.state.gov/historicaldocuments/frus 1964-68v14/d62> (last accessed 25 July 2015).

30. Foreign Office to Major Posts, 2 November 1962, FO 371/ 162398, TNA; Memorandum for the record, 7 May 1962, *FRUS 1961–1963 V*, document 190, <https://history.state.gov/historical-documents/frus1961-63v05/d190> (last accessed 25 July 2015); Norman Friedman, *The Fifty Year War: Conflict and Strategy in the Cold War* (London: Chatham, 2000), p. 374.

31. Dobrynin, *In Confidence*, p. 93.

32. State Department paper, 18 December 1967, *FRUS 1964–1968 XIV*, document 258, <https://history.state.gov/historicaldocu ments/frus1964-68v14/d258> (last accessed 25 July 2015).

33. See John Dumbrell, *President Lyndon Johnson and Soviet Communism* (Manchester: Manchester University Press, 2004), pp. 46–51, 77–80.

34. Editorial note, *FRUS 1964–1968 XI Arms Control and Disarmament* (1997), document 177, <https://history.state.gov/ historicaldocuments/frus1964-68v11/d177> (last accessed 25 July 2015).

35. See Schrafstetter and Twigge, *Avoiding Armageddon*, pp. 163–201.

36. Huizenga to Helms, 15 July 1968, *FRUS 1964–1968 XIV*, document 281, <https://history.state.gov/historicaldocuments/frus1964-68v14/d281> (last accessed 25 July 2015).

37. Note 2, *FRUS 1964–1968 XIV*, document 282, <https://his tory.state.gov/historicaldocuments/frus1964-68v14/d282> (last accessed 25 July 2015).

38. NSC Meeting, 19 November 1970, *FRUS 1969–1976 XXXIX European Security* (2008), document 37, <https://history.state. gov/historicaldocuments/frus1969-76v39/d37> (last accessed 25 July 2015).

39. Laurence Chang and Peter Kornbluh (eds), with foreword by Robert S. McNamara, *The Cuban Missile Crisis, 1962: A National Security Archive Documents Reader* (New York: The New Press, 1992), p. 344.

40. James G. Blight, Bruce J. Allyn and David A. Welch (eds), with foreword by Jorge I. Dominguez, *Cuba on the Brink: Castro, the Missile Crisis, and the Soviet Collapse* (New York: Pantheon, 1993), p. 214.

41. Ibid. p. 245.

42. Nicola Miller, 'The Real Gap in the Cuban Missile Crisis: The Post-Cold War Historiography and the Continued Omission of

Cuba', in Dale Carter and Robin Clifton (eds), *War and Cold War in American Foreign Policy, 1942–62* (Basingstoke: Palgrave, 2002), p. 229.

43. National Intelligence Estimate, 14 June 1963, *FRUS 1961–1963 XI*, document 347, <https://history.state.gov/historicaldocuments/frus1961-63v11/d347> (last accessed 25 July 2015).

44. Hal Brands, *Latin America's Cold War* (Cambridge and London: Harvard University Press, 2010), p. 52.

45. National Intelligence Estimate, 19 August 1964, *FRUS 1964–1968 XXXI South and Central America, Mexico* (2004), document 24, <https://history.state.gov/historicaldocuments/frus1964-68v31/d24> (last accessed 25 July 2015).

46. National Intelligence Estimate, 19 February 1964, *FRUS 1964–1968 XXXI*, document 522, <https://history.state.gov/historicaldocuments/frus1964-68v31/d522> (last accessed 25 July 2015).

47. James G. Blight and Philip Brenner, *Sad and Luminous Days: Cuba's Struggle with the Superpowers after the Missile Crisis* (Lanham, MD: Rowman and Littlefield, 2002), p. xxi.

48. Philip Brenner, '"A Mystery Wrapped in a Riddle and Kept in a Sphinx": New Evidence on Soviet Premier Alexei Kosygin's Trip to Cuba, June 1967, and the Turn in Relations between Cuba and the Soviet Bloc, 1967–68', *Cold War International History Project Bulletin*, 17/18, Fall 2012, pp. 792–4, <http://www.wilsoncenter.org/publication/bulletin-no-17-18> (last accessed 25 July 2015); Dumbrell, *President Lyndon Johnson and Soviet Communism*, p. 145.

49. Blight and Brenner, *Sad and Luminous Days*, pp. xxii, 31. See National Security Archive, Peter Kornbluh, 'The Death of Che Guevara: Declassified', http://www2.gwu.edu/~nsarchiv/NSAEBB/NSAEBB5/ (last accessed 25 July 2015).

50. National Intelligence Estimate, 2 September 1969, *FRUS 1969–1976 Volume E-10 Documents on American Republics, 1969–1972*, document 207, <https://history.state.gov/historicaldocuments/frus1969-76ve10/d207> (last accessed 25 July 2015).

51. Califano to Vance, 9 April 1963, in *FRUS 1961–1963 XI*, document 309, <https://history.state.gov/historicaldocuments/frus1961-63v11/d309> (last accessed 25 July 2015).

52. Memorandum for the Standing Group, covering letter of 10 May 1963, *FRUS 1961–1963 XI*, document 337, <https://history.state.gov/historicaldocuments/frus1961-63v11/d337> (last accessed 25 July 2015).

53. Memorandum for the record, 19 June 1963, *FRUS 1961–1963 XI*, document 348, <https://history.state.gov/historicaldocuments/frus 1961-63v11/d348> (last accessed 25 July 2015).

54. Chase to Bundy, 22 January 1963, in Mark J. White (ed.), *The Kennedys and Cuba: The Declassified Documentary History* (Chicago: Dee, 1999), pp. 306–7.

55. McCone to Kennedy, 10 April 1963, *FRUS 1961–1963 XI*, document 310, <https://history.state.gov/historicaldocuments/frus1961-63v11/d310> (last accessed 25 July 2015). On the prospective Cuban-American *détente*, see also Lars Schoultz, *That Infernal Little Cuban Republic: The United States and the Cuban Revolution* (Chapel Hill: University of North Carolina Press, 2009), p. 210; William M. LeoGrande and Peter Kornbluh, *Back Channel to Cuba: The Hidden History of Negotiations between Washington and Havana* (Chapel Hill: University of North Carolina Press, 2014), pp. 59–70; 'Kennedy Sought Dialogue with Cuba: Initiative with Castro Aborted by Assassination', National Security Archive, George Washington University, <http://www2.gwu.edu/~nsarchiv/NSAEBB/NSAEBB103/index.htm> (last accessed 25 July 2015); Helms to McCone, 5 June 1963, *FRUS 1961–1963 X-XI-XII*, document 685, <http://history.state.gov/historicaldocuments/frus1961-63v10-12mSupp/d685> (last accessed 25 July 2015).

56. Bundy to the NSC Standing Group, 21 April 1963, document 320, <https://history.state.gov/historicaldocuments/frus1961-63v11/d320>; Memorandum for the record, 24 June 1963, *FRUS 1961–1963 XI*, document 351, <https://history.state.gov/historicaldocuments/frus1961-63v11/d351> (documents last accessed 25 July 2015).

57. Shoultz, *That Infernal Republic*, pp. 209–10; Paper by the Bureau of Inter-American Affairs, 20 June 1963, *FRUS 1961–1963 XI*, document 349, <https://history.state.gov/historicaldocuments/frus 1961-63v11/d349> (last accessed 25 July 2015).

58. LeoGrande and Kornbluh, *Back Channel to Cuba*, pp. 64, 77.

59. Memorandum for the record, 12 November 1963, National Security Archive, <http://www2.gwu.edu/~nsarchiv/NSAEBB/NSA EBB103/index.htm> (last accessed 25 July 2015); Rabe, *John F. Kennedy*, p. 184; Note 6, *FRUS 1964–1968 XXXI*, document 3, <https://history.state.gov/historicaldocuments/frus1964-68v31/ch1> (last accessed 25 July 2015).

60. Memorandum of conversation, 26 November 1963, *FRUS*

*1961–1963* V, document 380, <https://history.state.gov/historical documents/frus1961-63v05/d380> (last accessed 25 July 2015).

61. Blight et al., *Cuba on the Brink*, p. 193.
62. Dumbrell, *Lyndon Johnson and Soviet Communism*, pp. 21–2, 137.
63. Memorandum for the record, 18 January 1964, *FRUS 1964–1968 XXXII Dominican Republic, Cuba; Haiti; Guyana* (2005), document 225, <https://history.state.gov/historicaldocuments/frus 1964-68v32/d225> (last accessed 25 July 2015).
64. Review of Current Programme of Covert Action against Cuba, undated, *FRUS 1964–1968 XXXII*, document 226, <https:// history.state.gov/historicaldocuments/frus1964-68v32/d226> (last accessed 25 July 2015).
65. Chang and Kornbluh (eds), *The Cuban Missile Crisis*, p. 394.
66. Review of Current Programme of Covert Action against Cuba, undated, *FRUS 1964–1968 XXXII*, document 226, <https:// history.state.gov/historicaldocuments/frus1964-68v32/d226> (last accessed 25 July 2015).
67. Editorial note, *FRUS 1964–1968 XXXII*, document 315, <https:// history.state.gov/historicaldocuments/frus1964-68v32/d315> (last accessed 25 July 2015).
68. Michael Beschloss (ed.), *Taking Charge: The Johnson White House Tapes, 1963–64* (New York: Simon and Schuster, 1997), p. 228.
69. Lyndon B. Johnson, *The Vantage Point: Perspectives of the Presidency, 1963–1969* (New York: Holt, Rinehart and Winston, 1971), p. 185.
70. Beschloss (ed.), *Taking Charge*, p. 228.
71. Verbal message from Castro to Johnson from Lisa Howard, 12 February 1964, National Security Archive, George Washington University, <http://www2.gwu.edu/~nsarchiv/NSAEBB/NSAEBB 103/> (last accessed 25 July 2015). For a full account of Howard's initiatives in 1963 and 1964 see LeoGrande and Kornbluh, *Back Channel to Cuba*, pp. 67–70, 81, 84–9, 93–6.
72. For US relations with Cuba from the Nixon administration onwards, see LeoGrande and Kornbluh, *Back Channel to Cuba*, pp. 119–484; Schoultz, *That Infernal Little Cuban Republic*, pp. 241–552.
73. NSC meeting, 28 July 1964, *FRUS 1964–1968 XXXI*, document 23, <https://history.state.gov/historicaldocuments/frus1964-68v31/d23> (last accessed 25 July 2015).

74. The administration's handling of the Cuban Crisis, 12 November 1962, CAB 21/5581, TNA.

75. Sean Greenwood, *Britain and the Cold War, 1945–91* (Basingstoke: Palgrave Macmillan, 2000), pp. 159–60. On Nassau, see also Ian Clark, *Nuclear Diplomacy and the Special Relationship: Britain's Deterrent and America, 1957–1962* (Oxford: Clarendon, 1994); Donette Murray, *Kennedy, Macmillan and Nuclear Weapons* (Basingstoke: Macmillan, 2000); Richard E. Neustadt, *Alliance Politics* (New York: Columbia University Press, 1970); Andrew J. Pierre, *Nuclear Politics: The British Experience with an Independent Deterrent, 1939–1970* (London: Oxford University Press, 1972).

76. Frederic Bozo, *Two Strategies for Europe: De Gaulle, the United States and the Atlantic Alliance* (Lanham, MD: Rowman and Littlefield, 2001), p. 88.

77. Embassy in France to Department of State, 4 January 1963, *FRUS 1961–1963 XIII Western Europe and Canada* (1994), document 263, <https://history.state.gov/historicaldocuments/frus1961-63v13/d263> (last accessed 25 July 2015).

78. For accounts of French foreign policy and its effects see Bozo, *Two Strategies*; James Ellison, *The United States, Britain and the Transatlantic Crisis Rising to the Gaullist Challenge, 1963–68* (Basingstoke: Palgrave, 2007); Garret Joseph Martin, *General de Gaulle's Cold War: Challenging American Hegemony 1963–1968* (New York: Berghahn Books, 2013); Christian Nuenlist, Anna Locher and Garret Martin (eds), *Globalizing de Gaulle: International Perspectives on French Foreign Policies, 1958 to 1969* (Lanham, MD: Rowman and Littlefield, 2010).

79. Frank Costigliola, 'The Pursuit of Atlantic Community: Nuclear Arms, Dollars and Berlin', in Thomas G. Paterson (ed.), *Kennedy's Quest for Victory: American Foreign Policy, 1961–1963* (New York and Oxford: Oxford University Press, 1989), p. 27.

80. Memorandum of conversation, 11 October 1968, *FRUS 1964–1968 XII*, document 85, <https://history.state.gov/historicaldocuments/frus1964-68v12/d85> (last accessed 25 July 2015).

81. Schlesinger, *A Thousand Days,* pp. 742–3.

82. Rostow to Rusk, 'The State of the World', 17 September 1963, *FRUS 1961–1963 VIII National Security Policy* (1996), document 142, <https://history.state.gov/historicaldocuments/frus1961-63v08/d142> (last accessed 25 July 2015).

83. See Effie G. H. Pedaliu, 'Transatlantic Relations at a Time When

"More Flags" Meant "No European Flags": the United States' War in South-East Asia and its European Allies, 1964–8', *International History Review*, 35: 3, August 2013, pp. 556–75.

84. The literature on the MLF includes Helga Haftendorn, *NATO and the Nuclear Revolution: A Crisis of Credibility, 1966–1967* (Oxford: Clarendon Press, 1996), pp. 110–45; Andrew Priest, 'The President, the "Theologians" and the Europeans: The Johnson Administration and NATO Nuclear Sharing', *International History Review*, 33: 2, June 2011, pp. 257–75; J. J. Widén and Jonathan Colman, 'Lyndon B. Johnson, Alec Douglas-Home, Europe and the NATO Multilateral Force, 1963–64', *Journal of Transatlantic Studies*, 5: 1, Autumn 2007, pp. 179–99.

85. Walt W. Rostow, *The Diffusion of Power: An Essay in Recent History* (New York: Macmillan, 1972), p. 394; Philip Nash, 'Bear any Burden? John F. Kennedy and Nuclear Weapons', in John Lewis Gaddis, Philip H. Gordon, Ernest R. May and Jonathan Rosenberg (eds), *Cold War Statesmen Confront the Bomb: Nuclear Diplomacy Since 1945* (Oxford: Oxford University Press, 1999), pp. 122–7.

86. Pedaliu, 'Transatlantic Relations', p. 566.

87. See Lawrence Freedman, *The Cold War: A Military History* (London: Cassel, 2001), pp. 82–6.

88. Telegram from the Brazilian Embassy in Moscow (da Cunha), 4:15 p.m., Monday, 5 November 1962, *Cold War International History Project Bulletin*, 5, Spring 1995, p. 263, <http://www.wilsoncenter.org/publication/bulletin-no-5-spring-1995> (last accessed 25 July 2015).

89. The Cuba Crisis: Its Course as seen from Moscow, 7 November 1962, FO 371/162405, TNA.

90. Raymond L. Garthoff, 'When and Why Romania Distanced Itself from the Warsaw Pact', *Cold War International History Project Bulletin*, 5, Spring 1995, p. 111, <http://www.wilsoncenter.org/publication/bulletin-no-5-spring-1995> (last accessed 25 July 2015); CIA memorandum, 18 February 1965, *FRUS 1964–1968 XVII Eastern Europe* (1996), document 10, <https://history.state.gov/historicaldocuments/frus1964-68v17/d10> (last accessed 25 July 2015).

91. Legation in Romania to State Department, 12 May 1964, *FRUS 1964–1968 XVII*, document 141, <https://history.state.gov/historicaldocuments/frus1964-68v17/d141> (last accessed 25 July 2015).

92. Csaba Békés and Melinda Kalmár, 'Hungary and the Cuban Missile Crisis', *Cold War International History Project Bulletin*, 17/18, Fall 2012, p. 413, <http://www.wilsoncenter.org/publica tion/bulletin-no-17-18> (last accessed 25 July 2015).

93. Lorenz M. Luthi, *The Sino-Soviet Split: Cold War in the Communist World* (Princeton, NJ: Princeton University Press, 2008), p. 227 [see also document 14, Appendix 4 in this volume for a Chinese perspective].

94. Documents provided by Shen Zhihua and Sergey Radchenko, translated by Zhang Qian and introduced by James G. Hershberg and Sergey Radchenko, 'Sino-Cuban Relations and the Cuban Missile Crisis, 1960–62: New Chinese Evidence', *Cold War International History Project Bulletin*, 17/18, Fall 2012, pp. 26–7, <http://www.wilsoncenter.org/publication/bulletin-no-17-18> (last accessed 25 July 2015).

95. Rostow, *Diffusion of Power*, pp. 262–3.

96. See Lorenz M. Luthi, *The Sino-Soviet Split: Cold War in the Communist World* (Princeton, NJ: Princeton University Press, 2008), pp. 340–4.

97. James F. Person, 'The Cuban Missile Crisis and the Origins of North Korea's Policy of Self-Reliance in National Defense', *Cold War International History Project Bulletin*, 17/18, Fall 2012, pp. 121–3, <http://www.wilsoncenter.org/publication/bulletin-no-17-18> (last accessed 25 July 2015).

98. Rostow to Rusk, 'The State of the World', 17 September 1963, *FRUS 1961–1963 VIII*, document 142, <https://history.state.gov/historicaldocuments/frus1961-63v08/d142> (last accessed 25 July 2015).

99. Report by the Deputy Director of the Vietnam Working Group (Heavner), 11 December 1962, *FRUS 1961–1963 II Vietnam 1962* (1990), document 328, <https://history.state.gov/historical documents/frus1961-63v02/d328> (last accessed 25 July 2015).

100. John Dumbrell, *Rethinking the Vietnam War* (Basingstoke: Palgrave Macmillan, 2012), pp. 52, 104–6.

101. Pierre Asselin, 'North Vietnam and the Cuban Missile Crisis', *Cold War International History Project Bulletin*, 17/18, Fall 2012, pp. 130–1, <http://www.wilsoncenter.org/publication/bulletin-no-17-18> (last accessed 25 July 2015).

102. Valuable general accounts of the Vietnam War include Mark Atwood Lawrence, *The Vietnam War: A Concise International History* (New York: Oxford University Press, 2010); George C.

Herring, *America's Longest War: The United States and Vietnam, 1950–1975*, 4th edn (New York: McGraw Hill, 2001); Robert D. Schulzinger, *A Time for War: The United States and Vietnam, 1941–1975* (New York: Oxford University Press, 1999).

103. Michael M. Dobbs, *One Minute to Midnight: Kennedy, Khrushchev and Castro on the Brink of Nuclear War* (New York: Knopf, 2008), pp. 346–7; Clark Clifford, *Counsel to the President: A Memoir* (New York: Random House, 1991), p. 411.

104. Roger Hilsman, *To Move a Nation: The Politics of Foreign Policy in the Administration of John F. Kennedy* (Garden City, NY: Doubleday, 1967).

105. David Milne, *America's Rasputin: Walt Rostow and the Vietnam War* (New York: Hill and Wang, 2008), p. 120.

106. Paul M. Kattenburg, *The Vietnam Trauma in American Foreign Policy, 1945–1975* (New Brunswick: Transaction Books, 1980), pp. 123–5.

107. Sheldon M. Stern, *The Cuban Missile Crisis in American Memory: Myths versus Reality* (Stanford, CA: Stanford University Press, 2012), pp. 148–9.

108. David M. Barrett, *Uncertain Warriors: Lyndon Johnson and his Vietnam Advisers* (Lawrence: University Press of Kansas Press, 1993), p. 36.

109. Henry A. Kissinger, *The White House Years* (London: Weidenfeld and Nicolson and Michael Joseph, 1979), pp. 633–4, 636.

110. Kissinger memorandum, 22 September 1970, *FRUS 1969–1976 XII Soviet Union, January 1969–October 1970* (2006), document 213, <https://history.state.gov/historicaldocuments/frus1969-76v12/d213> (last accessed 25 July 2015).

111. Kissinger to President Nixon, undated, *FRUS 1969–1976 XII*, document 194, <https://history.state.gov/historicaldocuments/frus1969-76v12/d194> (last accessed 25 July 2015) [document 16, Appendix 4 in this volume].

112. Senior Review Group Meeting, 19 September 1970, *FRUS 1969–1976 XII*, document 208, <https://history.state.gov/historicaldocuments/frus1969-76v12/d208> (last accessed 25 July 2015).

113. JCS paper, undated, document 211, <https://history.state.gov/historicaldocuments/frus1969-76v12/d211>; Kissinger to Nixon, 22 September 1970, document 212, *FRUS 1969–1976 XII*, <https://history.state.gov/historicaldocuments/frus1969-76v12/d212> (both documents last accessed 25 July 2015).

114. Kissinger, *The White House Years*, pp. 642–8; Raymond L.

Garthoff, *Détente and Confrontation: American–Soviet Relations from Nixon to Reagan* (Washington, DC: Brookings, 1994), pp. 88–90, 92; Schoultz, *That Infernal Little Cuban Republic*, p. 253. In 1978 and 1979 there were US alarms over the presence in Cuba of Soviet aircraft and troops respectively, but these had had no place in the 1962 settlement – although the matter reflected a long-standing concern about Soviet armaments in Cuba. See Raymond L. Garthoff, 'American Reaction to Soviet Aircraft in Cuba, 1962 and 1978', *Political Science Quarterly*, 95: 3, Autumn 1980, pp. 427–39.

115. See Dennis A. Crall and Thomas M. Martin, 'Cool Hand Luke: Lessons from the Quiet Diplomacy of the Cienfuegos Non-crisis', *Foreign Policy Analysis*, 9: 2, April 2013, pp. 189–201; Raymond L. Garthoff, 'Handling the Cienfuegos Crisis', *International Security*, 8: 1, Summer 1983, pp. 46–86; Patrick J. Haney, 'Soccer Fields and Submarines in Cuba: The Politics of Problem Definition', *Naval War College Review*, 50: 4, Autumn 1997, pp. 67–84; Asaf Siniver, 'The Nixon Administration and the Cienfuegos Crisis of 1970: Crisis-management of a Non-crisis?', *Review of International Studies*, 34: 1, January 2008, pp. 69–88.

# Conclusion

The anti-Americanism of Fidel Castro after 1959 always meant that Cuba and the United States would have been uneasy hemispheric bedfellows, but major difficulties in Cuban–American relations were not inevitable. American hostility, inspired by the left-wing complexion of the regime in Havana, was counterproductive, radicalising Castro and creating an opening for the Soviet Union. Against the background of Cold War rivalry, Nikita Khrushchev and his colleagues relished the opportunity to secure an ally so close to the United States in a region that had largely escaped Soviet influence.

US hostility towards Cuba, shown by the ill-starred Bay of Pigs invasion in 1961 and by sabre-rattling in the Caribbean the following year, gave rise to a reasonable – although not necessarily accurate – Cuban and Soviet expectation that another invasion was on the horizon, this time involving US troops. Khrushchev's chief motives for stationing nuclear missiles in Cuba were to defend the country while enhancing the Soviet Union's position in the nuclear arms race. We can assume that both goals counted because had the former been the only concern then Khrushchev might have relied on a well-publicised, substantial build-up of conventional armaments to deter an attack; long-range nuclear weapons were complementary but not vital to that objective. Stationing nuclear missiles outside Soviet territory was not entirely new, as for a period in 1959 the Soviet Union had placed such weapons in the German Democratic Republic. In American eyes, though, this was not as provocative as placing nuclear weapons in Cuba. Yet this act was entirely consistent with international law – the Soviet Union did not force the weapons on the Cubans, just as the United States had not used brute force to turn Italy, Turkey and Britain into nuclear missile bases. Moreover, the deception and denial shrouding the missile emplacements were nothing new in international politics, or indeed in US foreign policy.

The performance of American intelligence in response to the Soviet conventional and nuclear build-up in Cuba in the summer and autumn of 1962 was mixed. The discovery of the nuclear missile bases came as a shock given the ingrained perception that placing nuclear missiles in Cuba was at odds with the apparently low Soviet propensity for provocation and risk. There was also the gross underestimation of Soviet troop numbers in Cuba. However, the missiles were detected prior to their becoming operational, and there was an accurate supposition that Soviet forces in Cuba were armed with tactical nuclear weapons. Later, US intelligence was indispensable in helping to verify the removal of the Soviet missiles, although the removal of the warheads – given their modest size – had to be taken on trust.

Although the presence of the weapons in Cuba represented a significant shift in the nuclear balance of power, it was the political impact of the move that concerned President Kennedy and his ExComm colleagues the most. They felt it essential to eliminate the missiles because their continued presence would damage the administration's credibility among allies and foes alike, and in US domestic politics. American policymakers emphasised the Soviet move as an act of aggression and failed to appreciate that just as the United States had placed missiles abroad for defensive reasons, so could the Soviets. Kennedy and his advisers dismissed the idea that Soviet missiles in Cuba were simply the counterpart of US missiles in Turkey, in large part because of the secrecy and the deception around the stationing of Soviet missiles. A public agreement between the Soviet Union and Cuba about the missiles would have made the US position much weaker. Although in some ways comparable to American missiles in Turkey, the presence of Soviet missiles in Cuba – which had been under US domination until 1959 – was much more confrontational, given the implications for US politics and international relations. The Jupiters did not have a corresponding significance in the Soviet sphere, beyond the dismay of the

Soviet leadership about having US weapons of mass destruction located close to the border.

Understanding of what went on during the public face-off over the missiles – 22 to 28 October – is bedevilled by fables and 'spin', including the idea of an 'eyeball-to-eyeball' confrontation between Soviet and American vessels over the blockade line on 24 October, and by the administration's supposed use of the 'Trollope Ploy' to respond to Khrushchev's communications of 26 and 27 October. The fables stemmed from simple misunderstanding of what went on, along with the Kennedy administration's wish to enhance its standing. During the ExComm deliberations President Kennedy once appeared to have forgotten that the United States had missiles in Turkey, but generally he responded to the Soviet challenge in a calm and thoughtful manner. ExComm helped him to explore the options, but he abandoned the full ExComm group in the evening of 27 October in favour of a more select band of advisers. This was a clear expression of presidential leadership, given the general disinclination to sacrifice the Jupiter missiles in Turkey as a way out of the crisis. It was Khrushchev who appeared the most anxious as the week went on, but he too retained his composure.

Although Robert F. Kennedy had been one of the aggressive voices in ExComm, his backchannel discussion with Ambassador Anatoly Dobrynin during the evening of 28 October was of great importance to the resolution of the crisis. The use of the backchannel to strike a deal had a precedent with the resolution of the Checkpoint Charlie confrontation of 1961 exactly a year earlier. Both in October 1961 and October 1962 the backchannel helped to create what has been described as 'an atmosphere of mutual personal predictability' that facilitated crisis resolution.[1] The deal involved the Soviet removal of the missiles from Cuba, in return for a US pledge that there would be no invasion of the island, and a secret assurance that the Jupiters would be removed from Turkey within six months. In a limited sense, both the United States and the Soviet Union conceded more than they needed: evidence suggests that the US government could have avoided sacrificing the missiles in Turkey (they were outdated but their removal raised sensitive political issues), while the Soviet Union could have obtained a public deal over those missiles. This would have bolstered Khrushchev's claims of victory, complementing the non-invasion pledge. However, both leaders understood that matters could easily escalate out of control, so avoiding that outcome was the overriding priority. Neither leader wanted to push matters any further.

There is some ambiguity about who – to use the 'eyeball-to-eyeball' analogy – blinked first during the confrontation. US records indicate that Kennedy had at the beginning of the crisis raised the issue of sacrificing the Jupiter missiles. Although Soviet deliberations and threat perceptions during the confrontation are hard to reconstruct in any detail, the prospect of an American attack on Cuba and how it might escalate was on Khrushchev's mind from the outset. However, Cuban intimations of an impending invasion were decisive in leading Khrushchev to remove the missiles. Both Kennedy and Khrushchev – deeply conscious of what a nuclear war would entail – demonstrated a great deal of caution, a sense that permitting the confrontation to escalate to the use of nuclear weapons was not even a remotely acceptable option. Throughout his time in office President Kennedy had grown increasingly conscious of the unspeakable devastation that nuclear war would bring, with him once ruing that '300 hundred million Americans, Russians and Europeans' could be 'wiped out by a nuclear exchange'. He wondered if the survivors could 'endure the fire, poison, chaos and nuclear catastrophe'.[2]

Although Khrushchev had argued publicly that in a nuclear war with the capitalist states the socialist system would triumph, he recalled that once he 'learned all the facts about nuclear power I couldn't sleep for several days. Then I became convinced that we could never possibly use these weapons, and when I realised that I was able to sleep again.'[3] Emphasising the nuclear-inspired caution of Kennedy and Khrushchev does not mean that in a world of only conventional weapons the two leaders would readily have permitted a confrontation over Cuba to escalate violently, but the nuclear dimension was especially sobering. Nuclear anxieties led both to the missile crisis and its peaceful resolution. As well as underscoring the importance of personality when national leaders find themselves in dangerous confrontations, Kennedy and Khrushchev's nuclear caution helped to ensure that at the top level the confrontation was *relatively* easy to navigate.[4] Both sought to avoid war, and the channels of communication were open. Yet in recent years it has become clear that even with that caution in place at the top level, matters could still have escalated out of control because of command and control problems. These were apparent with the U-2 drifting into the Soviet Union on 26–7 October, the unauthorised destruction by Soviet troops in Cuba of another U-2 on 27 October, and the presence of nuclear-armed Soviet submarines in the Caribbean throughout the confrontation. The crisis was therefore difficult to manage operationally.

This book has stressed that the Cuban Missile Crisis was an international event, affecting and involving numerous other countries beyond the United States, the Soviet Union and Cuba. The US government worked hard to legitimise its policies by winning the public support of allies – although telling them what had already been decided was not the same as consulting them. American policymakers believed absolutely in their cause and appeared to feel that bringing allied advice into the decision-making process would only complicate matters. Although some countries rued Washington's unilateralism, the merits of the American case and the importance of close relations with the US government were such that allies provided important diplomatic, military and intelligence support. Evidence is more limited about Soviet relations with client states during the crisis, but it is clear that there was no consultation. In an issue that demonstrates the international complexity of the missile crisis, several neutral and non-aligned countries acted as intermediaries to end the dispute. The chief motive was to end the danger but there was also a wish to win diplomatic credit on the international stage. The global ripples of the crisis are also evident in how the incipient confrontation over Cuba may have led communist China to intensify its border confrontation with India, rightly expecting that international attention would soon be focused on the Caribbean. The Sino-Indian border war was second only to the missile confrontation on the list of American foreign policy concerns.

The United States and the Soviet Union were the chief protagonists in the origins, course and aftermath of the missile crisis, but Cuba was no mere pawn. The Cuban role in the origins of the crisis demonstrated, as Harold Macmillan suggested, that 'small countries and highly localized acute problems can endanger the peace of the world by bringing the powerful countries into competition and conflict with each other'.[5] The government in Havana encouraged the Soviets to provide greater support and accepted the missiles of its own free volition, despite misgivings about Moscow's insistence on secrecy and concerns about how the United States would react. During the confrontation, Castro's intimations of an imminent US invasion and above all his advocacy of a preemptive nuclear strike on the United States on 26 October unnerved the Soviet leader even more. The fact that an agreement was reached over Castro's head confirmed that the superpowers were the prime movers, but his hostility to a ground inspection regime shaped the character of the settlement and meant that the Kennedy administration did not achieve all that it had wanted.

The period from 28 October until 20 November – that is, from the agreement to the ending of the naval blockade and military alerts – can be considered 'round two' of the confrontation over Soviet armaments in Cuba. The terms that ended the crisis lacked the precision that might be associated with international agreements made in more relaxed circumstances. The Soviets agreed to remove 'offensive weapons', but they meant only the nuclear missiles, whereas the American government demanded the withdrawal of bomber aircraft, too. The Soviets conceded on this matter out of goodwill rather than obligation. The Kennedy administration did not provide a firm pledge not to invade Cuba – while there was no pressing desire to launch an invasion, the US government kept its options open. Khrushchev did not complain publicly about the 'evasive non-invasion' status of the pledge because he had no way of enforcing a more binding commitment. Also, by highlighting the limits of the US commitment he would have little to show publicly for his missile adventure. Moreover, he did not want to open up another matter for which his Cuban ally could berate him.

The imprecision in the terms that settled the crisis – specifically, what did or did not constitute 'offensive' weapons – became apparent in 1970, with the brief confrontation over the Soviet construction of a submarine base in Cuba. This episode represented round three of the conflict over Soviet weapons in Cuba, although it was contained and dissolved rapidly through dialogue. The terms of the 1962 deal were clarified and refined. Despite the ambiguities, the settlement had held up – the Soviets made no attempt to reintroduce nuclear weapons (other than submarine-launched missiles). Nor did the Americans invade Cuba.[6]

In many ways, the perception of victory in the missile crisis was subjective. John F. Kennedy basked in the glory of eliminating the missiles without violence, but the lustre of his success would have been tarnished had the sacrifice of the Jupiter missiles in Turkey, whatever their technological limitations, been a matter of public record. As Congressional critics and anti-Castro exiles pointed out, Castro stayed in power and Cuba remained a Soviet military base. The messiness of the settlement belied the impression of a clean-cut victory for the United States. Khrushchev obtained his putative non-invasion pledge, fulfilling his objective of ensuring Cuban security, and he gained a confidential agreement for the removal of the Jupiter missiles from Turkey. This was a gesture that he appreciated, given his need for face-saving concessions after his climb-down, although the Kennedy administration's insistence on secrecy muted the political value of the concession. There had never been any intention to remove the weapons as part of a deal, even in return for a non-invasion pledge. Khrushchev ended up worse off after the crisis than he would have been had he not placed missiles in Cuba.[7] Castro saw the Soviet retreat as cowardice and betrayal, and the communist Chinese condemned Khrushchev's climb-down as a 'Munich'. Furthermore, the missile misadventure provided fuel for the domestic opponents who overthrew the Soviet leader in 1964. But given the possibility of nuclear war, the peaceful resolution of the missile crisis was nothing less than a victory for the entire world.

The agreement that ended the confrontation over Cuba showed that arms control measures were possible, and the post-missile-crisis sense of sobriety and relief contributed to the signing of the Limited Nuclear Test Ban Treaty in 1963. Although Kennedy and Khrushchev showed some commitment to *détente*, neither was a zealot, with both having to accommodate conservative forces at

**233**

home and abroad. In fact, the missile crisis provided a reason for Kennedy *not* to pursue a more cordial relationship with Moscow, given how it showed that the Soviets were capable of opportunism and deceit; *actual* Soviet policies might contradict the *avowed* policies.

US policy towards Cuba remained almost as hostile as it had been before the confrontation. Although President Kennedy was not completely closed to Castro's peace overtures, he was deeply wary, given the sensitivity of the issue in US domestic politics and foreign policy. At the same time, there were Cuban–Soviet differences over matters such as the promotion of revolution, and increasingly there was a general sense in Moscow that Cuba was an expensive and awkward ally.

The Americans engaged in deception and dissimulation about the reason for removing the Jupiters from Turkey, conveying the impression that the step was part of a general modernisation of NATO forces. The withdrawal of the weapons did fulfil this goal, but the initiative stemmed mainly from what had been agreed secretly with Khrushchev. Although there had been intimations from some sources within the Turkish government that the removal of the Jupiter missiles would be acceptable, the issue was a thorny one given allied sensitivities. The lack of consultation both during the missile crisis and about the removal of the Jupiter missiles, the chief reason for which was widely suspected,[8] contributed to a general weakening of NATO after the missile crisis. So too did a perception of more restrained Soviet policies after the Berlin and Cuba confrontations. President de Gaulle was already pushing for greater independence from the United States, but the lack of consultation during the missile crisis bolstered his quest for autonomy. This was evident in France's withdrawal from NATO's military command structure in 1966. Meanwhile, Soviet relations with fellow communist states such as China and Romania were problematic after 1962 in part due to the impact of the missile crisis. The Chinese condemned the Soviet capitulation in October 1962, while the Romanians rued how Moscow had nearly brought war. The weakening of Soviet ties with other communist countries confirmed how the crisis accelerated the emergence of a more polycentric and complicated world.

Henry Kissinger commented that after 1962, the Soviet Union, keen to avoid finding itself in a position of weakness once more, launched a 'determined, systematic, and long term program of expanding all categories of its military power – its missiles and bombers, its tanks and submarines and fighter planes – in techno-logical quality and global reach'.[9] The arms build-up was in fact already under way prior to the missile crisis, with the stationing of nuclear weapons in Cuba as part of the quest for an improved status in the nuclear arms race. Nonetheless, Soviet authorities pursued the expansion with particular conviction after October 1962. By the late 1960s the Soviet Union had achieved parity. This made the missile crisis, as Kissinger put it, a 'historic turning point' in the Cold War. While the Soviets were keen to avoid further confrontations with the United States, they sought to negotiate from strength in the environment of *détente*.

From 1965 the United States was preoccupied with a futile war in Vietnam. While there is no indication that any post-missile-crisis sense of self-confidence led the US government to boost its commitment in South-East Asia, there is evidence that North Vietnamese disdain for Khrushchev's policies of peaceful coexistence and his climb-down in the face of US pressure over the missiles in Cuba led them to step up their commitment to the insurgency in the South. Therefore the missile crisis ensured that the US government had more to contend with in South-East Asia than would otherwise have been the case.

Despite decades of exploration and analysis, there are distinct limits to knowledge of the Cuban Missile Crisis. Many dimensions of US and especially Soviet military preparations are poorly accounted for, in large part because of limited primary source records. Changing judgements in Moscow about the threat of a US attack on Cuba during the confrontation, and policymaking and perceptions in Cuba are underexplored for the same reason. Historians have barely begun to account for the contributions and concerns of countries beyond the United States, the Soviet Union and Cuba. The archives of third-party countries offer an especially promising chance to expand knowledge of the Cuban Missile Crisis, and to present it in its proper perspective as a truly global event.

## Notes

1. Vladislav M. Zubok and Hope M. Harrison, 'The Nuclear Education of Nikita Khrushchev', in John Lewis Gaddis, Philip H. Gordon, Ernest R. May and Jonathan Rosenberg (eds), *Cold War Statesmen Confront the Bomb: Nuclear Diplomacy Since 1945* (Oxford: Oxford University Press, 1999), p. 157.
2. Philip Nash, 'Bear any Burden? John F. Kennedy and Nuclear Weapons', in ibid. p. 125.
3. Zubok and Harrison, 'The Nuclear Education of Nikita Khrushchev', pp. 146–7.
4. Lawrence Freedman, *The Cold War: A Military History* (London: Cassel, 2001), pp. 175–6.
5. Conversation between Kennedy and Macmillan, 29 June 1963, *FRUS 1961–1963 VII Arms Control and Disarmament* (1995), document 304, <https://history.state.gov/historicaldocuments/frus1961-63v07/d304> (last accessed 25 July 2015).
6. Kissinger to President Nixon, undated, *FRUS 1969–1976 XII*, document 194, <https://history.state.gov/historicaldocuments/frus1969-76v12/d194> (last accessed 25 July 2015).
7. R. Harrison Wagner, 'Bargaining in the Cuban Missile Crisis', in Peter C. Ordeshook (ed.), *Models of Strategic Choice in Politics* (Ann Arbor: University of Michigan Press, 1989), pp. 184–5, cited in Frank C. Zagare, 'A Game-Theoretic History of the Cuban Missile Crisis', *Economies*, 2: 1, January 2014, p. 38.
8. Effie G. H. Pedaliu, 'Transatlantic Relations at a Time When "More Flags" Meant "No European Flags": the United States' War in South-East Asia and its European Allies, 1964–8', *International History Review*, 35: 3, August 2013, p. 560.
9. Henry A. Kissinger, *The White House Years* (London: Weidenfeld and Nicolson and Michael Joseph, 1979), p. 197.

# Appendix 1: List of Persons

| | |
|---|---|
| Acheson, Dean | US Secretary of State, 1949–53, and consultant to the Kennedy and Johnson administrations. |
| Adenauer, Konrad | Chancellor of the Federal Republic of Germany. |
| Adzhubei, Alexei | Khrushchev's son-in-law and editor of *Izvestiya*. |
| Alekseev, Alexander | Soviet Ambassador to Cuba from August 1962. |
| Anderson, Admiral George W. | US Chief of Naval Operations. |
| Anderson, Major Rudolf | US U-2 pilot whose mission on 15 October 1962 discovered further Soviet nuclear missiles in Cuba, and who was shot down and killed over the island on 28 October. |
| Ball, George W. | US Under Secretary of State. |
| Bissell, Richard M. | CIA Deputy Director for Planning, 1959–62, in charge of covert actions against Cuba. |
| Bundy, McGeorge | US National Security Adviser. See Appendix 3. |
| Castro, Fidel | Prime Minister and Commander-in-Chief of the Revolutionary Armed Forces of Cuba. See Appendix 3. |
| Castro, Raul | Minister of the Revolutionary Armed Forces of Cuba. |

| | |
|---|---|
| Clifford, Clark | US Secretary of Defense, 1968–9. |
| Cordier, Andrew | Former senior UN official. |
| De Gaulle, General Charles | President of France. |
| Dean, Patrick | British Permanent Representative to the United Nations. |
| Dillon, C. Douglas | US Secretary of the Treasury. |
| Dobrynin, Anatoly | Soviet Ambassador to the United States. See Appendix 3. |
| Dorticós, Osvaldo | President of Cuba. |
| Dulles, Allen W. | CIA Director until November 1961. |
| Dulles, John Foster | US Secretary of State, 1953–9. |
| Eisenhower, Dwight D. | US President until January 1961. |
| Feklisov, Alexander S. | KGB official at the Soviet Embassy in Washington; also known as Alexander S. Fomin. |
| Fomin, Alexander S. | See Feklisov, Alexander S. |
| Fulbright, J. William | Democratic senator for Arkansas, and Chairman of the Senate Foreign Relations Committee. |
| Gilpatric, Roswell S. | US Deputy Secretary of Defense. |
| Goodwin, Richard N. | Assistant to the Special Counsel to the President of the United States and President of the Interagency Task Force on Cuba until November 1961; then Deputy Assistant Secretary of State for Inter-American Affairs. |
| Gribkov, General Anatoly I. | Official of the Main Directorate of Operations of the Soviet Central General Staff and representative of the Soviet Ministry of Defence within Soviet forces in Cuba in October 1962. |
| Gromyko, Andrei A. | Soviet Foreign Minister. |
| Guevara, Commander Ernesto Che | Cuban Minister of the Interior, 1961–5. See Appendix 3. |

| | |
|---|---|
| Harriman, Averell | US Secretary of State for Far Eastern Affairs. |
| Hilsman, Roger, Jr. | Director of the US State Department Bureau of Intelligence and Research. |
| Johnson, Lyndon B. | US Vice-President, 1961–3; President, 1963–9. |
| Johnson, U. Alexis | US Deputy Under Secretary of State for Political Affairs. |
| Keating, Kenneth | Republican senator for New York. |
| Kennedy, John F. | US President, 1961–3. See Appendix 3. |
| Kennedy, Robert F. | US Attorney General; brother of John F. Kennedy. See Appendix 3. |
| Kent, Sherman | Chairman, CIA Board of National Estimates. |
| Khrushchev, Nikita S. | Chairman of the Soviet Council of Ministers. See Appendix 3. |
| Kissinger, Henry | Consultant and academic; National Security Adviser to President Nixon. |
| Knox, William E. | President of Westinghouse International. |
| Kosygin, Alexei | First Deputy Premier of the Soviet Union until October 1964, thereafter Chairman of the Soviet Council of Ministers. |
| Kuznetsov, Vasili | Soviet Deputy Foreign Minister. |
| LeMay, General Curtis | Chief of Staff of the US Air Force. |
| Macmillan, Harold | British Prime Minister. See Appendix 3. |
| Malinovsky, Rodion | Marshal of the Soviet Union and Minister of Defence. |
| Marchant, Herbert | British Ambassador to Cuba. |
| Martin, Edwin M. | US Secretary of State for Inter-American Affairs. |
| McCloy, John J. | Presidential adviser and Chairman of the Coordinating Committee for Soviet–American Negotiations on Cuba in the United Nations. |

| | |
|---|---|
| McCone, John A. | Director of the CIA from November 1961. |
| McNamara, Robert S. | US Secretary of Defense, 1961–8. See Appendix 3. |
| Mikoyan, Anastas I. | First Deputy Chairman of the Soviet Council of Ministers. See Appendix 3. |
| Nitze, Paul H. | Assistant Secretary of Defense for International Security Affairs. |
| Nixon, Richard M. | US Vice-President, 1953–61; President, 1969–74. |
| Norstad, General Lauris | Supreme Allied Commander in Europe. |
| Ormsby-Gore, David (Lord Harlech) | British Ambassador to the United States. |
| Pliyev, General Issa Aleksandrovich | Head of Soviet forces in Cuba, 1962. |
| Roberts, Frank | British Ambassador to the Soviet Union. |
| Rostow, Walt | US State Department and National Security Council official. |
| Rusk, Dean | US Secretary of State, 1961–9. See Appendix 3. |
| Scali, John | ABC journalist. |
| Schlesinger, Arthur M., Jr. | Special Assistant to President Kennedy, 1961–3. |
| Sorensen, Theodore C. | Special Counsel to President Kennedy, 1961–3. |
| Stevenson, Adlai E. | US Permanent Representative to the United Nations. |
| Taylor, General Maxwell D. | President of the Cuba Study Group, April–June 1961; military representative to President Kennedy, June 1961–October 1962; Chairman of the Joint Chiefs of Staff in October 1962. |
| Thompson, Llewellyn | US Ambassador to the Soviet Union until July 1962; thereafter Ambassador-at-Large. |

| | |
|---|---|
| U Thant | Secretary-General of the United Nations. |
| Zorin, Valerian | Soviet Permanent Representative to the United Nations. |

# Appendix 2: Chronology

| | |
|---|---|
| 1823 | President James Monroe enunciates his 'doctrine' warning European powers against further territorial acquisitions or interventions in Latin America. |
| April 1898 | The United States declares war on Spain over Cuba, securing victory within four months. |
| December 1898 | Cuba is ceded to the United States under the Treaty of Paris. |
| 1902 | Cuba gains independence, although under the Platt Amendment to the Cuban constitution the United States retains the right of intervention in Cuban affairs. |
| 1904 | President Theodore Roosevelt's 'corollary' to the Monroe Doctrine claims the right to intervene in cases of disorder in Latin America. |
| 1928 | The Clark Memorandum (named after Under Secretary of State J. Reuben Clark) denies that the Roosevelt corollary to the Monroe Doctrine justified American intervention in Latin America, but stops short of denying the validity of intervention on other grounds. The Memorandum was published in 1930. |
| 1934 | The United States accepts Cuba's repeal of the Platt Amendment. |

| | |
|---|---|
| 1940–4 | First presidential administration of Fulgencio Batista in Cuba. |
| 1950–8 | Second presidential administration of Batista. |
| March 1958 | The withdrawal of American military aid to Batista. |
| 1 January 1959 | Fidel Castro assumes power in Cuba, after six years of insurgency. |
| 7 January 1959 | The United States recognises Castro's government. |
| 9 January 1959 | The Cuban government legalises the Communist Party. |
| 12 January 1959 | Execution of 'war criminals' begins in Cuba. |
| 24 January 1959 | Withdrawal of US military missions from Cuba. |
| 13 February 1959 | Castro becomes Prime Minister of Cuba. |
| 3 March 1959 | Law in Cuba confiscating property of persons who held office under Batista. |
| 11 March 1959 | Law in Cuba reducing rents by up to 50 per cent. |
| 15 April 1959 | Castro begins a visit to the United States, Canada and South America. |
| 17 May 1959 | Cuban Agrarian Reform Law forbids foreign land ownership and expropriates farm holdings over 1,000 acres. |
| 11 June 1959 | US ambassador expresses official concern about the method of compensation for expropriated American landowners. |
| 15 June 1959 | Cuban government rejects the United States' ambassador's note of 11 June. |
| 8 September 1959 | Che Guevara returns from a tour of Afro-Asian countries and Yugoslavia. |
| October 1959 | Turkish–American agreement for the stationing of US Jupiter nuclear missiles in Turkey. |
| 14 October 1959 | The US ambassador expresses further |

|  |  |
|---|---|
|  | concern about compensation for expropriated American properties. |
| 26 October 1959 | Mass meeting in Havana protesting against the 'bombardment' by US-based aircraft. Castro makes a violently anti-American speech. |
| 19 December 1959 | Two men executed in Cuba for counter-revolutionary activities, bringing the total number of executions to 553. |
| 31 December 1959 | Communist China agrees to buy 50,000 tons of Cuban sugar. |
| 4 February 1960 | Soviet Deputy Prime Minister Anastas Mikoyan visits Havana as part of a trade exhibition. |
| 13 February 1960 | Cuba and the Soviet Union sign a trade and economic aid agreement. |
| 29 February 1960 | Cuba signs a trade agreement with the German Democratic Republic. Throughout the year Cuba also signs trade agreements with Poland, Czechoslovakia, communist China, Hungary, Bulgaria and Romania. |
| March 1960 | President Dwight D. Eisenhower authorises an operation involving Cuban exiles to overthrow Castro's government. |
| May 1960 | Cuba and the Soviet Union establish diplomatic relations. |
| July 1960 | The United States suspends its quota of Cuban sugar purchases. |
| August 1960 | The United States imposes a trade embargo against Cuba. |
| September 1960 | The first large Eastern Bloc arms shipment reaches Cuba. Khrushchev and Castro meet and embrace at the United Nations in New York. |
| October 1960 | Cuba nationalises $1 billion of private American investments in Cuba. |

| | |
|---|---|
| 4 November 1960 | The CIA begins preparing a force of Cuban exiles that will launch an amphibious attack on Cuba. |
| 8 November 1960 | John F. Kennedy wins a narrow victory over Republican contender Richard M. Nixon in the presidential election. |
| 27 November 1960 | President-elect Kennedy is briefed about covert operations in Cuba. |
| December 1960 | Cuba aligns itself publicly with Soviet foreign and domestic policies. |
| 3 January 1961 | The United States ends diplomatic and consular relations with Cuba. |
| 4 January 1961 | Fidel Castro announces that an invasion is imminent, and orders full military mobilisation. |
| 20 January 1961 | Kennedy is inaugurated 35th US President. |
| March 1961 | Increase in the amount of sabotage activity in Cuba. |
| 13 March 1961 | Kennedy proposes the Alliance for Progress to raise living standards in Latin America. |
| March–April 1961 | Chinese industrial exhibition in Havana. |
| 15 April 1961 | Bombing of airfields at Havana, San Antonio de los Banos and Santiago de Cuba by US B-26 bombers piloted by Cuban exiles. Further air strikes are cancelled to conceal American involvement. |
| 15 April 1961 | Cuba complains to the UN Security Council of aggression by the US government. During a funeral oration for the victims of the air attack, Castro first proclaims the 'socialist' character of the Revolution. |
| 16 April 1961 | Beginning of wave of mass arrests, continuing over the next few days. |

| | |
|---|---|
| 17 April 1961 | Landing of US-backed Cuban émigrés at the Bay of Pigs, Playa Giron, Cuba. |
| 19 April 1961 | Khrushchev assures Kennedy that the Soviet Union has no intention of establishing bases in Cuba. |
| 20 April 1961 | Cuban armed forces have taken all the positions occupied by the invaders. |
| 5 May 1961 | President Kennedy tells the National Security Council that US policy will continue to seek the downfall of Fidel Castro. |
| 18 May 1961 | Castro offers to exchange for tractors the 1,113 prisoners taken at the Bay of Pigs. |
| 1 June 1961 | Soviet agreement to support the Cuban mining industry with a loan of 100 million pesos. |
| 3–4 June 1961 | Kennedy and Khrushchev meet in Vienna, where the latter delivers an ultimatum pressuring the Western powers to leave Berlin. |
| 24 July 1961 | Visit of Soviet astronaut Yuri Gagarin to Cuba. |
| 25 July 1961 | Kennedy addresses the nation about Berlin, and announces additional defence preparations and a civil defence programme. |
| 25 July 1961 | First public appearance of Cuba's Soviet-provided MIG fighters in fly-past. |
| 13 August 1961 | Soviet and East German forces erect a barbed wire barrier around West Berlin. Later, the barrier is reinforced to become the Berlin Wall. |
| 29 August 1961 | President Dorticós of Cuba leaves for the Belgrade Conference of neutral heads of state. Subsequently visits Prague, Moscow and Beijing, concluding agreements for the purchase of Cuban sugar. |

| | |
|---|---|
| 30 August 1961 | The Soviet Union ends a three-year moratorium by resuming atmospheric nuclear testing. |
| 11 October 1961 | Kennedy authorises the resumption of atmospheric nuclear testing by the United States. |
| 21 October 1961 | US Deputy Secretary of Defense Roswell Gilpatric states that the United States is in a position of overwhelming nuclear superiority over the Soviet Union, but also announces a substantial build-up of US nuclear and conventional forces. |
| 27–8 October 1961 | Soviet–American tank confrontation at 'Checkpoint Charlie' near the Berlin Wall. The confrontation is resolved through secret top-level communications between Washington and Moscow. |
| 3 November 1961 | East German trade exhibition in Cuba. |
| 30 November 1961 | Kennedy authorises Operation Mongoose to undermine Castro's government through a range of covert measures. |
| 1 December 1961 | Castro announces that 'I am, and shall always be, a Marxist–Leninist.' |
| 31 January 1962 | A conference of the OAS in Punta del Este, Uruguay, votes for the exclusion of Cuba from the organisation. |
| 3 February 1962 | US government ends all imports from Cuba; the main effect is to stop imports of Cuban tobacco. |
| 29 March 1962 | Beginning of trial in Cuba of Bay of Pigs prisoners. |
| April 1962 | Fifteen US Jupiter nuclear missiles in Turkey become operational. Khrushchev decides that Soviet nuclear missiles should be placed on Cuba. |
| 24 April 1962 | Fire (alleged sabotage) in the incomplete new National Bank building in Havana. |

| | |
|---|---|
| 25 April 1962 | Fire (alleged sabotage) in a chemicals depot near Havana. |
| May 1962 | Khrushchev offers to install nuclear-capable missiles in Cuba. Havana embassy KGB official Alexander Alekseev is appointed Soviet Ambassador to Cuba. |
| 8 May 1962 | The beginning of a series of US military exercises designed to test contingency planning for an invasion of Cuba. |
| 1 July 1962 | Cuban press begins publishing lists of alleged US violations of airspace. |
| 2–17 July 1962 | Raul Castro and an armed forces delegation visit Moscow to arrange the details of the missile deployments. |
| July–October 1962 | Over 100 Soviet shipments of troops and military equipment reach Cuba. |
| 26 August– 6 September 1962 | Cuban Minister for the Interior Che Guevara and key figure in Cuba's Revolutionary Armed Forces Emilio Aragonés Navarro visit Moscow to formalise the stationing of the nuclear missiles in Cuba. |
| 29 August 1962 | U-2 surveillance reveals evidence of Soviet SA-2 SAM sites in Cuba but uncovers no evidence of nuclear missile sites. |
| 31 August 1962 | Senator Kenneth Keating (Republican, New York) tells the Senate that the Soviets have placed nuclear missiles in Cuba. |
| 4 and 13 September 1962 | Kennedy warns publicly of grave consequences if Soviet nuclear missiles are found in Cuba. |
| 11 September 1962 | A TASS statement criticises US bases overseas and declares that the Soviet Union has no intention of introducing offensive weapons into Cuba. |
| 15 September 1962 | The first Soviet MRBMs reach Cuba on board the *Poltava*. |

| | |
|---|---|
| 19 September 1962 | The CIA's SNIE 85-3-62 notes that the Soviet Union could derive major strategic advantages from stationing nuclear missiles in Cuba but that the Soviet authorities were too cautious to take this step. |
| 14 October 1962 | A U-2 surveillance flight over Cuba photographs Soviet nuclear-capable missile installations. |
| 16 October 1962 | Upon receiving photographic evidence of Soviet nuclear-capable missile bases on Cuba, Kennedy establishes the Executive Committee (ExComm) of the National Security Council to help formulate a response. |
| 18 October 1962 | Soviet Foreign Minister Andrei Gromyko tells Kennedy that there are no offensive weapons in Cuba. |
| 20 October 1962 | Communist China launches its strongest attack to date in a border war with India. |
| 22 October 1962 | Kennedy announces publicly that the United States has discovered Soviet nuclear-capable missiles in Cuba, demands their withdrawal and imposes a naval 'quarantine' around the island. Briefings of ambassadors in Washington; of Prime Minister Harold Macmillan (Britain), Chancellor Konrad Adenauer (Federal Republic of Germany) and President Charles de Gaulle (France) in their respective capitals; and of the North Atlantic Council in Brussels. US forces move to DEFCON-3 – high nuclear alert. The beginning of Swiss efforts to mediate an end to the confrontation. Other countries that tried to mediate include Yugoslavia and Brazil. |

| | |
|---|---|
| 23 October 1962 | The OAS extends backing for the quarantine of Cuba. |
| 24 October 1962 | The US naval quarantine of Cuba takes force. Soviet ships en route to Cuba begin turning back. |
| | US forces move to DEFCON-2 – highest nuclear alert short of war. |
| 25 October 1962 | US representative to the UN Adlai Stevenson presents photographic evidence of the Soviet missile installations on Cuba during a Security Council debate with Soviet representative Valerian Zorin. |
| 26 October 1962 | Khrushchev offers to remove the missiles in exchange for a pledge not to invade Cuba. |
| | Castro urges Khrushchev to mount a nuclear first strike against the United States in response to an American invasion of Cuba. |
| 26–7 October 1962 | An American U-2 aircraft drifts over Soviet airspace above the Arctic circle. |
| 27 October 1962 | Khrushchev adds the removal of Jupiter missiles from Turkey to his demands. Soviet surface-to-air batteries shoot down a U-2 reconnaissance plane piloted by Major Rudolf Anderson over Cuba. Cuban anti-aircraft fire damages a low-level US reconnaissance plane. US warships confront a nuclear-armed Soviet Foxtrot-class submarine B-59 in the West Atlantic. Kennedy replies to Khrushchev's letter of 26 October, accepting its terms, while leaving scope for an agreement relating to 'other armaments', namely, US Jupiter missiles in Turkey. Robert F. Kennedy secretly meets Soviet |

|  |  |
|---|---|
|  | ambassador Anatoly Dobrynin and offers to remove Jupiter missiles from Turkey and Italy within 4–5 months. |
| 28 October 1962 | Khrushchev accepts US terms in a letter read out over Radio Moscow. Khrushchev writes a private letter to Kennedy setting out terms of agreement on Jupiter missiles. Robert F. Kennedy hands back Khrushchev's private letter to the President to Ambassador Dobrynin, on the grounds that the Jupiter deal must remain confidential. Castro announces that Kennedy's guarantee against an invasion of Cuba was worthless without the adoption of the 'five points' calling for an end to US economic and financial pressure; subversion against the Cuban government; pirate attacks from bases in the United States and Puerto Rico; violations of Cuban air and sea space; and demanding the evacuation of the Guantánamo naval base. |
| 30 October 1962 | U Thant arrives in Havana with advisers to encourage Castro to accept a ground inspection regime. |
| November– December 1962 | The Soviet Union removes its nuclear missiles and thousands of troops from Cuba, although 18,000 Soviet troops remain. |
| 1 November 1962 | Castro, in a speech describing his talks with U Thant, rejects ground inspection of Cuban territory, even under UN auspices. |
| 2 November 1962 | Mikoyan visits Cuba for three weeks to improve Soviet relations with Castro. |
| 4 November 1962 | The body of Major Rudolf Anderson, |

| | |
|---|---|
| | who was shot down over Cuba on 27 October, is sent back to the United States. |
| 8 November 1962 | The US government announces that the Soviet Union has dismantled its missile sites in Cuba. |
| 15 November 1962 | Castro addresses a letter to U Thant rejecting any idea of permitting ground inspection in Cuba and warning that any military aircraft violating Cuba's airspace will risk destruction. |
| 19 November 1962 | Castro sends a letter to U Thant stating that the IL-28 bombers are the property of the Soviet Union and that they are technologically out of date; but if the Soviet Union considers that their withdrawal will help solve the crisis, the Cuban government will not impede that decision. |
| 20 November 1962 | Kennedy lifts the naval quarantine of Cuba after Khrushchev agrees to remove IL-28 bombers from Cuba. He gives a qualified pledge not to invade Cuba. The United States and the Soviet Union end their military alerts. Communist China announces victory and unilaterally ends its war with India. |
| 25 November 1962 | Mikoyan makes a farewell speech to the Cuban people on television, describing the Cuban Revolution as 'the motivating factor in the revolutionary movements in Latin America'. Dorticós and Castro issue 'Cuba's reply to Kennedy', demanding that the UN verify sites in the United States and elsewhere where saboteurs are being trained against Cuba. |
| 24 December 1962 | 1,113 prisoners captured during the Bay of Pigs attack in April 1961 leave by air |

|  |  |
|---|---|
|  | for the United States, in exchange for children's food and medicine. |
| January 1963 | Turkey and Italy announce that Jupiter missiles stationed there will be withdrawn. |
| 4 January 1963 | US National Security Adviser McGeorge Bundy brings a formal end to Operation Mongoose. |
| 7 January 1963 | Soviet–United States joint letter to U Thant, agreeing to withdraw Cuban issue from the Security Council. Cuban letter to U Thant rejecting implication of 'Caribbean peace' and restating Castro's five points and need for a non-invasion pledge. |
| 6 February 1963 | US government publishes regulations designed to prevent free world shipping from going to Cuba. |
| 18 February 1963 | Khrushchev promises the US State Department withdrawal of 'several thousand' troops from Cuba by 15 March. |
| 1 March 1963 | The Director of the CIA reports that Cuba trained up to 1,500 Latin Americans in 1962. |
| 4 March 1963 | Communist China officially attacks the Soviet Union for softness on Cuba. |
| 21 March 1963 | Kennedy publicly condemns raids on Cuba by exiles. |
| April–May 1963 | Castro visits the Soviet Union, when he learns of the secret deal involving the removal of Jupiters from Turkey. |
| April 1963 | US Jupiter missiles are removed from Italy and Turkey. |
| 4 June 1963 | Castro returns from the Soviet Union. In a television broadcast, Castro describes his Soviet tour and expresses 'willingness to normalise relations' with the United States. |

| | |
|---|---|
| 10 June 1963 | Kennedy gives a speech at American University emphasising the need for better relations with the Soviet Union. |
| 19 June 1963 | Kennedy approves a CIA programme to bring about the downfall of the Castro regime. |
| 26 June 1963 | Kennedy's 'Ich bin ein Berliner' speech in West Berlin, condemning the communist system and the division of Germany. |
| 8 July 1963 | Cuban assets in United States – $33 million – frozen. |
| 24 July 1963 | Cuban government expropriates the US Embassy in Havana. |
| 5 August 1963 | The United States, Britain, and the Soviet Union sign the Limited Nuclear Test Ban Treaty. |
| 22 November 1963 | Kennedy is assassinated in Dallas, Texas, by Lee Harvey Oswald. |
| October 1964 | Nikita Khrushchev is overthrown by the Soviet Presidium. |
| 11 December 1964 | Che Guevara champions subversion while at the UN in New York. |
| Spring 1965 | The beginning of the Americanisation of the war in Vietnam. The last American troops would leave in 1973. |
| 27 March 1965 | Cuba joins the Soviet Union, communist China and Korea in promising military aid to North Vietnam. |
| 10 March 1966 | Charles de Gaulle announces that France is to withdraw from the NATO command structure. |
| 27 January 1967 | Signing of the Outer Space Treaty by the United States, the Soviet Union and the United Kingdom. |
| 14 February 1967 | Signing of the Treaty of Tlatelolco by twenty-one countries, banning nuclear weapons in Latin America. |

| | |
|---|---|
| 9 October 1967 | The capture and execution of Che Guevara by US-backed forces in Bolivia. |
| 1 July 1968 | The Soviet Union, the United States and fifty-three other countries sign the Nuclear Non-Proliferation Treaty. |
| 17 November 1969 | The beginning of Strategic Arms Limitation Talks between the United States and the Soviet Union. |
| September 1970 | The Nixon administration learns that the Soviets are constructing a base for nuclear-armed submarines in Cuba. Moscow backs down and affirms that it will abide by the October 1962 agreement not to station offensive weapons in Cuba. |

# Appendix 3: Biographies

*Bundy, McGeorge (1919–96)*

US National Security Adviser, 1961–6. A former army officer, foreign policy consultant and academic, Bundy advised John F. Kennedy during the election campaign of 1960, and in January 1961 he became Special Assistant for National Security Affairs (known less formally as National Security Adviser). He circumvented the slow-moving State Department and enjoyed a closer relationship with the President than did Secretary of State Dean Rusk. Bundy greatly strengthened the office of National Security Adviser, setting a precedent for the role. He backed the Bay of Pigs operation in April 1961. Late on 15 October the following year he was the first White House official to learn of the presence of Soviet missiles on Cuba, informing Kennedy of them early the next day and helping to establish ExComm. After supporting military action against the missiles, Bundy came to adopt a more moderate position. Later, he favoured a positive response to Castro's efforts at rapprochement with the United States. In 1964–5 he bolstered President Johnson's willingness to use force in Vietnam, but came to harbour growing doubts about the wisdom of US policy there. He resigned in 1966, acting as an occasional consultant on foreign affairs and teaching history at New York University.

*Castro Ruz, Fidel (1927–)*

Prime Minister and Commander-in-Chief of the Revolutionary Armed Forces of Cuba. Fidel Castro is the son of a former Spanish

**256**

colonial soldier who fought against Cuban and American forces during the Spanish–American War, and later became a plantation owner. As a law student at the University of Havana, Castro participated in radical student politics and in efforts to overthrow the dictator Rafael Trujillo in the Dominican Republic. In his early political career Castro's stance varied from radical to liberal, leaning mainly towards the former. He was consistently hostile to the United States, for what he saw as American exploitation of Cuba since the Spanish–American war of 1898. Castro and his associates tried to overthrow the US-backed dictator Fulgencio Batista, and after an attack on a military barracks in Santiago de Cuba on 26 July 1953, he was imprisoned for two years. He took refuge in Mexico, meeting revolutionary comrade-in-arms Che Guevara and establishing the 26th of July Movement. Castro became Cuba's commander-in-chief and prime minister after overthrowing Batista in 1959. In response to American hostility he welcomed Moscow's support, and agreed in the summer of 1962 that Cuba would host Soviet nuclear missiles. During the missile crisis he advocated the shooting down of American aircraft and even urged the Soviet Union to launch a preemptive nuclear strike in the event of an American invasion of Cuba. He was angered at how the Soviets made an agreement with Washington over his head to end the confrontation, and he prevented the establishment of a ground inspection regime to verify the removal of the Soviet missiles. Throughout the 1960s Castro's regime greatly improved literacy and health care in Cuba, while reducing the role of free enterprise. Castro sought to spread revolution in Latin America and Africa, supporting revolutionary efforts in dozens of states in the 1960s and 70s. The end of the Cold War brought hardship for Cuba as Soviet aid ended. Castro led the country until 2008, when his brother Raul took over.

*Dobrynin, Anatoly Fedorovich (1919–2010)*

Soviet Ambassador to the United States, 1962–86. After a career in engineering, Dobrynin joined the Communist Party in 1945 and held posts in the Ministry of Foreign Affairs' UN and American offices. At the beginning of 1962 he was appointed to the Washington post. He was not told that Premier Khrushchev had decided to place nuclear missiles in Cuba. During the missile crisis he played an important role in keeping Moscow informed of developments in the United States, not least through 'back-channel' meetings with Robert F. Kennedy. He warned his superiors that a US air attack on the missile bases or even a ground invasion of Cuba were real possibilities. On Saturday 27 October, RFK told Dobrynin that alongside a public pledge not to invade Cuba, the administration would provide a secret assurance to remove US Jupiter missiles from Turkey. The discussion helped to end the missile crisis. During the presidency of Richard Nixon in 1970, Dobrynin helped to defuse an incipient confrontation over the Soviet construction of missile bases in Cuba. Also in the Nixon period, he facilitated communication between the United States and North Vietnam in the context of peace negotiations in Paris, and he made an important contribution to Soviet–American *détente*. He helped to moderate tensions between the Soviet Union and the United States over the Soviet invasion of Afghanistan (1979), and he served as a foreign policy adviser to Mikhail Gorbachev (1986–91).

### Guevara, Ernesto 'Che' (1928–67)

Cuban Minister of the Interior, 1961–5. Born in Argentina, 'Che' graduated with a medical degree from the University of Buenos Aires, but undertook a revolutionary vocation out of the belief that society could only be improved through armed struggle. He maintained that popular forces could prevail against an army; that an insurrection could succeed even if conditions seem far from promising; and that insurgents should make particular use of the countryside as part of their strategy. Guevara served as a physician and military commander in Castro's guerrilla forces in Cuba during the late 1950s. After Castro took control of Cuba in 1959, he appointed Guevara as president of the National Bank. Guevara, one of most radical figures within the Cuban government, believed that Soviet backing was sufficient to deter an American attack, and was taken by surprise by the Bay of Pigs invasion in April 1961. In August Guevara tried to improve relations with the United States, but when visiting Moscow shortly after he is said to have probed Khrushchev about the possibility of placing Soviet missiles in Cuba. The following year he signed an agreement concerning the installation of the missiles and the presence of other Soviet military forces in Cuba, although he was concerned about how the US government might react to the discovery of the missiles. Like other Cuban officials, he was furious when during the missile crisis Nikita Khrushchev agreed with Washington to remove the weapons, but he strove to improve Cuban–Soviet relations when Anastas Mikoyan visited Cuba in November. In 1965, against the background of a power struggle in Cuba, Guevara left for Africa, where he helped to wage a revolt in the Congo. He then undertook similar efforts in Bolivia, where in 1967 he was captured and killed by the US-backed army. His death raised him to the status of a revolutionary icon.

### Kennedy, John Fitzgerald (1917–63)

US President, 1961–3. John F. Kennedy, the thirty-fifth president, was born into a large, privileged Irish family in Massachusetts, the son of businessman and politician Joseph P. Kennedy. JFK began his education in foreign affairs when traveling in Europe in 1937 and 1939. While at Harvard University he wrote a dissertation on the British response to Hitler's Germany, emphasising the need for military preparedness and firm leadership. The dissertation was polished (with the help of a journalist) and then published in 1940 as *Why England Slept*. It helped to present the young Kennedy as an intellectual and outlined what would become keynotes of his foreign affairs outlook. He served in the US Navy in the Pacific during the Second World War, winning medals and becoming known as a war hero. After working as a newspaper reporter in 1945, he was elected to the House of Representatives in 1946. He was a firm supporter of Cold War policies, backing the Truman Doctrine, the Marshall Plan and other key initiatives. As a senator from 1953, Kennedy emphasised the need to prevent the spread of communism in the postcolonial world, and criticised the Eisenhower administration for a lax approach towards US defences. After a slender victory in the election of 1960, Kennedy became the youngest elected US president in history, and the first Catholic in the office. He assembled a team of the 'best and brightest' foreign policy advisers, including McGeorge Bundy and Robert S. McNamara. His inaugural statement that 'we shall bear any burden, meet any hardship ... to assure the success and survival of liberty' was more cautious than the expansive language suggested. The 'New Frontier' was often more evident in style and rhetoric than policy, and Kennedy's presidential record was mixed. There was little progress on civil rights, and in foreign affairs there was the humiliation at the Bay of Pigs, renewed crisis over Berlin and a growing commitment in Vietnam. However, Kennedy resisted pressure to send combat troops there, and his administration was responsible for negotiating the neutralisation of Laos, so avoiding confrontation there. His successful handling of the Soviet challenge in Cuba in October 1962 is seen as a defining moment for him. Kennedy's assassination by Lee Harvey Oswald on 22 November 1963 meant that the growing promise was unfulfilled.

### Kennedy, Robert Francis (1925–68)

US Attorney General; brother of John F. Kennedy. After training as a lawyer Robert F. Kennedy served in the US Naval Reserve, 1944–6, and then worked as a journalist. He entered the government in 1951 as an attorney in the Department of Justice. In 1953 he worked for the anti-communist demagogue Senator Joseph McCarthy, but resigned after six months out of concern about his methods. Kennedy shared the conventional Cold War outlook that Soviet communism must be resisted firmly, and supported activist policies in the postcolonial world. He gained public attention in the late 1950s as chief counsel for the Senate committee investigating improper labour and management activities. He always discharged his duties with characteristic pugnacity. He managed his brother's campaigns for the Senate in 1952 and for the presidency in 1960, and generally acted as JFK's closest personal adviser. Kennedy junior was the driving force behind Operation Mongoose, the CIA effort to subvert the Fidel Castro government beginning in 1961. In contrast to the peaceable image conveyed in his memoir *Thirteen Days* (1969), he was among the chief belligerents in ExComm during the Cuban Missile Crisis, but he was also instrumental in negotiating an end to the crisis on 28 October. After the President's assassination in 1963, Kennedy continued as Attorney General under President Lyndon B. Johnson. There was a bitter rivalry between the two men, and Kennedy resigned in 1964 to run for the Senate. Although he was an early supporter of an expanded US commitment in Vietnam, he emerged from 1966 as a vociferous critic of Johnson's policies there. He was shot in Los Angeles on 5 June 1968 while campaigning for the Democratic nomination for president, and died the next day. The following year, Sirhan Sirhan, a Jordanian Arab, was convicted of the assassination.

*Khrushchev, Nikita Sergeyevich (1894–1971)*

Chairman of the Soviet Council of Ministers, 1953–64, and Soviet premier, 1958–64. Of peasant stock, Khrushchev rose through the ranks of the Communist Party, and during the Second World War he orchestrated resistance in the Ukraine and helped to move heavy industry to the east. After the death of Stalin, Khrushchev became party secretary in 1953 and premier in 1958. At the Twentieth Party Congress in 1956 he repudiated Stalin's brutal rule, even though he had participated in the purges of the 1930s. While he promoted liberalisation at home and in the Eastern bloc states, he used military force to crush a revolt in Hungary in 1956. Khrushchev challenged the West periodically over Berlin from 1958, and was responsible for the construction of the Wall in 1961. He placed nuclear missiles in Cuba in 1962 to protect the country against American attack and to improve the Soviet position in the nuclear balance of power. During the missile crisis in October he conceded the removal of the missiles in return for a US pledge not to invade Cuba, and for a secret US commitment to remove its Jupiter missiles from Turkey. Despite his provocative policies in Berlin and Cuba, generally Khrushchev favoured peaceful coexistence with the West. In 1963 the Soviet Union signed a Partial Nuclear Test Ban Treaty with the American and British governments. His time in office was also known for economic progress and for leadership in the space race, alongside growing strains in the relationship with communist China. After his overthrow in 1964 Khrushchev spent his retirement in seclusion, writing his memoirs. He was a contradictory character who often did not think through the consequences of his policies, but he was undoubtedly the most colourful of all Soviet leaders.

### Macmillan, Harold (1894–1986)

British Prime Minister, 1957–63. Born to a privileged background, Macmillan served as an officer during the First World War. He began his parliamentary career as a Conservative in 1924. During the Second World War he served in the Allied HQ in North-West Africa, where he met future president Dwight Eisenhower. Macmillan believed that Britain could act as Greece to America's Rome, providing a guiding influence in line with British interests. As Chancellor of the Exchequer during the Suez Crisis in 1956 he thought that the United States would stand by if Britain and France used force to reclaim the Suez Canal from Egypt. However, the US government vigorously opposed British policies, forcing a rapid withdrawal. Macmillan succeeded Anthony Eden as Prime Minister in 1957, and was successful in rebuilding Anglo-American relations. Although initially suspicious of the young John F. Kennedy and the thrusting ethos of the 'New Frontier', the two leaders soon forged a close relationship. During the missile crisis Macmillan made a point of staying in close touch with the President to provide moral support and guidance. Kennedy spent more time conferring with Macmillan (by telephone) than he did with any other foreign leader, but the British leader had no discernible influence on US policies and he was not told of the secret Soviet–American agreement to remove US Jupiter missiles from Turkey. Later in 1962 the United States cancelled its 'Skybolt' nuclear missile project, leaving the British, who were to buy some of the missiles, wondering what would become of their ambitions to remain a nuclear power. In December the US government decided to provide Britain with Polaris submarines on favourable terms. Macmillan resigned the following year, owing to domestic scandal and economic difficulties.

*McNamara, Robert S. (1916–2009)*

US Secretary of Defense, 1961–8. Of modest Californian background, and educated at the University of California at Berkeley and at the Harvard Business School, McNamara served in the Army Air Forces during the Second World War, when he applied statistical methods to the conduct of the global air war. He joined the Ford Motor Company in 1946, helping the company to regain success through the further application of statistical techniques. Through his Harvard contacts he came to the attention of John F. Kennedy and was appointed as Secretary of Defense, bringing business methods to the Pentagon and overseeing a substantial build-up of US nuclear and conventional forces. McNamara became one of Kennedy's closest advisers. He was responsible for the doctrinal changes in the US defence posture, notably the endorsement of Mutual Assured Destruction and the adoption of flexible response. He supported the attack on Cuba at the Bay of Pigs in April 1961, but during the missile crisis he considered that the Soviet missiles in Cuba were of mainly political rather than military significance, and was concerned about how an attack might escalate. McNamara was responsible for implementing the naval quarantine, and he oversaw the removal of the Jupiter missiles from Turkey in 1963. He enjoyed cordial relations with President Lyndon B. Johnson and was a leading advocate of a direct US combat role in Vietnam in 1964–5, but came to doubt the wisdom of the war. As President of the International Bank for Reconstruction and Development from 1968 he introduced measures to improve health, education and housing in poorer countries. He later admitted that he and other American policymakers had made mistakes in Vietnam, but declined to apologise for US involvement.

*Mikoyan, Anastas Ivanovich (1895–1978)*

First Deputy Chairman of the Soviet Council of Ministers, 1955–64; Chairman of the Presidium of the Supreme Soviet, 1964–5. He fought in the Russian Revolution, escaping captivity three times. Subsequently he occupied a number of eminent positions in the

Communist Party, including People's Commissar of Trade during the Second World War. In the period of post-Stalin collective leadership Mikoyan lent his backing to Nikita Khrushchev, endorsing the campaign of de-Stalinisation. In 1960 Mikoyan headed a trade delegation to Havana, which pioneered ties between the Soviet Union and Cuba and facilitated the survival of Castro's fledgling regime. Two years later Mikoyan opposed Khrushchev's decision to place missiles in Cuba on the grounds that Castro was unlikely to accept them, and even if he did, it would be impossible to keep their presence secret. During the missile crisis Mikoyan moderated the Soviet willingness to use tactical nuclear weapons against an American invasion of Cuba. After the confrontation had ended, Mikoyan was sent to Cuba to mollify Castro's anger about the agreement ending the missile crisis having been made without consultation. He won Castro's respect, although Cuban–Soviet relations remained strained. Mikoyan found himself increasingly isolated after Khrushchev's overthrow – to which he lent timid backing – in 1964.

### Rusk, Dean (1909–94)

US Secretary of State, 1961–9. Born and raised in the state of Georgia, in the 1930s Dean Rusk taught international law in California. During the Second World War he served in Burma and China, and in 1947 he joined the State Department, where he backed key Cold War initiatives. From 1952 until 1961 Rusk was president of the Rockefeller Foundation, a philanthropic organisation. Although John F. Kennedy did not know him, he offered him the post of secretary of state after Rusk published an article in *Foreign Affairs* extolling presidential power. However, the relationship was never close. The Secretary was reticent in large meetings, and did not provide the vigorous leadership of the State Department that the President wanted. Rusk tried to restrain the President from the invasion of Cuba in April 1961, but did not press his reservations. He favoured moderation during the Berlin Crisis of 1961, and in the Cuban Missile Crisis he contributed extensively by emphasising the diplomatic viewpoint. Initially, he opposed the sacrifice of the Jupiter missiles in Turkey because of his concern about Turkish and NATO sensibilities, but he was among the inner circle of advisers who were apprised of the secret agreement with the Soviet Union. Later he took steps to conceal the reasons for the removal of the Jupiters. Rusk enjoyed a closer relationship with President Johnson than he did with Kennedy, because both were of modest Southern origins and because the President greatly valued Rusk's discretion. He backed the use of military force in Vietnam, and always defended the American war there. He retired, exhausted, from government service in 1969 to resume an academic career.

# Appendix 4: Documents

## 1. Cuba and the United States in 1960

*The British ambassador in Havana, Herbert Marchant, accounts for the second year of the Cuban Revolution. He depicts the deterioration of Cuban ties with United States alongside developing bonds between Cuba and the 'Soviet/Chinese bloc', and maintains that as Soviet aid expanded, Castro was more inclined to antagonise the United States.*

... it is now evident that the Revolutionary Government has in the course of this year moved deeper and deeper into the orbit of the Soviet/Chinese bloc. Many of us here are still unsure how far this reorientation has been due to the influence of Marxist ideology and how far it stems from economic necessity. This is for discussion. The simple fact remains that the fast changing face of Cuba has in 1960 slipped abruptly sideways to the left ... relations with the United States are becoming more and more impossible, largely due to the atmosphere of hate – for the most part artificial – whipped up by press, radio and most efficiently of all by Fidel Castro himself. As the promise of aid from the Soviet bloc became more comprehensive, so the anti-United States campaign grew in intensity and daring. By May, with the Soviet trade agreement in his pocket, with a new Czechoslovak loan behind him and a new Chinese trade mission at his side in Cuba, Fidel Castro felt strong enough and bold enough to challenge the large foreign oil interests in this country. The three giants, Esso, Texaco and Shell, stood firmly together against the Cuban proposal that they should refine Soviet oil – and fell together a few weeks later.[1]

## 2. The Impact of the Bay of Pigs in Cuba

*Herbert Marchant notes how the US-sponsored attack on Cuba at the Bay of Pigs in April 1961 ended up strengthening the Castro government and its ties with the Soviet Union as never before. The Bay of Pigs greatly exacerbated the antagonism between the Cuban and American governments, and opened the door still wider to Soviet influence in Cuba.*

I doubt whether the United States' prestige has ever been lower in any country than it was here shortly after the invasion when, during a week of nationwide televised interrogations, prisoners from the invading forces told their stories and gave substance to an otherwise improbable fiction. The boost to the people's morale in general, to the stock of the Government and particularly to Fidel Castro himself was tremendous. It gave the authorities an excuse and confidence to arrest some 100,000 potential counter-revolutionaries, to close the schools, to throw out the priests, to introduce Vigilance committees and to set up a communist-style Ministry of the Interior. In brief, it was the perfect justification for past policies towards the United States and for the ruthless and public prosecution of the police state methods and regulations which now exist.

Having now discredited the arch-enemy, the United States, the next objective was to exalt the new Big Brother, the USSR. This time the operation was conceived to hinge around the visit of [Soviet astronaut Yuri] Gagarin for the 26 July celebrations. In the guise of homage to the Soviet hero, hammers and sickles began to appear on banners and flags. The 'Internationale' was introduced along with the Cuban national anthem, newspapers featured almost exclusively Russian science, art, literature, and thought. Even more Russian films came to Havana cinemas, more Russian technicians came to Cuba and more scholarships were offered for the study of the Russian language. The campaign was well-devised and well-executed and successfully broke down many of Castro's non-communist followers' natural instincts against Soviet Russia and all things Russian.[2]

## 3. Khrushchev's Motives for Placing Missiles in Cuba

*The British Foreign Office maintained that Khrushchev stationed
missiles in Cuba to help overcome American superiority in the
nuclear arms race. There was also the goal of strengthening the
Soviet bargaining position in relation to Berlin, and generally
undermining the standing of the United States. Historians also
acknowledge Khrushchev's desire to defend Cuba again further
American aggression.*

It seems likely that the Soviet Union has been anxious for some
time over the strategic nuclear imbalance in favour of the United
States and that this concern was heightened by President Kennedy's
messages to Congress on March and May 1961 requesting
increased appropriations to meet increased United States strategic expenditure, in particular for the Minuteman solid fuelled
ICBM programme. This concern has been reflected in increasing
Soviet defence expenditures. These rose from 9.3 milliard [billion]
roubles in 1960 to 11.9 milliard in 1961 and planned to rise to
13.4 milliard in 1962. This would represent an increase since
1960 of over 40 per cent.

But even this rate of expenditure could not hope to correct the
imbalance, at least in the short term. In these circumstances the
Soviet Government saw the need for some action which could
quickly provide an addition to their capability to strike at
the United States, in order to provide greater backing for their
pressures on the West on a wide range of issues, and in particular for them to apply adequate leverage upon the Americans for
settlement of the Berlin question on terms which would enable
Khrushchev to claim that he had carried out his promises. The
installation of missiles in Cuba was meant to provide the Soviet
solution to this problem. Their action if successful would have
conferred additional benefits such as undermining the confidence
of the Allies of the United States in United States determination to
use her power to resist Soviet encroachment.[3]

## 4. Kennedy Announces the Discovery of Missiles in Cuba

*In a live TV and radio broadcast, President Kennedy revealed the discovery of Soviet missiles in Cuba, explained why it was necessary to bring about their removal and outlined the American response.*

... this secret, swift, and extraordinary buildup of Communist missiles – in an area well known to have a special and historical relationship to the United States and the nations of the Western Hemisphere, in violation of Soviet assurances, and in defiance of American and hemispheric policy – this sudden, clandestine decision to station strategic weapons for the first time outside of Soviet soil – is a deliberately provocative and unjustified change in the status quo which cannot be accepted by this country, if our courage and our commitments are ever to be trusted again by either friend or foe ... further action is required – and it is under way; and these actions may only be the beginning ... Acting, therefore, in the defense of our own security and of the entire Western Hemisphere, and under the authority entrusted to me by the Constitution as endorsed by the resolution of the Congress, I have directed that the following initial steps be taken immediately: First: To halt this offensive buildup, a strict quarantine on all offensive military equipment under shipment to Cuba is being initiated. All ships of any kind bound for Cuba from whatever nation or port will, if found to contain cargoes of offensive weapons, be turned back. This quarantine will be extended, if needed, to other types of cargo and carriers. We are not at this time, however, denying the necessities of life as the Soviets attempted to do in their Berlin blockade of 1948.

Second: I have directed the continued and increased close surveillance of Cuba and its military buildup. The foreign ministers of the OAS, in their communiqué of October 6, rejected secrecy in such matters in this hemisphere. Should these offensive military preparations continue, thus increasing the threat to the hemisphere, further action will be justified. I have directed the Armed Forces to prepare for any eventualities; and I trust that in the interest of both the Cuban people and the Soviet technicians at the sites, the hazards to all concerned in continuing this threat will be recognized.

Third: It shall be the policy of this Nation to regard any nuclear missile launched from Cuba against any nation in the Western Hemisphere as an attack by the Soviet Union on the United States, requiring a full retaliatory response upon the Soviet Union.

Fourth: As a necessary military precaution, I have reinforced our base at Guantánamo, evacuated today the dependents of our personnel there, and ordered additional military units to be on a standby alert basis.

Fifth: We are calling tonight for an immediate meeting of the Organ of Consultation under the Organization of American States, to consider this threat to hemispheric security and to invoke articles 6 and 8 of the Rio Treaty in support of all necessary action. The United Nations Charter allows for regional security arrangements – and the nations of this hemisphere decided long ago against the military presence of outside powers. Our other allies around the world have also been alerted.

Sixth: Under the Charter of the United Nations, we are asking tonight that an emergency meeting of the Security Council be convoked without delay to take action against this latest Soviet threat to world peace. Our resolution will call for the prompt dismantling and withdrawal of all offensive weapons in Cuba, under the supervision of UN observers, before the quarantine can be lifted.

Seventh and finally: I call upon Chairman Khrushchev to halt and eliminate this clandestine, reckless and provocative threat to world peace and to stable relations between our two nations. I call upon him further to abandon this course of world domination, and to join in an historic effort to end the perilous arms race and to transform the history of man. He has an opportunity now to move the world back from the abyss of destruction – by returning to his government's own words that it had no need to station missiles outside its own territory, and withdrawing these weapons from Cuba – by refraining from any action which will widen or deepen the present crisis – and then by participating in a search for peaceful and permanent solutions.[4]

## 5. American Unilateralism

*British Ambassador in Washington David Ormsby-Gore notes how during the missile crisis the Kennedy administration showed little inclination to engage in serious consultation even with major allies such as Britain. Instead, there was a wish to win backing for policies that had already been decided.*

... although [much] care was taken to gain support for the President's decision [to implement a quarantine], the decision was his alone. It cannot be said that other Governments were consulted with any intention of their advice being taken into account. It would be wrong to conclude that this precedent would necessarily be followed in the handling of any future crisis which may arise in other parts of the world; but the fact remains that President Kennedy's Administration have had an important and, so far, successful experience in dealing on their own with a crucial aspect of Soviet–United States relations. It has been suggested in the Press that from now on foreign opinions of the United States' allies in the Atlantic Alliance will carry less weight in Washington than they have done hitherto. The President himself does not accept this implication but there is no doubt that the wearisome process of allied consultation is repugnant to some of the activists of the Administration.[5]

## 6. Was Kennedy Willing to Authorise a Preemptive Attack on the Soviet Union?

*General Kenneth Strong, head of Britain's Joint Intelligence Bureau, was on official business in Washington from 13 to 25 October. In a later conversation with Prime Minister Harold Macmillan and Foreign Secretary Alec Douglas-Home, he reflected on the American response to the discovery of the missiles in Cuba. In an alarming assertion, Strong maintains that the President was ready to launch a preemptive strike on missile bases in the Soviet Union if the dispute escalated. The account is entirely at odds with countless other items of evidence indicating Kennedy's*

**271**

*powerful commitment to ending the dispute peacefully. However, the excerpt is worth reproducing given the disturbing character of Strong's claim, and for how once again the issue of US unilateralism is in evidence.*

... The Americans were prepared to go it alone either without consulting their allies or irrespective of what their allies said *had the Russians reacted* against any action in Cuba by moving against Berlin. *General Strong* thought that the American Government were prepared for their action in Cuba to escalate into the nuclear. It seemed to him that the US Administration was overconfident that they had pinpointed the position of all the main sites of inter-continental ballistic missiles in the Soviet Union, and they hoped they would be able to take these out with a preemptive attack by their bombers. This point seemed to *the Prime Minister* and *the Foreign Secretary* to be of the utmost importance and would be a suitable subject for the Prime Minister to discuss at his next meeting with President Kennedy. He would warn the President of the dangers that would flow from overconfidence on this score.[6]

## 7. Khrushchev's Offer, 26 October 1962

*In a passionate letter to Kennedy, Khrushchev uses powerful imagery to underline the danger of nuclear war, and offers to remove the missiles from Cuba in return for a US pledge not to invade the island. This would allow him to retreat gracefully, as he could say that his stated goal of defending Cuba was fulfilled so the nuclear missiles were no longer needed.*

... Armaments bring only disasters. When one accumulates them, this damages the economy, and if one puts them to use, then they destroy people on both sides. Consequently, only a madman can believe that armaments are the principal means in the life of society. No, they are an enforced loss of human energy, and what is more are for the destruction of man himself. If people do not show wisdom, then in the final analysis they will come to a clash, like blind moles, and then reciprocal extermination will begin.

... I propose: we, for our part, will declare that our ships, bound for Cuba, are not carrying any armaments. You would declare that the United States will not invade Cuba with its forces and will not support any sort of forces which might intend to carry out an invasion of Cuba. Then the necessity for the presence of our military specialists in Cuba would disappear ...

If you did this as the first step towards the unleashing of war, well then, it is evident that nothing else is left to us but to accept this challenge of yours. If, however, you have not lost your self-control and sensibly conceive what this might lead to, then, Mr. President, we and you ought not now to pull on the ends of the rope in which you have tied the knot of war, because the more the two of us pull, the tighter that knot will be tied. And a moment may come when that knot will be tied so tight that even he who tied it will not have the strength to untie it, and then it will be necessary to cut that knot. And what that would mean is not for me to explain to you, because you yourself understand perfectly of what terrible forces our countries dispose.

Consequently, if there is no intention to tighten that knot and thereby to doom the world to the catastrophe of thermonuclear war, then let us not only relax the forces pulling on the ends of the rope, let us take measures to untie that knot. We are ready for this.[7]

## 8. Khrushchev's Offer, 27 October 1962

*For reasons that may never be confirmed, on 27 October the Soviet leader adds a demand to remove US Jupiter missiles from Turkey to his existing demand for a pledge not to invade Cuba. He sees the Soviet missiles in Cuba and the American ones in Turkey as analogous.*

... You wish to ensure the security of your country, and this is understandable. But Cuba, too, wants the same thing; all countries want to maintain their security. But how are we, the Soviet Union, our Government, to assess your actions which are expressed in the fact that you have surrounded the Soviet Union with military bases; surrounded our allies with military bases; placed military bases literally around our country; and stationed your missile armaments there? This is no secret. Responsible American personages openly declare that it is so. Your missiles are located in Britain, are located in Italy, and are aimed against us. Your missiles are located in Turkey.

You are disturbed over Cuba. You say that this disturbs you because it is 90 miles by sea from the coast of the United States of America. But Turkey adjoins us; our sentries patrol back and forth and see each other. Do you consider, then, that you have the right to demand security for your own country and the removal of the weapons you call offensive, but do not accord the same right to us? You have placed destructive missile weapons, which you call offensive, in Turkey, literally next to us. How then can recognition of our equal military capacities be reconciled with such unequal relations between our great states? This is irreconcilable . . .

I therefore make this proposal: We are willing to remove from Cuba the means which you regard as offensive. We are willing to carry this out and to make this pledge in the United Nations. Your representatives will make a declaration to the effect that the United States, for its part, considering the uneasiness and anxiety of the Soviet State, will remove its analogous means from Turkey. Let us reach agreement as to the period of time needed by you and by us to bring this about. And, after that, persons entrusted by the United Nations Security Council could inspect on the spot the fulfillment of the pledges made. Of course, the permission of the Governments of Cuba and of Turkey is necessary for the entry into those countries of these representatives and for the inspection of the fulfillment of the pledge made by each side. Of course it would be best if these representatives enjoyed the confidence of the Security Council, as well as yours and mine – both the United States and the Soviet Union – and also that of Turkey and Cuba.[8]

## 9. Kennedy's Demeanour during the Cuban Missile Crisis

*Ambassador David Ormsby-Gore provides a laudatory account of how President Kennedy conducted himself during the missile crisis. Although the Ambassador is clearly very much an admirer of the President, other assessments agree that Kennedy remained composed and calm throughout the confrontation.*

I saw the President four times during the course of the week of October 21, and on three of these occasions for long periods. I also had a number of telephone conversations with him. It has been suggested that he showed little or no signs of the pressures that were weighing upon him at this time, but this is inaccurate and foolish. He is an intelligent man with a deep understanding of his immense responsibilities not just to the United States alone but to the whole human race and he knew from the start that the decisions he was called upon to take might lead to global nuclear war. Although outwardly calm and although his characteristic quick flashes of humour never deserted him, he was in fact extremely tense and preoccupied. He acted very much in the way a captain is supposed to act when his ship is in danger. He put on a manner cool and collected. He never raised his voice. He spoke in clipped staccato. He kept in touch with every aspect of the whole operation, one moment asking Mr McNamara to check whether United States Air Force were properly dispersed in case of a surprise attack (they were not); choosing personally which aerial photographs should be released for the Press; checking the precise wording of [Valerian] Zorin's speech to the Security Council; advising on the precise manner in which Soviet ships should be intercepted. He telephoned incessantly but this extraordinary attention to detail did not prevent him from keeping the main issues clearly in focus.[9]

## 10. Castro's 'Doomsday' Letter, 26 October

*In a letter to Khrushchev that reached him after he had proposed the removal of US missiles from Turkey in return for the removal of Soviet missiles from Cuba, Castro intimates that an American attack on Cuba is imminent, and he appears to advocate a preemptive nuclear strike on the United States in the event of an invasion.*

From an analysis of the situation and the reports in our possession, I consider that the aggression is almost imminent within the next 24 or 72 hours.

There are two possible variants: the first and likeliest one is an air attack against certain targets with the limited objective of destroying them; the second, less probable although possible, is invasion . . . if the second variant is implemented and the imperialists invade Cuba with goal of occupying it, the danger that that aggressive policy poses for humanity is so great that following that event the Soviet Union must never allow the circumstances in which the imperialists could launch the first nuclear strike against it.

I tell you this because I believe that the imperialists' aggressiveness is extremely dangerous and if they actually carry out the brutal act of invading Cuba in violation of international law and morality, that would be the moment to eliminate such danger forever through an act of clear legitimate defense, however harsh and terrible the solution would be, for there is no other. . .[10]

## 11. Kennedy to Khrushchev: Resolving the Crisis, 27 October

*Kennedy's letter to Khrushchev outlines the elements of the deal that settled the dispute: the withdrawal of the Soviet missiles in return for a pledge not to invade Cuba. A US commitment to withdraw the Jupiter missiles was communicated orally from Robert F. Kennedy to Anatoly Dobrynin, but it is alluded to here by the reference to discussion about 'other armaments'.*

I have read your letter of October 26 with great care and welcomed the statement of your desire to seek a prompt solution to the problem. The first thing that needs to be done, however, is for work to cease on offensive missile bases in Cuba and for all weapons systems in Cuba capable of offensive use to be rendered inoperable, under effective United Nations arrangements.

Assuming this is done promptly, I have given my representatives in New York instructions that will permit them to work out this week and – in cooperation with the Acting Secretary-General and your representative – an arrangement for a permanent solution to the Cuban problem along the lines suggested in your letter of October 26. As I read your letter, the key elements of your proposals – which seem generally acceptable as I understand them – are as follows:

1. You would agree to remove these weapons systems from Cuba under appropriate United Nations observation and super-vision; and undertake, with suitable safeguards, to halt the further introduction of such weapons systems into Cuba.
2. We, on our part, would agree – upon the establishment of adequate arrangements through the United Nations to ensure the carrying out and continuation of these commitments – (a) to remove promptly the quarantine measures now in effect and (b) to give assurances against an invasion of Cuba and I am confident that other nations of the Western Hemisphere would be prepared to do likewise.

If you will give your representative similar instructions, there is no reason why we should not be able to complete these arrangements and announce them to the world within a couple of days. The effect of such a settlement on easing world tensions would enable us to work toward a more general arrangement regarding 'other armaments', as proposed in your second letter [27 October] which you made public. I would like to say again that the United States is very much interested in reducing tensions and halting the arms race; and if your letter signifies that you are prepared to discuss a *détente* affecting NATO and the Warsaw Pact, we are quite prepared to consider with our allies any useful proposals.[11]

## 12. Why Khrushchev Conceded: His Own Account

*The Soviet leader justified his decision to remove the missiles on the grounds that having secured a US pledge not to invade Cuba he had fulfilled his goal of defending the island. Khrushchev also emphasised how Castro's letter of 26 October confirmed his wish to end the crisis.*

We had to act very quickly. That is also why we even used radio to contact the president [on Sunday 28 October, indicating that the missiles would be removed], because the other means might have been too slow. This time we really were on the verge of war.

We received a letter from [Fidel] Castro in which he told us that the USA would attack Cuba within twenty-four hours. That would mean nuclear war. We could not be certain that they would not do so. The presence of our missiles provoked them too much; the Americans thus sensed the winds of war from up close. It was necessary to act quickly. That is why we issued the statement [on 28 October] that we would dismantle the missiles if the USA declared it swore not to attack Cuba . . .

In a letter, Fidel Castro proposed that we ourselves should be the first to start an atomic war. Do you know what that would mean? That probably cannot even be expressed at all. We were completely aghast. Castro clearly has no idea about what thermonuclear war is. After all, if a war started, it would primarily be Cuba that would vanish from the face of the Earth. At the same time, it is clear that with a first strike one cannot today knock the opponent out of the fight. There can always be a counter-strike, which can be devastating. There are, after all, missiles in the earth, which intelligence does not know about; there are missiles on submarines, which cannot be knocked out of the fight right away, and so on. What would we gain if we ourselves started a war? After all, millions of people would die, in our country too. Can we even contemplate a thing like that? Could we allow ourselves to threaten the world of socialism which was hard won by the working class? Only a person who has no idea what nuclear war means, or who has been so blinded, for instance, like Castro, by revolutionary passion, can talk like that. We did not, of course, take up that proposal, especially because we had a chance to avert war. What the Americans feared most, by the way, was that the missiles were in the hands of the Cubans and that the Cubans would start a war. That is why in our letter to the president we stressed also that the missiles were in the hands of our officers, who would not fire before receiving orders from the Soviet government. From our intelligence reports we knew that the Americans were afraid of war. Through certain persons, who they knew were in contact with us, they made it clear they would be grateful if we helped them get out of this conflict.

We agreed to dismantle the missiles also because their presence in Cuba is essentially of little military importance to us. The missiles were meant to protect Cuba from attack; they helped us to wrench out of the imperialists the statement that they would not attack Cuba, and they thus served their main purpose. Otherwise we can hit the USA from elsewhere, and we do not need missiles in Cuba for that. On the contrary, their deployment on our territory is safer for us and our technical personnel who look after them.[12]

## 13. Castro's Anger towards the Soviet Union

*Soon after the confrontation had ended, Fidel Castro complained to Soviet diplomat Anastas Mikoyan about the Soviet capitulation, and the lack of consultation. Castro's bitterness would have been still worse had he known of the secret agreement between the Soviet Union and the United States that American missiles would be removed from Turkey in return for the withdrawal of Soviet missiles from Cuba.*

. . . recent events have considerably influenced the moral spirit of our people. They were regarded as a retreat at the very moment when every nerve of our country had been strained. Our people are brought up in the spirit of trust in the Soviet Union. Nevertheless, many people do not understand the linkage between the Cuban events and the issue of the liquidation of American bases in Turkey. The unexpected withdrawal of Soviet missiles without consultations with the Cuban government has produced a negative impression upon our people. The Soviet Union gave its consent for inspections also without sending a notification to the Cuban leadership . . .[13]

## 14. Khrushchev's Surrender: A Chinese Perspective

*In an analysis drawn up immediately after the missile crisis, the Chinese embassy in Moscow maintains that the Soviet Union has compromised itself morally by conceding to American pressure. The deeply unsympathetic character of the assessment portends deterioration in Sino-Soviet relations.*

Khrushchev's reconciliation and submission to American imperialism constitutes a fiasco in the diplomatic struggle of the Soviet Union. Its influence on future development is bound to be extremely negative. Our preliminary views are as follows:

A development, extremely favouring the struggle against American imperialism, emerged at the moment when the American imperialists declared a blockade against Cuba. But just when the people were being mobilized and about to take action and the contradiction within imperialism was deepening, Khrushchev did not take advantage of the development, [which was at the time] extremely unfavourable to the US. He did not conduct a tit-for-tat struggle and push the development of the crisis [in the direction favouring anti-imperialism]. Instead, after performing [a few] gestures of struggle, he gradually backed down, and started to make a series of concessions, in the name of [being] cautious, calm, and rational, to the point of agreeing to dismantle and retrieve missiles previously deployed to Cuba, under United Nations supervision. This way, the Soviet Union had turned from initiative to passivity. From being a plaintiff condemning the US for threatening and invading Cuba, [it has now become] a defendant, admitting smuggling strategic weaponry and threatening US security. [The Soviet Union] abandoned the advantage [which resulted from] supporting Cuba, a sovereign country, in conducting a just struggle; it, instead, disadvantaged itself by deserting Cuba and accepting all

American conditions which were compensated by a guarantee of empty words. [By contrast,] the US has risen, from a pirate, condemned by the world with one voice, to a savior, defending the security of the Western Hemisphere and the peace of the world as a whole. The very situation encourages the arrogance of American imperialists while discouraging the global anti-American movement, indeed, to an unprecedented degree.[14]

## 15. Cuban Condemnation of American Policy

*On 25 November 1962, soon after President Kennedy had announced the lifting of the US quarantine, Fidel Castro and Osvaldo Dorticós reject the pledge that there will be no further invasion of Cuba, condemn the American disregard for Cuban sovereignty, and argue that US hostility played an important role in creating the missile crisis by forcing Cuba to defend itself.*

In his latest public statement, President Kennedy announced the lifting of the blockade of Cuba in return for the withdrawal by the Soviet Union of the intermediate-range ballistic missiles and IL-28 medium-range bombers stationed in Cuba. Nevertheless, the statements by the President of the United States contain the seeds of a provocative and aggressive policy against our country, which must be denounced.

In one part of his speech, President Kennedy said 'As for our part, if all offensive weapons systems are removed from Cuba and kept out of the Hemisphere in the future, under adequate verification and safeguards, and if Cuba is not used for export of aggressive Communist purposes, there will be peace in the Caribbean. As I said in September, 'We shall neither initiate nor permit aggression in this hemisphere.' We will not, of course, abandon the political, economic and other efforts of this Hemisphere to halt subversion from Cuba, nor our purpose and hope that the Cuban people shall some day be truly free. But these policies are very different from any intent to launch a military invasion of the island.'

The position of force adopted by the US government is wholly contrary to international legal norms. Above and beyond the outrages it has committed against Cuba, and that brought the world to the brink of war – an outcome avoided by means of agreements based on a commitment by the United States to abandon its aggressive and criminal policy against Cuba – it refuses even to give assurances that it will not again violate the United Nations Charter and international law by invading the Republic of Cuba, on the pretext that our country has not agreed to international inspection.

It is completely clear that Cuba has a sovereign right, based on the United Nations Charter, to agree or not to agree to inspection of its territory. Cuba has never offered or agreed to such verification . . .

President Kennedy's claim is groundless. It is merely a pretext for not carrying out his part of the agreement and for persisting in his policy of aggression against Cuba. As if that were not enough, even if permission were given for inspection, carrying with it all the guarantees that the US government might see fit to demand, the peace of the Caribbean would still be subject to the condition that Cuba not be used for 'the export of aggressive Communist purposes'.

What this means is that any effort by the peoples of Latin America to free themselves from the imperialist yoke could serve as a pretext for the US government to accuse Cuba of breaking the peace, and then to attack our country. Flimsier guarantees would be difficult to imagine.

To all this must be added one additional fact that speaks to the warmongering and domineering policy of the US government. In his latest statement, President Kennedy tacitly reasserted the 'right' – already claimed on several other occasions – for spy planes to fly over the territory of Cuba and photograph it from coast to coast. This too is a gross violation of international law . . .

The United States is trying to dictate what sort of arms we should or should not have. The US rulers, who compel us to expend enormous resources in order to defend ourselves against the aggression to which we have been subjected during the four years of our revolution's development, also claim to be judges of what the limit should be on the armaments with which we defend our freedom.

It was the US government that, by its repeated and overt attacks on our country, made it necessary for the Cuban people to arm themselves. It was President Kennedy himself who ordered an army of mercenaries to land at Playa Giron. It was under his administration that thousands upon thousands of US weapons were dropped on our country by parachute or unloaded by sea with the aim of encouraging bands of counterrevolutionaries, who committed the worst possible crimes against teachers, literacy volunteers, peasants, and workers.[15]

## 16. Shortcomings of the Understanding of 1962

*The agreement that ended the missile crisis was vague about what weapons the Soviet Union was permitted to have in Cuba. This is apparent in the following analysis by National Security Adviser Henry Kissinger, which he wrote against a background of concern about the Soviet construction of a submarine base in Cuba. Soon after, the 1962 agreement was clarified.*

The Khrushchev–Kennedy exchanges indicate clearly that there was an implicit understanding that we would agree to give assurances against an invasion of Cuba if the Soviet Union would remove its offensive missiles from Cuba under UN observation and would undertake, with suitable safeguards, to halt the reintroduction of such weapons systems into Cuba. However, the agreement was never explicitly completed because the Soviets did not agree to an acceptable verification system (because of Castro's opposition) and we never made a formal non-invasion pledge. The negotiations [in the UN in November 1963] between [John] McCloy and [Vasili] Kuznetzov, which were designed to work out a satisfactory means of formalizing the Kennedy–Khrushchev 'understanding' eventually just fizzled out. The 'understanding' we have with the Soviets, therefore, is an implicit one, which was never formally buttoned down . . .[16]

## Notes

1. Marchant to Home, 'Cuba: Annual Review for 1960', 17 January 1961, FO 371/156137, The National Archives (TNA), Kew, Surrey.
2. Marchant to Home, 'Cuba: Annual Review for 1961', 11 January 1962, FO 371/162508, TNA.
3. Foreign Office to Major Posts, 2 November 1962, FO 371/162398, TNA.
4. Radio and Television Report to the American People on the Soviet Arms Buildup in Cuba, 22 October 1962, John F. Kennedy Presidential Library and Museum, <http://www.jfklibrary.org/Asset-Viewer/sUVmCh-sB0moLfrBcaHaSg.aspx> (last accessed 25 July 2015).
5. Washington to Foreign Office, 9 November 1962, CAB 21/5581, TNA.
6. Note for the Record, 19 November 1962, PREM 11/3972, TNA. Emphasis in original.
7. *Foreign Relations of the United States (FRUS) 1961–1963 XI Cuban Missile Crisis and Aftermath* (Washington, DC: USGPO, 1996), document 84, <https://history.state.gov/historicaldocuments/frus 1961-63v11/d84> (last accessed 25 July 2015).
8. Khrushchev to Kennedy, 27 October 1962, *FRUS 1961–1963 XI*, document 91, <https://history.state.gov/historicaldocuments/frus 1961-63v11/d91> (last accessed 25 July 2015).
9. Washington to Foreign Office, 9 November 1962, CAB 21/5581, TNA.
10. Castro to Khrushchev, 26 October 1962, 'The Cuban Missile Crisis 1962: The 40th Anniversary', National Security Archive, George Washington University, <http://www2.gwu.edu/~nsarchiv/nsa/cuba_mis_cri/docs.htm> (last accessed 25 July 2015).
11. Kennedy to Khrushchev, 27 October1962, *FRUS 1961–1963 XI*, document 95, <https://history.state.gov/historicaldocuments/frus 1961-63v11/d95> (last accessed 25 July 2015).
12. Conversation between the delegations of the CPCz and the CPSU, 30 October 1962, *Cold War International History Project Bulletin*, 17/18, Fall 2012, p. 401, <http://www.wilsoncenter.org/publica tion/bulletin-no-17-18> (last accessed 25 July 2015).
13. Conversation between Castro and Mikoyan, 4 November 1962, *Cold War International History Project Bulletin*, 5 (Spring 1995), p. 95, <http://www.wilsoncenter.org/publication/bulletin-no-5-spring-1995> (last accessed 25 July 2015).

14. Chinese Embassy in Moscow, 'Khrushchev's Reconciliation with the United States on the Question of the Cuban Missile Crisis', 31 October 1962, *Cold War International History Project Bulletin*, 17/18, Fall 2012, p. 88, <http://www.wilsoncenter.org/publication/bulletin-no-17-18> (last accessed 25 July 2015).
15. Excerpts from a Statement by the National Directorate of the Integrated Revolutionary Organisations and the Council of Ministers of Cuba, 25 November 1962, reproduced in Tomás Diez Acosta, *October 1962: The 'Missile' Crisis as Seen from Cuba* (New York: Pathfinder, 2002), pp. 285–91.
16. Kissinger to Nixon, undated, *FRUS 1969–1976 XII Soviet Union January 1969–October 1970* (2006), document 194, <https://history.state.gov/historicaldocuments/frus1969-76v12/d194> (last accessed 25 July 2015).

# Index